Ursula K. Le Guin
Beyond Genre

CHILDREN'S LITERATURE AND CULTURE
Jack Zipes, Series Editor

Ursula K. Le Guin Beyond Genre

Fiction for Children and Adults

MIKE CADDEN

Routledge
New York • London

Published in 2005 by
Routledge
270 Madison Avenue
New York, NY 10016
www.routledge-ny.com

Published in Great Britain by
Routledge
2 Park Square
Milton Park, Abingdon
Oxon OX14 4RN
www.routledge.co.uk

Printed in the United States of America on acid-free paper.

Volume 33 in the Children's Literature and Culture Series.

10 9 8 7 6 5 4 3 2 1

Library of Congress Cataloguing-in-Publication Data
    Cadden, Michael.
        Ursula K. Le Guin beyond genre : fiction for children and adults /
    Mike Cadden.
            p. cm. -- (Children's literature and culture ; v. 33)
        Includes bibliographical references (p.) and index.
        ISBN 0-415-97218-3 (alk. paper)
        1. Le Guin, Ursula K., 1929- --Criticism and interpretation. 2.
    Children's stories, American--History and criticism. 3. Science fiction,
    American--History and criticism. 4. Fantasy fiction, American--History
    and criticism.   I. Title. II. Series: Children's
    literature and culture ; 33.

    PS3562.E42Z615 2004
    813'.54--dc22   2004014416

Contents

Series Editor's Foreword

Dedicated to furthering original research in children's literature and culture, the Children's Literature and Culture series includes monographs on individual authors and illustrators, historical examinations of different periods, literary analyses of genres, and comparative studies on literature and the mass media. The series is international in scope and is intended to encourage innovative research in children's literature with a focus on interdisciplinary methodology.

Children's literature and culture are understood in the broadest sense of the term "children" to encompass the period of childhood up through adolescence. Owing to the fact that the notion of childhood has changed so much since the origination of children's literature, this Routledge series is particularly concerned with transformations in children's culture and how they have affected the representation and socialization of children. Although the emphasis of the series is on children's literature, all types of studies that deal with children's radio, film, television, and art are included in an endeavor to grasp the aesthetics and values of children's culture. Not only have there been momentous changes in children's culture in the last 50 years, there have been radical shifts in the scholarship that considers these changes. In this regard, the goal of the Children's Literature and Culture series is to enhance research in this field and, at the same time, point to new directions that bring together the best scholarly work throughout the world.

JACK ZIPES

Acknowledgments

Like most young adults, I was a crossover reader—alternately reading Twain, Cormier, pulp fiction, Steinbeck, and young adult sports biographies. My first encounter with Ursula Le Guin was in 1980. I was a 16-year-old high school junior trawling my school library for something to read on my basketball team's trip to play a tournament in Boston. The trip from Oyster Bay, Long Island, to Boston would surely provide some down time during which I could avoid homework and enjoy a new book. It was there, somewhere on I-95, that I became a citizen of Earthsea. I was that young reader Parnassus Press asked Le Guin to target, and she hit her mark—a moving target heading across the Throgs Neck Bridge. Nice shot. Three points.

I didn't know it then, but Le Guin would catch me at various crossover moments—as a high school student looking for fantasy, as an undergraduate student rediscovering Le Guin the science fiction writer, as an instructor looking for something to use in a course on science fiction and fantasy (Is there a better author for such a mistaken combination course?), and as a doctoral student intent on studying children's literature in the field of English. In many ways I think my reading of Le Guin over time mirrored her production by genre, both of us concentrating more on the children's books later in our careers. It has been a joy to cross the bridges again and again.

Chapter 6 is a revision of "Speaking to Both Children and Genre: Le Guin's Ethics of Audience," which first appeared in *The Lion and the Unicorn*. It is reprinted here with permission of Johns Hopkins University Press.

I also want to thank Kent State University Press for permission to republish some material from "Purposeful Movement Among People and Places: The Sense of Home in Ursula K. Le Guin's Fiction for Children and Adults," which appeared in *Extrapolation*.

Portions of my article, "Speaking Across the Spaces Between Us: Ursula Le Guin's Dialogic Use of Character in Children's and Adult Literature," found in *Paradoxa: Studies in World Literary Genres* appear in this book. My thanks go to the people at *Paradoxa* for their kind permission.

I am grateful to Missouri Western State College for sabbatical leave and travel funds, which were wonderful gifts vital to the completion of this project.

I appreciate Michael Levy, Maria Nikolajeva, and Roberta Seelinger Trites for their generous responses to drafts of this manuscript. I relied on Marilyn Hunt for her expert advice on the art of interviewing, and of course on Roe Gnuschke for her invaluable help in finding materials through interlibrary loan.

Ursula Le Guin proved to be a generous respondent. My thanks to her for granting me interview time and for making notes on essay drafts. Her interaction made the process both more enjoyable and immediately enlightening.

Ultimately, however, this effort is dedicated to LuAnn, Rose, and Lillian —the three brown-eyed ladies on Lovers Lane, St. Jo.

Preface

He had now made unscathed, for the first time, that crossing-over and return which only a wizard can make with open eyes, and which not the greatest mage can make without risk.

Ursula K. Le Guin
A Wizard of Earthsea

The epigraph alludes to the wizard Ged's crossing from the land of the living to the Dry Land, the land of the dead in Ursula K. Le Guin's *A Wizard of Earthsea*. It is a perilous crossing, to be sure, and such a crossing in the third book in the Earthsea series will cost Ged his powers. Other wizards in the series lose their lives as a result of that crossing. Wizards cross that wall separating the two worlds with various motives. Some wish power in and over both realms, others cross in a selfless attempt to rescue someone, and then there is Ged, who would seem to cross because it is his destiny, as foretold in Earthsea lore.

Ursula K. Le Guin, a wizard of sorts herself, made her own crossover by publishing *A Wizard of Earthsea* in 1968. She had, by then, established herself as a writer of science fiction with her first three novels. When Herman Schein of Parnassus Press convinced Le Guin to write something for young adult readers, she made the crossover not only to a different audience, but to the genre of fantasy. Since childhood, Le Guin crossed genres as a reader: "I never read only science fiction, as some kids do. I read everything I could get my hands on, which was limitless."[1] As a writer she continues, through her fiction, poetry, and in her critical commentary, to investigate the legitimacy of categorizing her "thought experiments." She delights in "genre-busting," as she puts it, and is an exception even among crossover writers: Sandra Beckett notes that "the extensive list of dual-audience authors is greatly reduced, however, when limited to those whose works have made it into both the children's literature canon and the canon for adults."[2] Le Guin has won major awards as a writer for both children (Newbery Honor Book and the National Book Award), young adults (The Margaret Edwards Award and Arbuthnot Lecturer), and adults (Nebula and Hugo awards, a Pushcart prize, the prestigious Harold Vursell Award from the American Academy & Institute of Arts & Letters, and runner-up for both the National Book Award and the Pulitzer Prize), a situation that Helma van Lierop-Debrauwer claims "breeches traditional boundaries and helps to establish a positive image" for the children's writer.[3] And her reputation as a literary theorist on the genres of fantasy and science fiction would be secure whether she wrote fiction or not. In fact, she won the Pilgrim Award, given by the Science Fiction Research Association for an outstanding body of *critical* work on science fiction.

Le Guin is a writer who has trafficked much among the genres (both of fiction and nonfiction), but she is much more interested in continuity than separation. She is interested in the connection of points, of ideas, rather than in the discrete and autonomous nature of categories nurtured so fondly by those of us in the business of literary exposition. She routinely thumbs her nose at the border guards of genre as she speeds by in a vehicle that is at once spaceship, stroller, family wagon, and dragon. She's a writer more interested in matters of degree than kind, which is why she rails against the dividing lines critics, bookstores, and libraries impose on the literary world.

Genre crossing is almost as perilous a journey as it comes in the publishing world, since one can't be certain that one's readers will follow. Fans might not know that something is being offered by a favorite writer in what amounts to an entirely different section of the library or bookstore—which might as well be in a different world. She has made that crossing, seemingly unscathed, many times now—from science fiction to fantasy to realism, from fiction to poetry, from essays to editor's introductions, from adult to young adult to children's literature. And the subtexts that critics identify in her work are present in all of her work, though very infrequently are those connections made because of the real barriers of genre in the production of literary criticism. This is no fault of the critic whose work is in studying specific literary contexts. It is the nature of literary study itself that has resulted in the tendency of Le Guin's fantasy to be ignored by her science fiction fans and critics, and of her realism, young adult, and children's stories to be ignored by just about everyone.

This collection of essays pays attention to Le Guin's lines of vision—not so much the lines that divide, but those that connect her work. I invite the reader to regard less the vertical lines of genre (well, at least until the sixth essay) and consider instead the horizontal lines that intersect and, arguably, blur those verticals. I argue that rather than crossing to avoid critical pursuers, or merely to try out a new type of fiction, Le Guin traces lines of thought and follows lines of vision that simply employ the different metaphors that different genres offer. With the exception noted in the volume's sixth chapter, these lines don't mark the movement from one genre to the next as much as they mark the moves from one idea, one type of character, a certain plot, a particular relationship, a specific reader to another; they allow us to see her trying out ideas in subtle variation rather than only in completely different literary contexts.

She isn't so much inviting us to leap across literary chasms as pointing to the next stone in the stream to step on. The last stone might have been science fiction, the one we stand on might be realism, the next children's literature, but the line is one that traces the idea of, say, anthropomorphism, or degrees of character connection, or ways of coming home—and we sometimes have each foot on a different stone. We tend to want to take those strings of stones and make big genre rock piles out of them. Like her characters, Le Guin wants to travel in the company of others, and the regrouping of rocks into piles has potentially isolated her readers from each other and herself. I think there's an invitation in her work to follow her one step at a time along lines of vision. As we see in the latest volume of Earthsea, Le Guin will tear down the wall between worlds and reestablish a continuous line of existence. "Something there is," Robert Frost tells us, "that doesn't love a wall." Le Guin's body of work is one such thing.

The first three essays deal with questions of character in different ways. The first proposes a continuum of sentience in Le Guin's work—from the alien to the human, from the animal to the dragon, and the points between. She ultimately privileges an examination of difference through a dialogue among different types of being rather than through a synthesis of types, which is often the case in science fiction. The next essay then asks the reader to consider the continuum of connections possible among characters, of how they connect and what the implications are for complete connection at one end and utter isolation on the other. I argue that character viewpoint and focalization strategies are the means by which Le Guin achieves character connection or isolation. The second essay argues that Le Guin's work features dialogue among different points of view rather than presenting monologue. Suzanne Reid comments on reasons that Le Guin should be at home presenting various points of view in so many contexts: "Ursula learned early from her family and their many acquaintances to look beyond the boundaries of a single viewpoint."[4] In fact, she devotes a section in her book on creative writing, *Steering the Craft*, to polyphony: "one of the marvelous things about that marvelous thing the novel is its many-voicedness, its polyphony. All kinds of people get to think, feel and talk in a novel, and that great psychological variety is a part of the vitality and beauty of the form."[5]

In the third essay, I examine how characters move through time and place. Although the first two essays argue for continua of existence and character connection, respectively, the third examines those characters' movement through time and place with others as a means of finding "home." As there is a line charting sentience and degrees of character connection, there is a line of possibilities for chronotopic movement in the pursuit of home. How do characters move across time and place in her fiction? What are the chronotopic possibilities? There turns out to be a rather long line of subtle gradations irrespective of genre that account for how, or whether, characters find a sense of home.

The fourth and fifth essays examine particular contexts—the alternative world of Earthsea and the future world of *Always Coming Home*, respectively—and examine multiple lines of thought and vision in each of those. Rather than considering one line across many works, as I do in the first three essays, these two essays show how specific works employ multiple continua. In the Earthsea sextet, I look down lines such as the movement from epic to novel, the gradation of age-based genres, the shift in viewpoint and dialogue strategies, the change in protagonist focus, the line of character relation (as discussed in the first two essays), and the chronotopic continuum in the series (as discussed in the third essay). In *Always Coming Home,* similar continua are present regarding genre and character viewpoints and relationships, as well as a continuum of implied readership.

The sixth essay is a reconsideration of Le Guin's relationship to genre. In this essay I argue that what appear to be separate works by genre (fantasy, science fiction, realism) can be reconsidered as a continuum of hopeful fiction that corresponds to Le Guin's notion of age-based implied readerships.

Following that last essay is an interview in which I ask Ursula K. Le Guin about these crossings-over by genre and her journeys along lines of thought and vision. Here Le Guin discusses her work as a crossover writer—or writer for multiple audiences—as well as her writing practices and the genesis of some of her work. The interview covers ground not previously considered in her other interviews to date.

These seven chapters attempt to show the ways Le Guin "steers the craft" of fiction—to borrow from the title of her handbook on writing—along the lines of ethics, genre, narration, character, plot, and audience. And in keeping with Le Guin's practice of observing continua of many kinds all through her fiction, I offer these essays in a line of sorts. So, as the essays progress, the line narrows in scope regarding the number of texts considered but broadens in terms of the number of textual, subtextual, and contextual continua entertained.

My approach in these essays is to consider features of narrative, though a narrative approach is ultimately in the service of arguments about her subtexts of connection and continuity. I think it's important not only to note the presence of themes or subtexts as they exist in different works in different genres, but to show the narrative strategies that mark the relationship among works outside the context of genre. Her ideas can be considered in an alternative structure.

The work of Mikhail Bakhtin informs much of this work because the continuum is a highly dialogic metaphor. Any one point in a line is in conversation with the ones next to it; a line isn't a random collection of independent points, after all. In order to see a line as a continuous form, we have to recognize the connection of point to point. As the line "fills in," the importance of any individual point diminishes in service to the creation of that line. And unless a line has an arrow at one end, or is curved to suggest a movement up or down, it doesn't imply progression or regression. Indeed, Le Guin's thought experiments ask us to consider the continuum as a whole, as a series of relationships that demand consideration, not the ends of lines. As I argue in one of the essays, "home" isn't a point of arrival or departure—an either end of a line—but a movement along a line under certain important conditions. The line is a sum of its points; Le Guin's larger mission is to present a sum of points not to be separated from each other in their consideration. Bakhtin also makes it clear, unlike many narrative theorists, that one cannot tear asunder form and content, text and subtext, in order to determine what is at work in a literary text. For these reasons I cite Bakhtin's ideas throughout these essays.

I've commented on the significance of the title, but let me say something as well about the subtitle of this book. Le Guin once wryly observed, "with the agreed exception of *Alice in Wonderland*, books for children are to be mentioned only dismissively or jocosely by the adult male critic."[6] An important aspect of this book is the discussion of Le Guin's children's books, or of the child reader, in each of these essays. I hope that this critical adult male will show that Le Guin makes it impossible for us to dismiss or laugh her children's works off of center stage. Donna White, for instance, has discussed in her fine book on Le Guin's treatment by the critics, *Dancing with Dragons*, how Ursula Le Guin's work for children has been ignored in scholarship in some journals that focus on speculative fiction, while her adult work gets short shrift in children's literature journals.[7] We often disregard what Le Guin has to say across the body of her fiction. The children's book is an important form of fiction to consider, and by illustrating the relationship between them and her works for young adults and adults we both recover her larger body of fiction and further the argument that children's literature, and its study, cannot be dismissed as unimportant or irrelevant. Richard Erlich recently wrote that Le Guin's work is "an interrelated set whose individual members are mutually illuminating and defining."[8] It is my hope to add to the discussion by highlighting that mutual illumination through a juxtaposition of all of her fiction along various lines. Because this book entertains all of Le Guin's fiction, by genre and by readership of all ages, the audience for this book is potentially quite large.

It is perhaps best to consider the audience for this collection of essays by halves. The first three essays in this collection will be most rewarding to those familiar with Le Guin's work since the purpose of those essays is less to provide close readings of individual texts than to chart phenomena that cross most of her fiction. There are portions of those essays that necessarily allude to works rather than delve into them, especially the short fiction contained in her story-suites *Orsinian Tales, Searoad,* and *Four Ways to Forgiveness*. The fourth and fifth essays treat many fewer works and provide much closer reading as a result; these two—which examine the Earthsea series and *Always Coming Home*, respectively—I believe, are quite accessible to readers less familiar with those stories. The sixth chapter, because it discusses Le Guin's relationship to genre rather than specific works by the author, should also prove profitable to a general reader interested in the relationship between children's and adult literature, as well as the reader intimate with Le Guin's body of work. Through this shift in scope, and therefore a shift in (or reconfiguration of) implied reader, I attempt to make the collection useful for a variety of readers. Indeed, as the book examines continua in Le Guin's work, there is an invitation to several continua of readers: critics of the genres of fantasy, science fiction, and realism; critics of adult, young adult, and children's literature; and readers familiar with Le Guin's work to those unfamiliar with it.

Le Guin is a writer of continua who is coincidentally shelved in rather different places— in libraries, bookstores, classes, and professors' bookcases. The goal of this project is to help her readers cross from one shelf to another or one bookcase to another—to make those wooden shelves more porous than they already are. The characters in her children's book *Soloman Leviathan's Nine Hundred and Thirty-First Trip Around the World* pursue the horizon, not a destination. They know they won't ever get there, but they marvel at the points of interest along the way. So it is with Le Guin. She's still traveling and we along with her.

1

Le Guin's Continuum of Anthropomorphism

In no case is a higher third born of the confrontation of opposites.

George Slusser
The Farthest Shores of Ursula K. Le Guin

Only when the Man listens, and attends, O Best Beloved, and hears, and understands, will the Cat return to the Cat's true silence.

Ursula K. Le Guin
Buffalo Gals and Other Animal Presences

[The dialogic text] is constructed not as a whole of a single consciousness, absorbing other consciousnesses as objects unto itself, but as a whole formed by the interaction of several consciousnesses, none of which entirely becomes an object for the other.

Mikhail Bakhtin
Problems of Dostoevsky's Poetics

Harold Bloom compliments Le Guin as a writer of "precise, dialectical style."[1] Le Guin does not seem to value dialectic, however. There are many different unreconciled ideas in Le Guin's work. In the Earthsea books alone, Le Guin purportedly draws on Taoism, Jungian psychology, various feminisms, different models of anthropology, "the Hermetic and Neo-Platonic traditions and some elements of Zen,"[2] Sartre's existentialism, and "Buber's I-Thou relationship and some of Martin Heidegger's ideas on speech and being."[3] We would have trouble synthesizing these many systems, to be sure. I don't think Le Guin is asking us to.

Dialogue, while concerned with interdependence, does not insist upon a synthesized or reconciled position but revels in simultaneous, separate, and equally powerful positions in concert with each other. Le Guin engages in "thought experiments" in the parallel lines of different genres regarding the way worldviews relate to each other. Rather than address the dialogue among formal philosophies like those described above, I want to examine the way Le Guin uses anthropomorphism to show the limits of binary and dialectic. She establishes a continuum that plots points on the line for humans, animals, aliens, and dragons and then examines the spaces between those points. Even when it seems that Le Guin is synthesizing different positions on the continuum of sentience by providing us with characters like the eponymous Tehanu, Myra from "Buffalo Gals" (1987) and Selver in *The Word for Word is Forest* (1972),[4] she is really showing us how those positions, or characters, on the line are in conversation with each other—any character is a platform for dialogue rather than a determined identity.[5] There is a line that stretches between the binary of self and other, and Le Guin is interested in the degrees between those end points.

The Human and the Animal

Hailing the other across distance is important in Le Guin's work. The space between us is the most vital part of a relationship because it is what allows relationship to occur—it signifies the need for relationship and establishes a place for it. Michael Holquist asserts that even "the very capacity to have consciousness is based on *otherness*. This otherness is not merely a dialectical alienation. . . . On the contrary: in dialogism consciousness is otherness" (1990, 18). Synthesis removes the space between and fragmentation proclaims it to be unbridgeable—or it simply ignores the gaps entirely. One cannot create a self or a round literary character by destroying the other, synthesizing it with the self, or eschewing contact with it.[6] In each of these cases we are left with only part of the story of existence, and a skewed one at that.

Le Guin recognizes the necessary separation of the self and the other, but she tries to get characters as close to the other as possible and mediate a gap that cannot simply be closed. What Le Guin says of people might be said of her characters: "If you deny any affinity with another person or kind of person, if you declare it to be wholly different from yourself . . . you may hate it or deify it; but in either case, you have denied it spiritual equality and its human reality."[7] Le Guin repudiates the ultimate fragmentation of characters as "wholly different," yet she doesn't suggest the equally simplistic notion that we're all really just the same deep down. As she says in the introduction to her collection *Buffalo Gals and other Animal Presences*, "this conversation, this community [of animals] is not a simple harmony. The Peaceable Kingdom, where the lion and lamb lie down, is an endearing vision not of this world. It denies wilderness. And voices cry in the wilderness."[8] She argues for difference by degree—real and potentially dangerous differences, but differences that are not insuperable. There are many stops between self and other.

Roger Sale argues that animal characters are "the major source of the power of the best children's literature."[9] The animal character provides the writer of children's and adult literature with yet another way to approach the question of identity. Ann Swinfen observes that "this urge to leap the gulf which divides men from animals is shared by the writers of all animal tales, . . . whatever may be the other motives behind their work" (14). Margaret Blount claims that all writers who use animals as dramatic material are attempting to cross "the great gulf between human and animal."[10] In attempting to cross this gulf, the author "may leap, build bridges, or even pretend the gulf isn't there" (Blount, 17). And authors have provided us with everything from people in fur, as we see in *The Wind and the Willows* and *Angelina Ballerina*, to the animal represented with the consciousness that the author believes is peculiar to its species, such as in *Call of the Wild* and *Black Beauty*.[11] William Magee marvels that certain writers for children, especially Elizabeth Sewell, achieve in their writing a "distinctive and credible nonhuman point of view."[12] Different authors attempt to represent the animal at various distances from the human, and they have different beliefs about how far from the human they can go.[13]

Useful anthropomorphism should go beyond a random use of animals as people. Many contemporary children's picture books depict characters as animals with no apparent purpose except the obvious belief that the implied audience likes animals. The nature of the animal often isn't part of the rationale for the choice (the fox and hen as natural enemies, for instance), nor is the animal supposed to have some metaphoric value (foxes are crafty). At best animal characters often merely serve as costumes for characters almost childlike themselves; at worst they are part of a strategy to erase race, class, and gender from what might otherwise be stories depicted in realistic settings. Ducks and cats paint houses together and spiders have tea parties for insects. In her fiction works, Le Guin's animal choices are always purposeful. In her *Solomon Leviathan* (1983) a giraffe and boa constrictor take to the waves in a rowboat. While this might seem like a set of odd character choices, it's important to note that the absurdity of the relationship matches the absurdity of their quest to find the horizon. In other words, the characters are purposefully absurd.

Nor should anthropomorphism be a thoughtless mixture of animal and human, or what Le Guin describes as "just tacking a few tentacles or queer mating habits on to a standard Anglo-Saxon cardboard man and calling it a Pxzquilchian Native."[14] Such pasting of parts or swapping of heads Barbie/G.I. Joe-fashion serves not to put the animal and human (or different kinds of animals) in relation with each other but to point out the failure of synthesis. Le Guin plays with this failure on purpose when she creates her woefully designed Milts in *The Adventure of Cobbler's Rune* (1982). The characters are meant, as an odd mixture of creatures, to seem both ridiculous and monstrous. Purposeful mixture of animal and person can be done, and must be since we are limited in our ability to imagine what is truly other. C. S. Lewis challenges us "to imagine a new primary colour, a third sex, a fourth dimension, or even a monster which does not consist of bits of existing animals stuck together. Nothing happens."[15] Le Guin, for her part, thinks of the animal as something neither to equate with nor divorce from humanity. Rather, she asks us to consider it along with the child and the woman as points increasingly distant from "man," neither in opposition to him nor in search of blending into him. It is her opportunity to get us to play with how the vertical line of status intersects the horizontal line of sentience. "So long as 'man' 'rules,' animals will make rude remarks about him" (1990c, 12).[16] Le Guin asks us to move from the vertical to horizontal line as we consider difference; she encourages us to rethink status by using anthropomorphism as the metaphor of difference.

Of Synthesis and Connection Denied

In a few of her stories reproduced in *Buffalo Gals and Other Animal Presences* (1987) Le Guin plays with the problems of animal-human relationships and the related difficulty of adult-child, man-woman relationships. These are stories about betrayal across gender, age, and species. Two of the tales deal with transformation and two with separation. "The Wife's Story" and "Horse Camp" each show us a transformation: the former is about the transformation from wolf to man and the latter is about the transformation from girl to horse. In "The Wife's Story" we are told of a mysterious problem that a She-wolf's husband is having. He acts strangely, and their children don't seem to recognize him: "Make it go away!" shouts the youngest in her father's face.[17] It turns out that the husband changes into a man "in the dark of the moon" and is caught in the transformation at the story's end (68). According to his wife, he had "turned into the hateful one" and his destruction by the pack is necessary if regrettable (70). The wife waits to see if he will resume his wolf form at the end or perhaps come back to life in his wolf form with the death of the human, but the human corpse remains. The two forms die together. From H. G. Wells to Le Guin, it is clear that trying to synthesize man and animal and erase difference is not the answer. The man-wolf ends up betraying himself and his family; the pack and his wife betray him; all betray the children. There is no way to combine, erase, or ignore difference without betrayal and destruction.

In "Horse Camp" the transformation is subtle and gradual, and more figurative than literal. Norah, off to horse camp with her friends and older sister, identifies more and more with the horses. By the last third of the story Norah begins to see herself as a horse, identifying with the horses that run free, feel beautiful, and are disciplined by Meredy the handler.

At the end of the story, however, she sees her older sister Sal, now also a horse, "walking lightfoot and easy, fresh, just starting up to the high passes of the mountain. On her back a young man sat erect, his fine, fair head turned a little aside, to the forest. One hand was on his thigh, the other on the reins, guiding her."[18] Adolescent Sal is heading into the dark forest of sexuality in horse form—reined in and reigned over by the erect young man. "No, no, no, no!" Norah calls, feeling betrayed in some ineffable way by change, her sister, the boy, and her own future (147). The horse and woman are analogous here as two who are subject to handling by man. It is a comparison made to show us what awaits the beautiful, the free, the strong girls in a world where the axis of power is vertical, where she and the horse are both ridden.

Two other stories that deal with animals and betrayal feature different thought experiments. Rather than having the gaps erased, as in "The Wife's Story," they are made unbridgeable. This is the betrayal. In "The White Donkey" young Sita encounters a unicorn as she takes her goats to a field to graze. The unicorn can be approached, we know from folklore tradition, only by a virgin. Sita finds the "donkey" beautiful and, after a little hesitation on the unicorn's part, establishes a relationship of trust and appreciation. Sita doesn't know that the animal is a unicorn; to her it is a singularly beautiful white donkey with a curious horn on its forehead. As it is with "Horse Camp," this story is about the girl-horse bond that Le Guin recognizes as both typical and instructive regarding empathy; it illustrates the dramatic irony of these innocent girls reaching out to the other in a man's culture.

Sita's uncle arranges her marriage and she has to say goodbye to her white donkey, for as a married woman she will move to her new husband's home, and her brother will take over the goats. She has been "sold" for "one bullock and one hundred rupees cash."[19] She cries when she says, "'Goodbye, white donkey.' The white donkey looked at her sidelong, and slowly, not looking back, moved away from her and walked into the darkness under the trees" (142). Her uncle, who sends her off to a man at whom she wouldn't look earlier, betrays the relationship and mediation between the girl and the mythical beast. Separation is forced and the gap is made impassable.

In "May's Lion" there is another case of man cutting off the mediation between woman and beast, though betrayal might be seen in multiple ways. In Aunt May's account given by her niece, the story's narrator, we learn that a mountain lion has come out of the woods and rests beneath the fig tree in the yard. The cat is sick, May determines. She doesn't know what to do. She is concerned that she has to milk her old cow Rosie and that time is running out for her to make a decision. After consulting with Miss Macy on the telephone and being made to worry about rabies, May calls the sheriff. Two carloads of men respond and May concludes, "I guess there was nothing else they knew how to do. So they shot it."[20] The vertical relationship is chosen—shoot the wild thing. They don't know any other way.

Betrayal is complicated, as complicated as the relationships that exist in the story: "I didn't want him shot. But I didn't know what to do for him. And I did need to get to Rosie" (183). The men betray May by shooting the lion, a sick lion that May gives water to and wishes no harm. May betrays the lion by turning it in. Rosie the cow, whose attention is made a priority because she is a part of the system, betrays the lion with her need. The cow betrays May by forcing her to make a decision. May betrays herself by deciding not to go on to Rosie in spite of the lion in the yard. Nobody escapes blame in this tale.

But the narrator offers us an alternative. After she relates May's story to us there is a gap in the text—a gap as significant as that between animal, woman, and man in the story. Across that gap the narrator offers another way. The narrator wants to tell the story again as fiction, "yet without taking it from [May]; rather to give it back to her, if I can do so" (183). In this version the woman in May's position decides to walk by the mountain lion in order to milk the cow. Later the mountain lion dies beneath the fig tree. The cow is milked, the lion dies on its own terms, and there is no betrayal: "It's still your story, Aunt May; it was your lion. He came to you. He brought his death to you, a gift; but the men with guns won't take gifts, they think they own death already. And so they took from you the honor he did you, and you felt that loss. I wanted to restore it" (188). Le Guin speculates that "perhaps it is only when the otherness, the difference, the space between us is perceived as holy ground, as the sacred place, that we can 'come into animal presence'" (1990c, 13).

Neither synthesis nor separation is satisfying, and the notion of having to make a choice between the two is unacceptable. In two other tales Le Guin experiments with trying to allow characters to have insight into both the human and the animal while being both and neither simultaneously.

Human and Animal Eyes in *Tehanu* and "Buffalo Gals"

Myra from "Buffalo Gals, Won't You Come Out Tonight" (1987) and Tehanu and Tenar from *Tehanu* (1990), the fourth book in the Earthsea series, are involved in character bridging.[21] What can we make of the relationship between animals and people in these texts? How are the animal others, as well as our human selves, constructed in the narratives, and by whom? While Margaret Chang asserts that "Buffalo Gals" and *Tehanu* are connected in terms of their "integration of wildness into the whole of human experience,"[22] I would say that the "integration" of the one trait into the other bears critical investigation. Is the animal, alien, and human melded in the same character? Are these different parts actually integrated and reconciled? Or is there, rather, a dialogue going on about wildness among and within characters along the continuum of animal sentience?

Animality is extensive in *Tehanu*, despite the fact that relatively few animals are found in the novel other than some sheep and a few goats. Animality is a tool used for understanding relationships, nonetheless. Roger Sale points out that "if the [narrative] handling [of animal characters] becomes fixed or settled too soon, a kind of paralyzed storytelling can result" (252), a paralysis not unlike the allegorical limitations of fable. This limiting condition, this animal stasis, is not found in either *Tehanu* or "Buffalo Gals." We see various and shifting "animal presences" in the character of Tehanu.[23] She who is other, Tehanu, is seen to have animal qualities by Tenar, Tehanu's foster mother, and the external narrator. Tehanu is given various animal contexts that provide multiple ways to think of who she is, which range from the domestic animal to the feral child or the dragon itself. No gap between two selves is definitively filled, only temporarily bridged or loosely woven in several places. Identity remains slippery.

In *Tehanu*, the narrator focalizes through Tenar, observing Tehanu as "a little ruined butterfly" (8), "docile animal" (35), a "mousing cat" (32), one with a "crab's claw" (37), as a "bird" (72), and as a "little animal" (179, 199).[24] A relatively detached narrator, in this case, gives us Tenar's impression that Tehanu "vanish[ed] in the evening light beyond the dark doorframe, flying like a bird, a dragon, a child, free" (*Tehanu,* 103). Tehanu is like all of these things at once and yet she is not any one of them. Tenar calls Tehanu her "birdlet" (*Tehanu,* 52–53, 111) and her "little bird, flame" (*Tehanu,* 119). Interestingly, a young Tenar/Arha has a dream in *The Tombs of Atuan* (1970), the second book in the Earthsea series, in which "her despair grew so great . . . like a bird of fire,"[25] first giving us that image in relation to herself. Tenar links the images in ways that invite us to think not of a bird-flame, a phoenix rising from the ashes of an old world order, or even of a dragon, but as both bird and flame unblended, unreconciled in form or purpose despite the promise of a new Earthsea that will be revealed in *The Other Wind* (2001), the sixth and currently last book in the series.[26]

It is Tenar's vision of Tehanu that helps Tehanu redefine herself as someone more than the burn scars she bears on her face and body (*Tehanu,* 172). In the book, Tenar gives "the nameless child" (*Tehanu,* 8) the portentous Kargish name "Tehanu," which means "burning, the flaming of fire" (9). Tenar, the namer, herself is multiple: "All her former selves are alive in her: the child Tenar, the girl-priestess Arha, who still thinks in Kargish, and Goha the farmwife, mother of two children. Tenar is whole, but not single."[27] Tenar does not name from a position of singularity, as do the wizards, but names as a dialogue of selves, which explains the multiple ways she sees and names Tehanu.[28]

As Tehanu acts as a bridge between the dragon, the animal, and humanity, so too does Tenar act as bridge between Tehanu and the human world. Tenar, then, is a spider like Grandmother in "Buffalo Gals"—one who is to hold the fabric together. For the woven holds form without requiring that all strands touch. In her dreams, Tenar is allied with the birds and the dragons, as she so positions Tehanu for herself and for us. In her dreams, Tenar sees herself as "seabird" (*Tehanu*, 61–62) as well as both "dragon" (50) and a conduit for dragon expression (64). Tenar recognizes dreams as portents of change in a world whose fabric is changing, but which is not unraveling altogether (*Tehanu*, 68, 111). With her "animal sense" (*Tehanu*, 138), her multiple humanity as thinker in True Speech, Kargish, and Hardic (82), and her dragon empathy born of dreaming, she becomes a weaver of viewpoints; "Goha," after all, "is what they call a little white web-spinning spider on Gont" (1). Tenar is "an excellent spinner" (*Tehanu*, 34) who sits in the middle of a web connecting, but never fusing the different worldviews found on the continuum of animal sentience. Tenar sees that "there was a gap, a void, a gulf, on beyond the right and the truth. Love, her love for Tehanu and Tehanu's for her, made a bridge across the gap, a bridge of spider web, but love did not fill or close it. Nothing did that. And the child knew it better than she" (*Tehanu*,172–3). Tenar's web does not obliterate that dialogic space between self and other, but emphasizes that space through its presence even while crossing it.

Tenar can speak from different "perspectives," from different points on the spectrum of identity. She is limited in her vision across that spectrum, however, as everyone is. Some are simply less limited than others. She and Tehanu each see from slightly different spots on the continuum, each a bit to one side of center. In "Buffalo Gals," however, Myra sees from two places simultaneously; she straddles the middle, giving us a vision of two worlds that occupy "*simultaneous but different* space."[29] "Buffalo Gals" attempts to provide this narrative representation of simultaneity and difference in one character, however—something that the later *Tehanu* uses several characters to accomplish. Even Tehanu, presumably double visioned, isn't able to give voice to her terrible sight in the narrative, though she shares the spectrum with others who can help mediate the spaces. The two novels represent Le Guin's different and developing narrative attempts to weave across the spaces between points on the continuum.

The young girl Myra is hurt following a plane crash. She has lost one of her eyes. The narrator describes for us the way Myra sees before receiving what is described in *Tehanu* as "second sight" or "the third eye"[30] from a coyote: "She hobbled after the coyote. She could not see it. She kept her hand pressed over the right eye socket. Seeing with one eye there was no depth; it was like a huge, flat picture" (18). With the "new" eye, cleaned for her by coyote and replaced with one made out of pine pitch by Jay, Myra can see "a line, a straight, jerky line drawn across the sage brush plain, and on the far side of it—nothing? Was it mist? Something moved there— 'It's cattle!' she said'" (40). The narrator tells us that "If she shut the hurting eye and looked with the other, everything was clear and flat; if she used them both, things were blurry and yellowish, but deep" (28). But the lost eye and the kept one suggest the limits of Myra as a site for sight both as human and as animal. She sees the animals, though as in a dream she invests them with humanity. Myra's limits regarding seeing and being the other, and ours both through our alliance to her and the narrator, are evident in the following interchange:

> "I don't understand why you all look like people."
> "We are people"
> "I mean, people like me, humans."
> "Resemblance is in the eye," Coyote said.
> "But—like you wear clothes—and live in houses—with fires and stuff"
> "That's what you think." (31)

The animals look like humans to her, and she looks like a young animal of their own kind to them.[31] It is difficult for Myra to see herself from the perspective of the other, and difficult for her to see the animals through her one eye. Even when she is given her new eye it doesn't help her go beyond unsatisfactory synthesis. The mother chipmunk is called "Mrs. Chipmunk" by Myra (24), which not only imposes humanity upon her, but marital status and hence reproductive propriety as well. What Myra sees in her "animal eye" is informed by who she is, no matter how her eye might be altered. Contact with the other must be mediated more delicately, it seems. Myra gives us two visions housed in but one site of self. When the continuum is reduced to one point, it demands artificial synthesis. Le Guin demonstrates in *Tehanu* that the continuum of self to other needs more careful mediation that represents the simultaneity of the human, animal, and alien (dragon) while it also acknowledges their separation at the same time. Le Guin trades in the move from "Buffalo Gals" to *Tehanu* multiple narrative vision for multiple narrative sites in order to accomplish the same dialogic effect.

Tenar, through the narrator, voices concern over what Tehanu sees out of that "other" eye: "At that moment Tenar first asked herself how Tehanu saw her—saw the world—and knew she did not know: that she could not know what one saw with an eye that had been burned away" (*Tehanu*, 112). Tehanu's right eye, the eye Myra also "loses," is as inaccessible to us as it is to Tenar and a narrator that is kept out of Tehanu's consciousness, but Tenar continues to try to bridge that gulf in order to know how Tehanu sees the world. The very attempt is the successful first step away from the monolithic vision of the world and of the self that the wizards have, or the unsatisfying synthetic view Myra has, and heralds the new order in Earthsea. The narrator can only guess at the view from Tehanu's "good" eye: "Her one eye seemed to look up at Goha" (*Tehanu*, 5). This identity of Tehanu's identity as bird, or even as witch's familiar, is challenged by eyes through which neither the narrator nor we can truly see, keeping Tehanu's identity from being fastened by our gaze. The powerful eyes of dragons, witches, and wizards see or identify Tehanu differently than do ours, even if we can't see through their eyes because of the limitation imposed by the narrative strategy. Ogion, the respected wizard and Tenar's foster father—and even Moss and Ivy—recognize in Tehanu a vague resemblance to themselves in terms of power, though this recognition is disturbing to them. This resemblance in power is one of degree, not of kind. The witch Ivy says that "when [Tehanu] looks at [her] with that one seeing eye and one eye blind [she doesn't] know what [Tehanu] sees" (*Tehanu*, 181), even though Ivy sees power in her. We only know, through the narrator and Tenar, how Tehanu appears when she is looking: how she looks, not what she sees. Tehanu's face, "scarred and whole, seeing and blind" is dragged over to the human side of the continuum of self/other by Tenar's vision. Myra, to the contrary, tries to bridge the gap alone as human in the narrative. Tenar sees that "when [Tehanu] was excited or intent, even the blind eye socket seemed to gaze, and the scars reddened and were hot to touch" (*Tehanu*, 199). Anthropomorphism, the testimony of the powerful, and Tenar's dreams all provide us with other eyes, though clouded, through which to see Tehanu; the blind eye socket's gaze, however, reminds us that the gap remains despite the several bridging strands of web cast across. That inscrutable gaze, in concert with their aggregate of vistas of Tehanu, is part of what helps Tenar and the others "author themselves" while avoiding simple binaries.

The textual shift from Tenar's perspective to that of Tehanu's late in the novel *does* give us a little more insight into what Tehanu sees, however. In the novel's concluding chapter we are told by our narrator who now focalizes through Tehanu that she "looked into the west with the other eye, and called with the other voice the name she had heard in her Mother's dream" (245). Nothing more is shared about Tehanu's ability to see. Tehanu's eye remains hers to see through, though it is paralleled with Kalessin's glance, which looks "sidelong like a bird from one long, yellow eye" (*Tehanu*, 248) —and here we see Le Guin inviting us to consider dragon as bird—as both and neither. We move through the more accessible, though multiple Tenar to the more remote Tehanu who gives us as much as we can know, or bear, about that which is truly other. Rather than having Tenar or Tehanu try to be the one site of dialogue as Myra is in "Buffalo Gals," Le Guin makes Tenar one eye and Tehanu another, and those eyes, as well as the wizards', dragons', and villagers', see in myriad ways. The dialogue works better because it acknowledges and respects the spaces between each view.

Le Guin tells us that she had to see the story through Tehanu: "Until I saw Tehanu, until she chose me, there was no book. I couldn't see the story till I could look through her eye. But which eye, the seeing or the blind?" (1993, 19) The novel, as much a re-vision of the perspective of the earlier "Buffalo Gals" as it is a revision of Earthsea, answers Le Guin's question in different ways. *Tehanu* shows us that we need more mediation than we are given in Myra's story—more versions of self and other to mediate gaps, more narrative sites and voices. We need stronger supports in our bridges between the self and other. One stanchion won't do. Tenar stands just on our side of the middle; Tehanu barely over the middle toward the other; the dragon and Ged seem to be at the extreme ends of the spectrum between which Aunty Moss, Tenar, animals, and Tehanu mediate.[32] We don't have a meeting in the middle in one simple way: there is no one "middle."[33] Le Guin, through *Tehanu* at least, avoids the attempt to isolate an absolute middle in which an impossible synthesis would take place; what, after all, is dead center between self and other? By placing characters on either side of an indeterminate "center" that never needs naming, Le Guin gives us all that can be given: a vision of those who are closer to one side than the other.

As Le Guin uses Tehanu's animality as a means of mediating the dragon and the human, so does she use the animal as a vehicle for understanding the other in her children's picture books.

Of Cats and Dragons

In children's literature the dragon offers us a different context for considering the gradations of humanity. The animal is a part of our real world, the alien a part of an extraterrestrial vision, but the dragon is the creature in the entirely alternative world of fantasy, which is the province of the psyche, fear, desire, and children's literature. What Le Guin says of the unicorn is true also of the dragon: "the creature in question is not an 'alien' or extra-terrestrial, but just the opposite. It is an animal whose habitat is restricted to the human imagination."[34] The dragon is our imagination's symbol for the other end of the continuum of sentience. And we share dragons with children.

The dragon of western tradition symbolizes the dark side of human beings externalized for convenient slaying. It is on the losing end of the binary of good and evil. The dragons described in the first three books of Earthsea tend toward that evil representation, as we see when Ged calls them "baneful lizards"[35] or when they are described as having "sinister grace."[36] We aren't typically asked to consider that the enemy is us—or at least children aren't. Margaret Blount assures us that "the [western] dragon will amass all the wealth it can find or steal, keep it forever and kill all comers or other dragons" (117). Blount offers an antidote, however: "The dragonish character must be changed so that the dragon is small, young, friendly, funny, or reluctant—de-natured in some way, otherwise it cannot be approachable, cannot exist except as a thing for which death is violent and inevitable" (117).

The dragon has a history of being tamed in literature for children, as Blount notes. While Jane Yolen's *The Dragon's Boy* neutralizes the dragon by eliminating the fantasy element in the story (the dragon turns out to be mechanical), C. S. Lewis asks us to think of the dragon as a small boy in *The Voyage of the Dawn Treader* when Eustace is transformed. These dragons become "approachable" for the reasons Blount names. They are really neither externalized evil nor our fear of otherness worthy to consider. The dragon-Eustace in *Dawn Treader* is simply a boy in a magical costume. Eustace is "a dragon's body and a human soul" (Blount, 125). In contrast, Ogion and Ged believe dragons are the blending of "human mind and dragon heart" (*Tehanu*, 13). But the Woman of Kemay remarks to Ogion: "'If only it were that simple!'" (14). The project of *The Other Wind* as begun in *Tehanu* is to force us to confront the dragon as part of the mysterious continuum of existence by forcing us to see our relation to it. It isn't the other half of an irreconcilable binary; it's on the other end of the tether. It isn't to be integrated and it isn't to be vanquished. It is to be recognized and hailed through the mediaries between us. In order to keep us from the danger of holding the dragon by the tail, Le Guin uses the animal or animal behavior as mediation. In her work for young children, however, Le Guin softens the dragon in a way that she doesn't in the Earthsea series, which includes books for young adults and adults. Le Guin's favorite animal for mediating among points on the continuum of life is, without a doubt, the cat. Le Guin tells us that the cat, like the dragon, is "entirely strange, / a messenger to all indoors / from the gardens of danger."[37] She confesses that despite the fact that they are entirely strange (or because of it), "all cats guide [her]" (1990c, 151). The cat is our mammalian dragon—the one that seems domesticated but isn't, the one who "steadfastly denied ever having had any name other than those self-given, unspoken, effanineffably personal names."[38] But because Le Guin believes that there is a "natural, universal, and mysterious" connection between the child and animal, it makes sense that cats are used as the familiar of the other for children (*Buffalo Gals*, 139). The cat will guide the child to the other. Despite the earlier Earthsea dragons serving as representatives of the other side of a binary, the Earthsea series does introduce the dragon-as-cat as a way to soften that dragon other. In *A Wizard of Earthsea* we find that Yevaud, for instance, offers us a useful analogy, comparing himself to cats, for which "it is very common . . . to play with mice before they kill them" (*Wizard*, 91). In *The Farthest Shore* there are several dragon-to-cat allusions: the dragon Orm Embar's voice is said to be "soft and hissing, almost like a cat's when she cries out softly in rage" (*Farthest Shore*, 130); at one point Orm Embar's head is "low like an angry cat's and his breath [comes] in gasps of fire" (167); the eldest dragon, Kalessin, "leapt like a cat up into the air" (194). It is the cat's cradle song in *Tehanu*, after all, that feature's Tehanu's call of "'Come, dragon, come!'" (*Tehanu*, 37) The cat is the closest mammal we have to the dragon as inscrutable other, unlike the ridiculous, human-like dog found in Le Guin's "Schrödinger's Cat." Cats are never truly domesticated in Le Guin's fiction, or probably anywhere, for that matter, as the old saw goes about trying to herd them.

The most direct use of the cat as mediary to the other is found in Le Guin's *Catwings* books (1988–1999)—written over the course of time Le Guin was experimenting in "Buffalo Gals" and *Tehanu*. Ged asks of dragons: "What do we know about them? Would they teach as we do, mother to child, elder to younger? Or are they like the animals, teaching some things, but born knowing most of what they know?" (*Tehanu*, 218) Perhaps the "catbirds" of the Catwings books provide some answers. While "the dragons of Earthsea remain mysterious to" Le Guin (1993, 22), it may be that catwings are, for their being cats-made-dragon rather than dragons-made-cats, ultimately more knowable for both her and us. As the allusions to cats make the dragons in Earthsea more accessible to us, the wings and otherness of cats in *Catwings* (1988), *Catwings Return* (1989), *Wonderful Alexander and the Catwings* (1994), and *Jane on Her Own* (1999) push the cat further out along the continuum from self to other.[38] Until the arrival of Jane and Alexander gives us more mediation between people and the other, however, the catwings run the risk of being one more example of the paste-together character.

The catwings are Le Guin's most playful, though not her least important "thought experiment." They are not people in fur, as are Mole, Rat, Badger, and Toad in *The Wind in the Willows*, nor are they exactly actual animals equipped with accessible human consciousness, as are the rabbits in *Watership Down*. The winged cats, as animals with accessible human consciousness and speech, bridge the one span between human and animal; the addition of wings on the cats forms a bridge between the cat and the dragon. Although the tradition of children's literature enables Le Guin to, "without explanation or apology, make cats and birds talk, as Aesop and Beatrix Potter did" (Chang, 4), the use of talking cats with wings goes beyond either Aesop or Potter in the employment of animal character.[40]

In the third book of the Catwings series, *Wonderful Alexander and the Catwings*, Alexander (more typical as a wingless anthropomorphized cat) serves as a point between people and other in order to connect with Jane, who is a speechless, winged cat. With the arrival of Alexander we have a more mediated spectrum that includes people, traditionally anthropomorphized cats (Alexander's family), talking cats with wings, and a silent, winged cat who comes remarkably close to Kalessin in description. Alexander is a familiar construction in children's literature and provides a comfortable first step toward the other. A "normal" cat with human thoughts and consciousness is something that allows us to move from the self toward the other without the false impression that we have actually gotten all the way there. Jane is without speech, which dehumanizes her and pushes the

winged cat closer to the dragon-other. Alexander is our narrative focus in
Wonderful Alexander, and continues the move other-ward in his reaching out
to the traumatized Jane.[41] In this way, Alexander plays a role similar to
Tenar's, and Jane comes close to both Tehanu's and Kalessin's functions,
though in the Catwings series the ultimate other—the dragon—is only
implied.

Jane appears on page 12 of what is otherwise a familiar story about the
anthropomorphic and infantilized cat Alexander Furby. She appears in the
picture on page 12 as a black, distant, and unnatural figure winging its way
toward Alexander, who has been treed by dogs. Alexander at first takes the
figure to be "a bird flying straight towards him, coming nearer and nearer"[42]
—just as Tenar sees Kalessin as an albatross in *Tehanu* as he is still miles
from the Gontish shore. The original catwings are less significant in this
story, though they provide an additional site of mediation between
Alexander and Jane. Alexander, Jane, and the collection of other catwings
have become three different points of mediation between the human and the
other rather than there being a single site of synthesis to house them all.
Margaret Chang argues convincingly that *Wonderful Alexander and the
Catwings* "plays out the drama of Ged and Tehanu beyond *Tehanu*" (8), and
employs the strategy of dialogue.

While it might be reductive to assert that *Wonderful Alexander* is simply
Tehanu for younger children, or to simply equate Alexander with Ged or
Tenar as drawers-out of others, the subtextual connections are there, as they
are across all of Le Guin's fiction. This is what makes her a crossover writer,
after all. For across Le Guin's work for young children different combina-
tions of animal-human relations exist. In the two books about Kroy, *The
Adventure of Cobbler's Rune* and *Solomon Leviathan's Nine Hundred and
Thirty-First Trip Around the World*, there are only anthropomorphic animals
and no humans. In *Fire and Stone* we have a dragon that can at least say the
word "rocks" (though it is misheard as a roar). In *Tom Mouse* (2002), *Leese
Webster* (1979), and the Catwings books we have anthropomorphic animals
that are unable to communicate with humans though speech. In *A Visit from
Dr. Katz*, (1988) there are realistic cats portrayed, so there is no admission
into their consciousness. And in *Fish Soup*, (1992) there is no animal that
figures into the story line. She experiments with the mutual presence of animal and human in her fiction across literature for all ages.[43]

We have considered the animal-human connection in general and based
on gender. The animal also serves as mediary between the human and the
more distant other for both children and adults. Now I'd like to consider the
alien as the site of dialogue between the animal and the human in an early Le
Guin novel, which shows her interest in this continuum over almost three
decades. I discuss it last here, however, because of the way it integrates the
alien into what I discuss above.

The Alien as Animal and Human

The Word for World Is Forest shows us characters that display degrees of discomfort about each other's relative humanity and animality. Raj Lyubov, the Terran specialist on "high intelligence life forms," or "hilfer," on the planet Athshe (known as "New Tahiti" by the Terrans) is both a site of interaction between Captain Davidson, a Terran officer, and Selver, the Athshean leader —and a site of various dialogues himself. [44] Lyubov inspires no reconciliation, integration, or dialectic between himself and Davidson; rather, all Lyubov manages is "confusion," "failure," and "uncertainty." [45] The narrator raises the question of Lyubov's efficacy in terms of action and participation: "It was not in Raj Lyubov's nature to think, 'What can I do?' Character and training disposed him not to interfere in other men's business. His job was to find out what they did, and preferred to be enlightened, rather than to enlighten, to seek facts rather than the Truth. But even the most unmissionary soul, unless he pretends he has no emotions, is sometimes faced with a choice between commission and omission" (*Word*, 107).

This is a choice between doing and being put in another way. Lyubov, unlike either Selver (5) or Davidson (106), does not "do" but "is"—a quality extolled in much of Le Guin's fiction, especially by Ogion the Silent, Ged's teacher and his and Tenar's foster father in Earthsea. In Lyubov's case, however, inaction is made to seem a type of failure. Lyubov fears he has failed in his attempts to be accepted by either side, his own or the aliens'. Lyubov considers himself both a "traitor" (*Word,* 110) to his people and a failure in his attempt to get Selver to see that he, Davidson, Selver, and the Hainish and Cetian envoys are ultimately all alike as human. They are and they aren't. Again, Le Guin eschews the easy answer of "but we're all the same deep down inside." It is Lyubov as site for simultaneous feelings and understandings as Terran and Athshean, incomplete as either in the way the novel portrays those conditions, that makes him useful. He isn't supposed to serve as point of synthesis but as a somewhat confused site for dialogue among positions. [46]

Lyubov himself implores Selver to see a dialectical situation, a similarity with Davidson, with Lyubov himself, but Selver doesn't. In a conversation similar to the one between Myra and Coyote cited above in "Buffalo Gals," Lyubov wants Selver to believe what he himself believes, erroneously, about the sameness of all "humans":

> "Lyubov, why aren't you like the others?"
> "I am like them. A man. Like them. Like you."
> "No. You are different—"
> "I am like them. And so are you. Listen, Selver. Don't go on. You must go
>   back . . . to your own . . . to your roots"
> "When your people are gone, then the evil dream will stop." (117)

Selver doesn't go back, doesn't see a link beyond the recognition that both Davidson and he are "gods" (*Word,* 162). Lyubov is genuinely trying to reconcile what he, a Terran, knows of Selver as a "hilf" and his own response to what he calls "the Teddybear Reaction"—his Terran response to the Athsheans' size, furriness, and general appearance—their animality. Lyubov reacts to the "Freak Reaction," which he explains is the "flinching away from what is human but does not quite look so" (98). Keith Hull raises this issue as well when he wonders about Le Guin's fiction, "Which is sufficient to define humanness, appearance or behavior?"[47] In Lyubov's case it seems that neither is quite enough, for Davidson is as inhuman in a behavioral sense as Selver is in appearance.[48] For Davidson the issue is more clearly based on appearance, though Selver's "human" behavior bothers him. For Selver, it seems mostly an issue of behavior: Davidson and the others are insane, and therefore are clearly not human. Again, the issue is to reject an either/or imposition in the aggregate of views put forth by all characters—all reasonable in their own *separate* lines of thought.

Lyubov and Selver both fail; they both succeed. Lyubov is successful as a dialogic character arguably, for the very reason he sees himself as a failure: he achieves no reconciliation. He is an embodiment of the dialogue in the narrative. Lyubov's role as bridge between the space of Terran and Athshean, human and animal, self and alien, makes him useful in the narrative in a dialogic sense, despite any judgments regarding his depth or morality as a character.

Selver—"creechie," Athshean, "Man," "hilf," alien, god, and dreamer—is, like Lyubov, a bridge, though in other ways. His "human" behavior and his "teddybear" appearance—unreconciled—cause difficulty for the two Terrans. It doesn't take Captain Davidson long to supply us with the term "creechies" (*Word,* 3) for the Athsheans. "Creechies" is the first name applied to the indigenous population and, therefore, makes a strong first textual impression regarding their identity in the text. The label "creechies" does more than point to the Athsheans as alien-other. The Athsheans are constructed as animals, "creatures," and therefore their status as animal-other is, from a western, European, male perspective, quite a bit lower than human beings. This explains that one should, as Davidson does, "see things in perspective, from the top down, and the top, so far, is humans" (*Word,* 5). Creechies aren't slaves to Davidson, as Kees proposes, but beasts of burden, like cattle (*Word,* 10), and so there is neither moral transgression nor economic downside in their use. These beasts of burden speak Pidgin English, which suggests that subhuman is the equivalent of sub-standard English. It is when Selver addresses Davidson in flawless English, learned at the tutelage of Lyubov, that the Athshean "reminded Davidson of someone human" (*Word,* 18). This disturbs him as much as it does the cruel slave driver when he hears "we must talk, Mr. Gosse" in plain, unfettered English (*Word,* 122).

Despite evidence of Selver's, and therefore Athshean intelligence, Davidson still finds the Athsheans "a bust as men" because of Davidson's limited and limiting notion of what it means to be "a man"—a selective view in dialogue with both Selver's uncertain definition and Lyubov's all-encompassing definition of humanity (8).

Davidson, the most one dimensional and monologic character in the mix, is important for establishing one set of positions in a dialogic reading. The reader gets Davidson's view of other humans in Le Guin's universe: the Cetian envoy is a "little grey ape" and the Hainish envoy a "big white fairy" (*Word*, 76) who are seen as "humanoids" just a green hair above the creechies. Davidson's vision of humanity is balanced with Selver's as well as the Ekumenical envoys', who maintain that Cetians, Terrans, as well as Athsheans are all descendants of the ancient Hainish race. This "theory" is never proven, however, which leaves room for some doubt on all sides. Since Davidson finds irreconcilable the qualities of the animal and the human in Selver, he chooses to assign the former category to Selver and acts accordingly toward him. Davidson forces himself to make a choice between two opposites. Selver, conversely, given what he knows of his own humanity, finds the Terrans' humanity questionable: "No one can say certainly whether they're men or not" (*Word*, 45). There will never come an answer that satisfies anyone fully, which seems to be the point.

Selver is "a god, a changer," and "a bridge between realities" (*Word*, 35). The two realities include two states that even the Athsheans can't fully synthesize but must negotiate: dream and reason. The Athsheans, Lyubov tells us, "balance [their] sanity not on the razor's edge of reason but on the double support, the fine balance, of reason and dream" (*Word*, 99). Even "their words were not only two-syllabled but two-sided" (105)—double-sided reality and language befitting that dissolved "fine balance" rather than a dialectical existence. This becomes the Athsheans' model of a dialogic existence as well as their measure for humanity. It is because "yumens" can't dream right —or can't control their sleeping or hallucinogen-induced dreams—that their humanity is questioned. The single–visioned people are monsters.

The dream/reality split is a different way Le Guin tries to achieve double vision in one character than the one she will try later with Myra and Tehanu. Selver sees in two ways—through waking and dream vision, which is different from Myra's two eyes. Selver moves back and forth rather than trying to see both realities simultaneously. It is the ability to see in two ways that, for Selver, marks the human. It is an important matter. The gap between positions is respected because he shifts vision only when he moves between parallel (not hierarchical) planes. In this way, and in his role as animal/human/alien on the continuum, he acts as a mediary different from the single Myra or the multiple characters in *Tehanu* or the Catwings books.

Dreams, as complicated and unresolved dialogue, do not come so easily, and Selver does not easily control them. The movement between reason and dream is still movement, after all, and qualifies as movement between two different ways of seeing—from one leg of the balance of sanity to the other:

> "Do you hold the dream in your hands?"
> "Yes."
> "Do you weave and shape, direct and flow, start and cease at will?"
> "Sometimes, not always."
> "Can you walk the road your dream goes?"
> "Sometimes. Sometimes I am afraid to."
> "Who is not?" (*Word*, 40).

Selver acknowledges that it is only sometimes that he, a superior dreamer himself, seems in control as weaver. Later in the story, the reader sees such difficulty: "Selver, struggling with a sleep-dream beyond his control, cried out as if in great fear, and woke" (*Word*, 41).

Selver, as one who travels between two ways of seeing, strikes a balance between Davidson and Lyubov as people with rather single ways of seeing the world. Selver, as weaver, doesn't try to synthesize the two visions he has, or choose only one. He realizes that he isn't in control of that, nor should he be. He doesn't try to make the waking world the same as the dream world, or the dream world the same as the waking world. They inform each other. One of the realizations Selver has in his traffic between visions is that the Terrans have brought "a new way to do a thing, or a new thing to be done"—in this case, killing (168). Selver acknowledges to Davidson that the two have brought "each other gifts as gods bring. You gave me a gift, the killing of one's kind, murder. Now, as well as I can, I give you my people's gift, which is not killing. I think we each find each other's gift heavy to carry" (*Word*, 160).

The Word for World Is Forest is Le Guin's examination of gradations on the continuum of the human, alien, and animal. Nothing is synthesized by the end of the work. Le Guin offers no conclusions about the nature of humanity, identity, or difference. Through examining essence and action in the characters, we come away with a sense of difference by degree and an appreciation of the implications of making absolute choices.

Texts that feature anthropomorphism present different ways to mediate between points on the continuum of animal sentience. Those that offer more points of contact on the continuum, if not more narrative perspective, seem to have fewer difficulties avoiding the problem of synthesis. However, each tale teaches us something about seeing each other. Le Guin eschews the binary when it comes to understanding the differences between "people." Coyote tells Myra that there are only two kinds of people. "Humans and animals?" Myra ventures. "No," Coyote answers, "the kind of people who say, 'There are two kinds of people' and the kind of people who don't" ("Buffalo Gals," 32).

It's a joke . . . but it isn't. Each individual stands somewhere along the continuum of existence. To be conscious is to define yourself not strictly in opposition to but in concert with other conscious beings, both close to and distant from yourself in a variety of ways. From *Word*, "Buffalo Gals," and *Tehanu* to the Catwings books, Le Guin experiments with the best ways to reconcile the differences between self and other over the range of texts in the genres of adult and children's literature and over the decades of her writing life.

2
Connecting Characters on the Continuum of Viewpoint

So I wrote this book for my friend, with whom I have lived and will die free.

Ursula K. Le Guin
"A Woman's Liberation"

In the last essay, I discussed the ways that Le Guin employs anthropomorphism as a strategy for mediating between points on a continuum of sentience. In this essay I want to examine Le Guin's continuum of character connection and isolation, which parallels her continuum of narrative and focalization strategies. How close can characters get to each other through the author's use of different viewpoint strategies?

Le Guin uses narration (who tells a tale) and focalizers (viewpoint characters) to show how characters connect to find a purpose. Narration and focalization are used to control how close characters can get to one another. Without others, characters fail to realize goals—or even to develop a clear sense of themselves—so it matters how close they can get to other characters. Le Guin makes it clear through all of her fiction that the character that stays isolated—by choice or circumstance—is least happy and ultimately without much sense of self or purpose. And it is character connection that will make possible the sense of home discussed in the next essay.

So there are a few lines to follow. One continuum (or horizontal line) measures character relationships—more specifically, character closeness. Since closeness is a function of narration and focalization, I examine the continuum of closeness by examining Le Guin's parallel continuum of narration and focalization. I move from those works that employ multiple focalizers through external narration to those with fewer and ultimately to Le Guin's character narrations, or first-person work. It is *mostly* true that the more focalizers the more connection, but nothing is that convenient, especially in Le Guin's work. Without exceptions there is no standard, after all. In any case, I will show how those books use (or are limited by) the strategies of narration and focalization in their bid to establish character closeness and distance.

The last set of lines is the vertical, by which I also organize this discussion. I organize this discussion by genre—the lines that purport to divide literary texts and contexts. I do this in order to illustrate the degree to which Le Guin's generic contexts evince the same narrative strategies to achieve or deny character relationships. Do the vertical lines actually divide, or are they simply different contexts, more parallels, for the same line?

The Novels

I begin with the genre with which Le Guin has had the most critical success.[1] An interesting quality of Le Guin's novels is that they almost all employ external narrators.[2] Most often the external narrator in a Le Guin novel will look (or "focalize") through two or three characters. Characters speak for themselves infrequently.

The Anomaly: Many Focalizers, Little Connection

Malafrena (1979)[3]—Le Guin's first novel, though her thirteenth published— juggles the most character focalizers, and, as Le Guin's earliest attempt at a novel, strains under the weight of that crowd. I begin then, with an exception to the rule promised above. *Malafrena* has the most focalizers, but because Le Guin doesn't use the narrative strategies I'll discuss below to create character connection, this mass of characters remains a collection of isolated individuals.

    Malafrena is unique among Le Guin's novels in terms of narration, for the author employs what she calls "Involved Author" or "Omniscient Author" narration.[4] It is the voice that is so close to everyone that it sacrifices the chance at real intimacy with one or a few characters. This narrative technique makes characters as distant to us as the other end of the continuum of narrative consciousness—the fly-on-the-wall narration in which no character's viewpoint is entertained. Extremes are isolating, in both narration and society, and it is for this reason that Le Guin ultimately avoids narrative extremes in her portrayal of societies in her novels. However, in *Malafrena,* set in the imaginary Eastern European nation of Orsinia following the French Revolution, we gradually lose intimacy with the protagonist, Itale Sorde, as we gain limited access to so many others in the course of this tempestuous novel. He is lost in the crowd, a part of a large, yet limited consciousness. While it is a compelling story—a real potboiler involving revolution and romance—it keeps other characters (and us) too far from Itale. The effect is that Itale is kept from either connecting with another character or finding a lasting purpose. Most of Le Guin's other novels, whether set in the future, in an alternative world, or on our own Earth, avoid these extremes of narration and employ external narration with only a few focalizers.

Three Focalizers: Connection and Isolation

Planet of Exile (1966), *The Lathe of Heaven* (1971), *The Word for World Is Forest* (1976), and *The Eye of the Heron* (1978) rotate chapters among only three focalizers.[5] *The Lathe of Heaven* and *The Word for World Is Forest* provide us one important character that we are likely to find unsympathetic. This character is an important catalyst used to enable the other two characters to connect. However, because Le Guin doesn't care for creating character binaries, she uses a particular narrative technique to make such a character more sympathetic and connected to the reader. She blurs the distance between the narrator and the focalizing character. Narratologists call the total blur between the external narrator and the viewpoint character free indirect discourse.[6] The more the narrator blurs with the character along the continuum that stretches from external to character narration, the more it seems that the thoughts of the focalized character are offered both by the character and the narrator at the same time. Since the weighty authority of the external narrator is part of that blend, it can be used to make us feel that the character's impressions are at most "objective"—and at the least the character deserves some sympathy, a hearing out on his or her own ground. Le Guin uses it in her first three Earthsea books when important young adult characters—Ged, Tenar, and Lebannen, respectively, need to be portrayed as sensible even as they engage in rash actions as a result of naïve thinking. Going about it that way rather than using first person achieves two important things: it enables other focalizers to exist in the text, and it heightens the sense of reliability of the ideas reported.[7]

Captain Davidson in *The Word for World Is Forest*, for instance, is almost a caricature of the testosterone-laden military officer who would just as soon rape and murder the natives of the planet Athshe as look at them. He is someone even Hemingway might find too aggressive and self-assured. Dr. Haber, the psychologist and George Orr's antagonist in *The Lathe of Heaven*, is the self-assured, well-meaning, egomaniacal scientist who ultimately wishes to use George Orr's dreams to change the world to suit his own vision of utopia. In each case, the character focalizer is, as compared to the other two in the respective novels (or to most anyone), less sympathetic to the reader and other characters and less distant from the narrator. Free indirect discourse is used to make such a character's worldview seem more objective to the reader without resorting to comment by a narrator. For instance, early in *The Word for World Is Forest,* the story of Terran colonization of a pre-Industrial world, Davidson's thoughts are being reported by the narrator from very close range. Davidson is musing on how the planet Athshe is "made for" the Terrans: "Cleaned up and cleaned out, the dark forests cut down for open fields of grain, the primeval murk and savagery and ignorance wiped out, it would be a paradise, a real Eden. A better world than worn-out Earth. And it would be his world. For that's what Don

Davidson was, way down deep inside him: a world-tamer. He wasn't a boastful man, but he knew his own size. It just happened to be the way he was made" (*Word*, 3–4). The reader is less likely to dismiss such a character because of the presence of the objective authority of the external narrator. If we reject the character *too* soon (for indeed we ultimately will) we may fail to understand the conditions that lead him to isolation, and it's important in Le Guin's fiction for us to understand isolation as the ultimate failure, deserving the pity we afford a tragically ironic tale. Haber's and Davidson's respective purposes are egomaniacal—monologic rather than dialogic. Davidson needs what seems to be corroboration and validation from the external narrator. We witness this "objectivity" when the character is referred to by name rather than as "I." Le Guin uses free indirect discourse to help put speakers on a more equal ideological footing with other characters and her implied readers, which helps keep the stories from becoming too single voiced or ideologically polarized. We are helped to understand that all characters have their reasons, and their choices seem reasonable to them. Some are surprised at their ultimate isolation, and while we may not be surprised we can understand their astonishment.

When the characters Lyubov or Selver from *The Word for World Is Forest* are the focalizers, we are given more narrative markers like "he thought" or "he said" to make it clear that the narrator is simply reporting on the character. These characters don't need the public relations work of free indirect discourse to make us consider with fairness their more mainstream, humane worldviews. Dr. Haber from *The Lathe of Heaven*, however, does need the help of free indirect discourse. The three chapters in which Haber is the focalizer are characterized by the intense use of that narrative strategy. This is necessary to make him more real and less like a one-dimensional evil scientist. Late in this novel about George Orr and his ability to literally change the world through effective dreaming, the narrator and Haber's consciousness merge on the subject of George Orr's talent for altering reality. Le Guin writes, "Why had this gift been given to a fool, a passive nothing of a man? Why was Orr so sure and so right, while the strong active, positive man was powerless, forced to try to use, even to obey, the weak tool?" (*Lathe*, 123) Again, Orr himself and Heather Lelache, the other two focalizers, are portrayed with more narrative distance, much like Lyubov and Selver in *The Word for World Is Forest*.

Just as free indirect discourse makes some otherwise unsavory characters more accessible and sympathetic in the above tales with three focalizers, the use of the three viewpoint characters in both *Planet of Exile* and *The Eye of the Heron* make different positions more clear to the reader, which will help us understand how connections are made. Each novel provides us, as in *Lathe* and *Word*, three viewpoints on world events; two of those viewpoint characters use each other as a way to make sense of the world while one remains more isolated by contrast. These isolated third wheels tend to either fall away or meet with bad ends: Haber, Davidson, Vera, and Wold all end up left behind in one way or another in their respective stories. By having only a few focalizers, these novels provide a focus on a few important characters and help us to understand in some detail how each perspective is informed by the other(s). Meaning and purpose are negotiated. The real point of the game is to ally at least two of the characters in a purpose—to make it clear that alone we are not likely to find home. Egotism is a dead end and a short road traveled without companions.

In *Planet of Exile*, Le Guin's first published novel and the first in the Hainish space series, two of the three focalizers—Agat the Terran and Rolery the Werelian—become lovers. Wold, Rolery's father and a clan elder, is that third-wheel focalizer. His vision remains fixed on the past; he is unwilling to see a combined future for their two societies, and he dies only as he begins to envision such a future at the end of a very long, very conservative village life. We are shown how the two young people see each other, which evolves throughout the novel. They even engage in mind-speech and mind-hearing—extreme forms of shared narrative consciousness, to be sure. The aggregate effect of the constant shift in focalization is that we appreciate their growing love for and reliance on each other because we see it from each of them as well as from Wold's point of view, which at least helps the reader pull for them. They become joined in the purpose of helping each other's communities survive in the face of attack from a third group (an unfocalized and, therefore, necessarily alienated group).

In *The Eye of the Heron*, another in the Hainish series, two of the three focalizers are young, would-be lovers; the third, Vera, is an older woman who is more closely connected to the older way of life. In the case of the two young ones, however, it is the thought of the one that helps the other character proceed, and gives courage or vision. As Agat and Rolery represent the next stage of the journey of civilization on their planet, Luz and Lev represent the shared vision of a new journey in their own world. Before he dies, Lev gains hope from Luz that dialogue is possible between the city folk and the agrarians; Luz takes her memory of Lev with her as she and a group of Lev's people search for a new settlement. Each character uses another to help define his sense of purpose and to gain the strength to move. Because we are so connected to the characters' minds through their alternating focalizations, we can get past the fact that they actually share the same space in the novel only briefly. Vera, the third wheel, stays behind to start a new colony, but she is not alone. She stays with the old group that lives under the thumb of a more powerful colony. There is, then, a sense of stasis in the old world that is clear in comparison to the world of the new, pioneering group.

Even in *The Lathe of Heaven* and *The Word for World Is Forest* two of the three focalizers are highly connected, though not always physically present to each other. In *The Lathe of Heaven,* George Orr and Heather Lelache become close over the course of the novel. Haber, the third wheel, goes mad from trying to change the world alone through his dreams. In the four chapters focalized through George following Heather's appearance in the novel, she is a grounding force and keeps him focused as his dreams continue to reconstitute reality. In the two chapters in which Heather focalizes, she helps us see George in a way he can't see himself—as a strong and purposeful man. Their mutual viewpoints and their presence in each other's chapters tighten their bond and make it abundantly clear to the reader how they help each other cope with their constantly changing and potentially maddening world—even when they can't be together, which is often.

The Lathe of Heaven makes it abundantly clear that one needs help in order to construct a world on any level. At one point George is distressed at having dreamed Heather away. He receives a gift from one of the aliens who is having trouble communicating his point about community to George—a copy of the Beatles' "With a Little Help from My Friends" (*Lathe,* 154). The alien, limited in speech to English clichés, spouts "One swallow does not make a summer" and "many hands make light work" as a way to try to make his point clear (*Lathe,* 154). George taps into what the aliens, adept at dream weaving, call "*Er'perrehnne,*" a form of group reality formation used during "effective" dreaming (*Lathe,* 178). His first reaching out to the collective unconscious, so to speak, returns him to a world with Heather in it. His success is achieved through help from his "friends," and is why he can find home. Contrast this to Haber, doomed to go mad in his attempt to remake the world through solitary dreams.

Selver and Lyubov form a bond in *The Word for World Is Forest* that is made stronger through their mutual focalization of each other. Davidson ends up banished on an island—alone as at least two of the other third wheel characters end up. Lyubov and Selver see each other from the outside, giving the reader inner and outer views of each. The appreciation and understanding each feels for the other enables both to do the work they have to do in order to free Athshe from Terran exploitation: Lyubov writes a revealing ethnography of the Athshean people and Selver stages an armed revolution against the Terran military. They travel separate roads toward a common destination, keeping each other in mind and deed all the while.

Le Guin's *The Beginning Place* (1980) is the story of Hugh and Irene, adolescents discovering themselves and each other in their travels to the alternative/dream world of Tembreabrezi.[8] The narrator alternates focalization between these two focalizers. This is another exception in Le Guin's work—her only work with two focalizers, but the role of the third focalizer discussed in the novels above seems to be replaced by Hugh's and Irene's initial views of each other, views radically different from where they end up. They begin the novel seeing each other wrongly in the dimness of the twilight land of Tembreabrezi. They consider each other as obstacle rather than an ally, and it is the use of shifting focalization that helps us see how their views change over the course of the novel. In other words, the antagonizing world-view—the third position that will be left behind—is their own early view of each other.

Le Guin is a bit extreme in how parallel she makes those shifting focalizers. Chapters 1 through 8 alternate between Hugh's and Irene's perspectives, giving each character four chapters of focalization. Chapter 9, the last chapter, begins with Hugh, shifts to Irene, moves to the strict mimesis of dialogue without external narration, and ends with one brief paragraph of external narration. While this might seem to be a process of synthesis, the two young people remain separate while also establishing a commitment to one another.[9] By shifting focalizers, Le Guin allows us to learn how the two characters come to value each other and to see each other more truly. The development of their sympathy for each other enables them to construct a purpose in their last important journey from Tembreabrezi back to the real world. They grow from mutual resentment to mutual affection and interdependence and end up leaving their respective dysfunctional families on the way toward a new life together.

Single Focalizers: Isolation

There are four novels in the Hainish series that have single principal focalizers: *Rocannon's World* (1966), *City of Illusions* (1967), *The Dispossessed* (1974), and *The Telling* (2000).[10] In all of these novels the principle subtext is about isolation and its defeat. So it is important that though secondary characters will serve as partners, and only then from the distance of memory, we see through only one set of eyes. In *The Dispossessed* and *The Telling*, the power of memory—or the illusion of it through chronological displacement—helps the solitary protagonist connect to a loved one. Notice, too, that the publication dates of these novels in relation to the others discussed above indicate that Le Guin was experimenting with different ways to focalize throughout her writing history. This, in other words, is not a continuum of development on the part of the author, with the exception of the argument that *Malafrena*, her first novel, is unique in its narrative extremity.

The Dispossessed and *The Telling* are quite similar. Each is about a lone figure that finds himself or herself working underground to try to bring two societies together. Not only are the two novels similar in plot, they are similar in the way their stories are arranged to allow a solitary figure to connect with someone who provides a sense of purpose.[11] In *The Dispossessed,* that connection is achieved through alternating chapters that stagger the Anarres and Urras chapters; all of the Anarres chapters would come before the Urras chapters if they were placed in chronological order. Le Guin offers thematic parallels between the anachronic chapters as a way to provide transition, but the most important parallel is the general one between Shevek's study of simultaneity in temporal physics and the arrangement of the chapters. The alternation between place and time creates simultaneity of place and time in the reading experience.[12] Because of this structure, Shevek becomes connected to his "partner," Takver, throughout the book rather than only in the beginning. They are on different planets but still co-exist because of the constant narrative shift between past and present. While early stages in Shevek's childhood on Anarres mirror and alternate between the early chapters of his life as an alien on Urras, he is purposeless and a wanderer only. Shevek is a man on a mission with a clear sense of direction late in the book, when chapters depicting Shevek with Takver on Anarres mirror later chapters and alternate between his relationship with Takver and his fomenting the revolution on Urras.

In *The Telling* the use of narrative juxtaposition is more traditional. In this tale, Sutty, the Ekumen's envoy, finds that she must help a world retain its memory, which a new regime is trying to wipe out.[13] Sutty's memories of her lover, Pao, and of her aunt and uncle are interspersed in the narrative within different chapters but are a clear and constant source for her understanding and sense of commitment in the novel: "once the memory began, she could not stop it. She had to go through it until it let her go" (*Telling*, 2). Those memories never really let her go, however, nor she them—though she fears that she will ultimately lose them, and with them the words that will help her make sense of her new circumstance. She discovers, however, that "the . . . words were there, not lost, waiting in the darkness, ready to come when she called them" (*Telling*, 89); their "presence filled her" (89). The memories ground Sutty and enable her to think about the somewhat different, somewhat similar human relationships on Aka. Memory enables her to understand the implications of homophobia on Aka and the lifelong bond of the Maz couples.

Memory is a type of focalization, after all, and it allows the author to give us insight into the way that a character sees the world. Memory is also a less reliable source for filling in narrative gaps in a story. Sutty's memories of Pao are chosen not because they are a way to fill important gaps in the story, but because they facilitate her understanding of Aka in relation to Earth, which helps her define her purpose of protecting the threatened Akan culture. The memory of Pao fills Sutty with a sense of purpose in her work against regimes that repress free thought and free love. Memory keeps her from isolation. "Memory is also the joint between time and space," Mieke Bal tells us (147), and so operates like the narrative simultaneity of *The Dispossessed*. Even isolated spies can connect with partners through different types of anachrony. But it is clear in both cases that until the partners are "called up," the single focalizers are adrift in time and space, borne by the current without purpose and vulnerable to the egomania of a Haber or a Davidson.

City of Illusions and *Rocannon's World* also feature single character focalizers and protagonists on dangerous missions; however, both novels do
far less than other novels in terms of creating important and grounding partners in the narrative. While Rocannon has some native "hilfers" (highly in-
telligent life forms) accompanying him on his journey, they remain rather
one-dimensional and inaccessible to the narrator and the other characters.
And though in *City of Illusions* Falk travels a good distance with Estrel, a
woman he meets along the way, we never enter her consciousness or come to
believe that she influences (much less defines) his purpose. Indeed, it turns
out that she is a spy who is leading him to the enemy. Their partnership is a
lie, and Falk is left without any real companion to help him—unusual in a Le
Guin story. However, Falk's memory of companions from his past cause him
to feel loyalty to those people, and that knowledge inspires him to double his
efforts to confute the Shing. The memory of characters important in grounding Falk and defining his purpose makes his situation much like those of the
other "spies" Shevek and Sutty, though that influence is explored much less
in this novel, and the mission remains rather abstract and impersonal. It is as
if, in these early novels, Le Guin discovered an important feature of "home"
that would evolve over the course of her later work. I will pursue this idea in
the next chapter.

Among Le Guin's novels with external narration, focalizers tend to be
multiple in order to facilitate character connection and help us to appreciate
the reasons and implications for holding isolating ideological positions.
Even in cases when the focalizer is singular, Le Guin finds ways through
anachronism to create partners that help in the fundamental purpose of each
novel, as we have seen above. Richard Erlich is right when he says, "Le
Guin distrusts loners."[14] For with past or current partnership comes dialogue,
and from that comes a reliable and healthy sense of connection.

Character Narrators: Connection and Isolation

Two novels with character narrators are *The Left Hand of Darkness* (1969)
and *Very Far Away from Anywhere Else* (1976).[15] The first is Le Guin's Hugo
and Nebula-winning fourth book in the Hainish cycle; the second is her
fourth young adult novel and her first published realistic novel. Each gives
us the direct viewpoint of characters. The two books differ from each other
in how they handle the challenges of creating character pairs that define purpose. *The Left Hand of Darkness* achieves character closeness despite being
written in first person because the chapters alternate between two character
narrators as well as among different source texts, such as an Orgotan creation narrative, a biological report on Gethenian sexuality by the First
Observer, and folk tales. Genly Ai, Envoy of the Ekumen, begins the narrative by reporting that "the story is not all mine, nor told by me alone. Indeed,

I am not sure whose story it is; you can judge better" (*Left Hand*, 1). He and Estraven, the deposed Prime Minister of Gethen, share fifteen of the novel's twenty chapters and a mad weeks-long trek across a glacier to escape their pursuers. In *The Left Hand of Darkness,* Le Guin takes her more usual strategy of employing an external narrator with two or three character focalizers and removes the external quality entirely. The result is, not surprisingly, a difference in degree rather than kind. Through the character narration we are given deep insight into two characters from within and without, and their resulting intimate, narrative connection enables them to complete the larger purposes of the novel. Estraven's narration comes later in the book in the form of journal entries, and is used to help us revise our (and Genly's) opinion of his character, and of Genly's own. Le Guin chooses to allow the characters to speak to us from the same narrative distance, unlike in either *The Lathe of Heaven* or *The Word for World Is Forest* in which the external narrator and character focalizers were separated by different degrees of proximity. John Stephens claims that "the preponderance of first-person narrative in the second half of this century, with an especially strong form in the fad for double first-person narration in the late 1980s and early 1990s . . . overtly suggests that events are perceived and resolutions reached through a dialogic and negotiative process, thus affirming a confluence of perspective and, hence, validity of outcome."[16] This seems to be true of *The Left Hand of Darkness*—though it predates the "fad" Stephens observes. There is, ultimately, only misunderstanding between Genly Ai and Estraven, not ideological difference—exactly as it is with Hugh and Irene in *The Beginning Place*. Similar to *The Beginning Place*, *The Left Hand of Darkness* is the record of the correction of an important misunderstanding between like-minded characters. Genly Ai and Estraven both believe in the Ekumen (the union of all Known Worlds) and the petty provincialism of the two nation–states of the planet Winter. Both want them dead. The characters' different notions of pride keep them from communicating with any success in the beginning. Neither character needs to be made more empathetic to us, or to each other, ultimately.

Very Far Away from Anywhere Else is at the other end of Le Guin's narrative continuum from *Malafrena*. Although, since Malafrena is equally isolating, the books form a sort of circle. *Malafrena* contains an omniscient narrator and a protagonist who doesn't succeed in connecting in a lasting and fundamental way to another character, *Very Far Away from Anywhere Else* features a single character narrator, Owen, who constantly combats isolation by trying to connect to one other character.[17] "People are necessarily alone," Owen opines early on, and the narrative strategy used in this novel emphasizes that isolation (*Very Far*, 3–4). Natalie, Owen's chance at romance and friendship, is represented only through Owen. This is the price the narrative pays for reinforcing Owen's heightened sense of isolation through character narration. But it is clear throughout the novel that it is Natalie's shared belief in the importance of ideas that helps Owen survive adolescence. Natalie is, like Owen, passionate about ideas and engages Owen in dialogue about the connections between music (her interest) and cognitive psychology (his). Ideas connect them. It is the pressure of group-think—so depressing to Owen—that isolates him as an outsider, as different. While the narrative strategy isolates Owen, his relationship with Natalie helps provide him with the companion necessary for him to become secure with himself. "What I realize now is that she needed me just as badly as I needed her," Owen observes in retrospect (38).[18]

It is important that characters connect with one another in Le Guin's fiction. The novels that don't succeed so well in enabling characters to connect with other characters tend to be those that haven't received much critical attention, such as *Malafrena, Rocannon's World,* and *City of Illusions.* With the notable exception of *Malafrena,* the novels that show us multiple consciousness through multiple focalization or multiple character narration, achieve the greatest degree of character connection, which is vital for characters to achieve a sense of purpose and identity in Le Guin's fiction. The novels that form strong bonds between characters and have those characters accompany each other in some important way are the novels most critically acclaimed.[19]

The Suites

"Suite" is Le Guin's own term for her linked stories published in book form. She compares these books to the way a musical suite forms a whole through what seem to be separate parts.[20] Sutty remarks in *The Telling* that "short stories are only pieces of the long one" (226), which seems to be Le Guin's philosophy regarding story-suites. Her story-suites include *Orsinian Tales* (1976), *Searoad* (1991), and *Four Ways to Forgiveness* (1995).[21] I add to *Orsinian Tales* the most recent tale from that land, the eponymous tale from *Unlocking the Air and Other Stories.*[22] Also, since *Four Ways of Forgiveness* was published Le Guin has come out with a fifth way: "Old Music and the Slave Women"; I discuss this along with the suite to which it rightly belongs.[23]

The suites need to be set apart from Le Guin's other short story collections. *The Wind's Twelve Quarters* (1975), *The Compass Rose* (1982), *A Fisherman of the Inland Sea* (1994), *Unlocking the Air* (1996), *The Birthday of the World* (2002), and *Changing Planes* (2003) are collections of stories in which the tales have little to do with each other beyond being published since the last collection.[24] *Buffalo Gals and Other Animal Presences* (1987) is focused on animals, and includes new and previously published tales and poems that examine animals.[25] However, there is no narrative thread that unites them. [26]

Connecting Characters in Tales of Orsinia: Orsinian Tales
and "Unlocking the Air"

Orsinian Tales is a story cycle that examines different moments in the history of the fictitious East European nation of Orsinia. Mostly ignored by critics, the Orsinia stories are individually beautiful in their brevity, a true suite in concert. [27] The first of them to be published was "An die Musik" (1961)—in fact, it was Le Guin's very first published story. Le Guin published "An die Musik" along with ten previously unpublished tales to form the collection *Orsinian Tales* fifteen years later. The novel of Orsinia, *Malafrena*, came out three years after the story collection and focused exclusively on a few years in the third decade of the nineteenth century. [28] The latest Orsinia story is the eponymous tale from *Unlocking the Air*. It was first published in 1990, immediately after the fall of the Soviet Union. Le Guin has not been back to Orsinia since—at least not in print. [29]

Of the twelve short stories about Orsinia, all but "Ile Forest" employ an external narrator. This is not unusual for Le Guin, but Orsinia tales (and, indeed, all of her story-suites) differ from her novels by having mostly single focalizers. More than half of the twelve use single focalizers, and only two tales have more than two focalizers. One explanation is that like *The Dispossessed, The Telling, Rocannon's World*, and *City of Exile*, these tales of Orsinia tend to be about isolation. Even further, they are sad but hopeful tales of the attempt to connect to others in a country whose history is one long failed journey quest for identity. It isn't until "Unlocking the Air," in which the communist bloc crumbles, that Orsinia seems to have a chance at sovereignty and the ability to have regular relationships with its neighbors. In the stories of Orsinia, the country is as isolated as its inhabitants.

"The Fountains" features the most isolation in the collection; it is the story of how Dr. Kereth defects for only an afternoon. After eluding his watchers while at an academic conference in France, Kereth wanders about Versailles and Paris. There is only free indirect discourse in the tale, depicting his excitement and fear as he wanders, but he is alone in his temporary reverie, playing at freedom. A loyalist to the Orsinian cause, he returns to his captors eventually. There *are* individual tales of Orsinia that feature character pairs joining in order to find purpose, but those pairs don't always stay together. Usually a journey is undertaken alone.

There are partners in "The Barrow," but they are hardly supportive of each other. In this tale, set in the year 1150, the Lord Freyga, the focalizer, sees a visiting Catholic priest as "a fat black spider" and blight on the good fortunes of his house. [30] The free indirect discourse lets us see as Freyga does that "ropes and webs of darkness tangled thicker and thicker around the man-spider in the corner of the hearth. A tiny glitter showed under his brows. The lower part of his face moved a little. He was casting his spells deeper and deeper" (14). Free indirect discourse eliminates distance and helps us see how this man, distraught over his wife's struggle to give birth, can see this man as an evil demon in his home. He ultimately drags the priest out and sacrifices him on a pagan altar away from all other eyes. Freyga returns alone to his home, to a well-born son, and to a manor house overseeing a land divided between Christian and pagan rites. He is isolated and ultimately, we assume through guilt, becomes a patron of the church. It is a tale of a conflicted time in Orsinia, as all Orsinia tales are. It is a tale of a dark time when the partner on the journey is to be sacrificed rather than embraced in order for purpose to be found—and a dark purpose it is.

In "The Road East" we see through Maler's eyes alone. The year is 1956, and he has lost a friend who fought in the Resistance. Maler secludes himself away in his house with his mother. Provin, a co-worker, tells Maler that "there's nothing left to us now but one another."[31] Maler balks at the proffered connection with others and clings to his mother—his silent partner in stasis. A countrywoman who needs help leaving the city echoes Provin's sentiment when she says to Maler "when you turn your back on me, when you won't speak to me, my dear, then you're rejecting not only me, but your true self. After all, we have no one but each other" (79). He is ultimately moved to try to help her leave the city and return to her home. Though they are stopped at the bridge that leads out of the city, he seems to have been inspired by the attempt and the failure at the hands of a simple guard asking for papers. He comes home to inform his mother that he's going out alone in the besieged city to join the Resistance. The story is remarkably like Hugh's story in *The Beginning Place*, though Hugh finds a partner to help him in the journey to the city and in life. Maler is resigned more to what will likely be a violent end; though not hopeful, he is now at least not hopeless. He has a purpose that joins him to his fellow Orsinians.

Both "An die Musik" and "The Lady of Moge" are similar in that they shift focalizers, though only to emphasize isolation. In these stories the shift in focalization provides us with the points of view of main characters, but the shift only serves to show us that they won't understand each other, though we can understand each, making the story all the more ironic and bittersweet. We've seen Le Guin use two focalizers in both *The Beginning Place* and *Left Hand of Darkness* for the chance to show us misunderstanding remedied, but in these tragic-ironic tales in Orsinia the two focalizers keep their distance. In each story the main focalizer—the one whose eyes we see through at the end—is left alone and resigned to a life of unfulfilled dreams. In both cases, their own honor conspires to defeat them. We sympathize with these characters that are struggling not with villains, but with a world that seems to conspire against them and itself.

In "The House," "Ile Forest," and "Conversations at Night" there is some character connection. In "The House," Mariya returns to the city in 1965 to try to get back together with her ex-husband, Pier. Mariya, the single focalizer, deserted him years before, but she has found no solace. She returns to the city, alone, to find Pier left destitute by one of the many repressive regimes that pop up in Orsinian history. They cling to each other facing a journey toward an uncertain future in a politically dangerous time. She tells him at the end that he is "the house to which [she] comes home."[32] They find purpose in each other, and though they have more hope than they had, they don't have much. "Ile Forest" focuses on the lives of the narrator's sister and her new husband, Galven. The narrator's sister and brother-in-law live in a ruined home on the edges of the man's all-but-ruined life. The newlyweds work on building a new life together, but much of this new life is to be spent rebuilding the brother's life. The narrator seems more resigned to his sister's fate than he is hopeful about it. In "Conversations at Night," which takes place in 1920, the two focalizers, one left blind by war, ultimately lean on one another, but as in "Ile Forest," one sacrifices in order to help the other build a life. This means, in the characters' own words, "a long chance."[33] "Conversations at Night" is a story that comes close to hopefulness. Each character sees the presence of freedom in their union— in Mariya and Pier's case, him from isolation, her from her static life in the city. In any case, the stories feature attempts at purposeful movement with significant others, but achieving purpose and home is limited by the place.

The most hopeful of the stories are the three that are directly linked through the family Fabbre: "Brothers and Sisters," "A Week in the Country," and "Unlocking the Air." As a group this is by far the most hopeful, and the character couplings don't lead to isolation but to purposeful movement. The first, "Brothers and Sisters," is set in 1910. In the story, the principle focalizer, Stefan, leaves the city and a ruined life in search of a woman who he believes to be his best chance at a new life. He finds Ekata at her farmhouse at the end of his trek. He knows it is a risk: she may well rebuke him. She clings to him, however, signaling hope, and they ride off together the next morning: "running away, they laugh."[34]

The very next tale features Stefan's grandson, also named Stefan. It is 1962 and the grandson, a student in physics at the University in Krasnoy, travels with his friend Kasimir who is off to the countryside to visit his family. Stefan travels under some protest, for his friend Kasimir wants to get him away from his studies and visit his family and farm. Stefan travels out unwillingly, and after a long illness suffered on the farm, he comes to love Kasimir's sister Bruna. As the two friends ready to go home and walk through town, Kasimir is shot as a suspected freedom fighter. After being imprisoned for some days, Stefan is released and plans a solitary trip back, but Bruna finds him and holds fast to him. They decide to marry and return, we assume, to Krasnoy.

The trio of stories ends with the last tale of Orsinia, "Unlocking the Air." Krasnoy in 1990 is reeling under the collapse of the Soviet Union, and Orsinia is finally on the brink of freedom and cohesion for the first time. Stefan and Bruna's daughter Stefana is part of the coalition to help form a government when the time comes. Stefan and Bruna find themselves in the city square at the end. "They stood on the stones in the lightly falling snow and listened to the silvery, trembling sound of thousands of keys being shaken, unlocking the air, once upon a time."[35]

The implied partner in many of these tales is the country of Orsinia itself. The characters in the tales of Orsinia embark on a journey together that is marked by a sense of hope that flies in the face of reason—a purpose that Orsinia did not really dare hope to for until "Unlocking the Air." Characters sometimes find the partner for constructing purpose, but the larger story of place, in this case a country without a sense of identity, shapes those attempts at connection in ways that make them tales about battling isolation and despair. Some don't escape the fate of the land and stay alone, some find some solitary purpose with their embattled country, and a few find solace in the eye of the maelstrom with the ones to whom they cling.

Connecting Characters in Searoad

Or not. *Searoad*, a collection of stories set in the fictional Northern California coastal town of Klatsand, stresses the tragedy of character isolation even more than the tales of Orsinia do. Nobody really connects. Unlike its use in the novels, focalization here is used as a way to illustrate the links that are never made, but which would be of great value; we see this in the Orsinian tales "The Lady of Moge" and "An die Musik." What the shifts from single to multiple external focalizers and then to character narration by one or several characters illustrate, however, is that there are a variety of ways to show the same self-enforced and ironic seclusion. The irony of missed opportunity is more common and almost palpable in this story-suite. Each tale gives us access to the consciousness of one or more characters as a way to reinforce the fact that those in Klatsand share place but not personal space—the sum of the stories presents us with the same ultimate problem of connection seen in *Malafrena*. Klatsand is a place in which characters are surrounded by potential help but never reach out for it—they are each Tantalus starving in the midst of plenty. The characters in Klatsand remain isolated because they don't reach out to others in their land—or do so feebly and too late because of the dramatic irony that characterizes the tales. The sympathy due each by other characters is shared only with and by the reader. As Orsinia is a land desperately reaching out for a future, its characters reach out with equal desperation; Klatsand is a town isolated on the coast, its characters emulate their community by staying isolated as individuals hemmed in by sea and mountains.

There are the single focalizers in Klatsand stories. Each of them chooses not to connect with the outside. Rosemarie in "The Ship Ahoy" shuts herself in one of the rooms of her motel and reads science fiction novels. She hears crying through the wall: one of her patrons suffers untold heartache. She sympathizes through the wall, but "she was afraid. She thought as hard as she could, trying to send the energy through the door, to send the words to him: 'It's all right. It will be all right.'"[36] Her fear keeps her in her room. "She could not help him" (13). It is the feeling, here and throughout, that reaching out beyond a tentative gesture is actually beyond the emotional capabilities of the characters.

Warren, a solitary traveler to Klatsand, finds himself associated with "The Sightseeing Seniors of Cedarwood," much to his displeasure. He decides, however, to cling to his isolation by denying the association: "'I'm not with them,' Warren said with a flash of irritation. He wanted not to be *involved* with them."[37] He finds himself interested in connection by the end, but by then it is too late.

In "Bill Weisler," the protagonist stays away from the beach "these days" because of all the people. "These days there was always somebody else . . . The only way to keep away from them was to stay in and work."[38] Bill Weisler fears contact, especially with women: "if there were things to say to women, he did not know them" (61). He has contact with characters from two other stories in the collection, but fails to make any real connection with them. While the tale ends with a hopeful conversation between Bill and Jilly from "In and Out," the preceding story in the collection, we know that Jilly's own situation will probably mean that little more contact will happen, but we can hope.

"Texts" is the brief tale of a woman, Johanna, who is either mad or a visionary—or both. The narrator gives us insight into her consciousness and allows us to understand how she sees writing in the world all around her—in things like sea foam and lace collars. We never leave her consciousness and we're never shown her in contact with another soul. Her gift or curse is her own burden to bear.

Shirley in "Quoits" is, like Bill Weisler, able to make some sort of contact with another, but, like Bill, will have to settle with a gesture rather than real connection. As she mourns the loss of her lover, Barbara, Shirley has to contend with Barbara's daughter, Jen.[39] The tale chronicles the uneasy truce established between them. But Shirley "had not done what should be done" with Jen: "they must weep together if need be" ("Quoits,"103). After Jen has gone through Barbara's things she leaves the next day, "fierce and tearful" ("Quoits,"108). Shirley, left alone, walks the beach. She is left with a strong sense of who she is, but a good part of that is "lonely." At the end of her walk "the wind blew through her. Her feet were cold in their damp socks and wet shoes, and she was hungry" ("Quoits,"109).

Character narration, or first-person address, doesn't necessarily force character isolation, as *The Left Hand of Darkness* proves, but it certainly creates the right conditions for it. In these stories it gives us a different way to see isolation. The nameless librarian in "True Love" finds her new lover, Antal, connecting with another woman—Rosemarie, whom we met in "Ship Ahoy." We might be hopeful that Rosemarie has found a real connection with someone since the death of her inattentive husband over the course of the four stories between "Ship Ahoy" and "True Love." But when we consider that Antal is also currently seeing the librarian, surely unknown to Rosemarie, we can't hope for any real relationship between any of them. When the librarian deduces that Antal and Rosemarie have slept together, it reinforces both the librarian's loneliness and Rosemarie's impending return to isolation.

Two of the tales that employ character narration that precede "Hernes" are, perhaps, the most hopeful regarding a character's ability to make a connection. In "Crossroads" the character has to leave town to have that saving relationship. Ailie carries the burden of her mother's life in her mind. Terina, another waitress, tells Ailie that she sees the specter of Ailie's mother around her on two separate occasions. Ailie tells Terina, "It's my mama," and Terina says she "thought maybe."[40] "I have been carrying her around lately," Ailie admits, and this provokes her to call her own daughter in another town (118). Ailie tells her, "I was thinking I wanted to see you" and Irma, her daughter, arranges for Ailie to move in (118). What makes this tale different from the others is that a character succeeds in making a connection, but that means leaving Klatsand. To stay in Klatsand is to remain isolated. Travelers and residents in Klatsand both find it impossible to forge connections within this land of isolation. Klatsand is a jealous partner.

"Sleepwalkers" introduces us to five speakers, who are all staying at or running Hannah's Hideaway, another motel in Klatsand. The story's title comes from the first speaker's perception that the people in Klatsand are all sleepwalkers—people who live "a mass-produced existence, stereotypes, getting their ideas from TV."[41] He, the dramatist John Felburne, misreads them. Clearly the people of Klatsand, the people of these twelve tales, are not types, but he sees only the external effects of their isolation. We come to find that Ava, the maid and principle interest of the narrative, is regarded differently by each speaker. Only one of the speakers knows about Ava's secret —the murder suicide of her husband who killed her daughter. We never hear from Ava herself, however, and each speaker addresses an external narratee. While Katherine McAn keeps contact with Ava after Ava has confided in her the story of her family, Katherine can only offer sympathy. Katherine wonders to herself, "Why do I want her to get a better job, nicer work, higher wages—what am I talking about? The pursuit of happiness?" (98) as if she realizes that there are some conditions that can't be fixed by "success." If

Ava grows from her contact with Katherine we aren't going to see it. At the end of the story, Ava thanks Katherine for their talk and tea—"I really enjoyed talking with you" (98)—and goes "down the neatly raked path that winds between the cabins, among the dark old spruce trees, walking carefully, one foot in front of the other. No sudden movements" (98). Ava is left among the dark old trees of Klatsand, a solitary figure still.

"Hernes," the sixty-five-page novella that concludes the suite, gives us four character-narrators—but heartache won't be alleviated by numbers.[42] As we saw in "Sleepwalkers," this story provides numbers to underscore the degree to which isolation occurs despite the presence of company. In this case the isolation is within generations of family. Five generations of women are shown, four of which speak. The youngest, Jaye, is not old enough to enter her monologue—it surely hasn't been a conversation. There are conversations recorded, surely, but the constant fragmentation provided by the monologue form keeps any sense of dialogue from developing.

Two of Le Guin's tales provide more than one perspective through an external narrator, much as the author's novels do: "In and Out" and "Hand, Cup, Shell." The effect is the same, however: increased perspectives only reinforce the ironic degree to which they miss the chance to connect with empathetic souls. In the first of these two, the tale shifts from Jilly's perspective to Kaye's, back to Jilly's, and lastly returns to Kaye's. The movement back and forth shows us their ironic failure to connect despite similar losses in life. Kaye has lost a daughter; Jilly is losing her mother to cancer. While Kaye sees a kinship between them regarding loss, Jilly only sees her own problems. Each woman works to transform a house into a space of comfort, though one wants stasis and the other transformation. Jilly works on a clay model of a Chinatown house while her mother is busy dying of cancer in the house they share. Kaye, in contrast, has begun the process of transforming her dead daughter's room from a museum (what her husband wants—a monument to changelessness) to a room that is clean and full of healthy memories. Jilly needs what Kaye has to offer—an empathetic ear willing to listen. Jilly won't see it; she only resents the woman who comes "here with [her] dead daughter."[43] Jilly can't even go into the same room with her mother. She remains afraid of one person, resentful of the other. Jilly denies both herself and Kaye the chance to heal through dialogue.

The other tale in external narration that gives us insight into the consciousness of more than two characters is "Hand, Cup, Shell." This story shows us the thoughts of three generations of women—May, Rita, and Gret. It is, then, closest to the story "Hernes" as a cross-generation narration that fails to show us real communication. Le Guin writes, "Having come to be together over the weekend, they fled one another without hesitation, one to the garden, one to the kitchen, one to the bookshelf, two north up the beach, one south to the rocks."[44] The three women focalizers share their insights *about* each other but not *with* each other. Only the narratee and, by extension, the reader, knows the whole story.

Le Guin uses focalization and character narration in these stories in order to highlight isolation while allowing the reader to understand and appreciate the ironic and unnecessary separation that persists in people's lives. Readers connect with characters through pity and sympathy; yet the characters remain distant. In Klatsand the land is a partner, but it is a jealous partner. It is a land full of stories of isolation. Each character that stays there shares him- or herself with the land, but not with another soul. Others who dare connect must leave to do it. The sad irony of Klatsand is paralleled by the tragic–ironic Orsinia, a land where the individual struggles with the land in the hope of finding identity and connection. Those in Orsinia who find a partner in struggle do so only when Orsinia is forgotten as the focus, but the land is always in the background making the connection between characters a "long chance" indeed.

Five Ways to Connect Characters: Four Ways to Forgiveness *and "Old Music and the Slave Women"*

Le Guin's most recent story-suite is comprised of a combination of *Four Ways to Forgiveness* (1995) and the story "Old Music and the Slave Women" (1999). "Old Music and the Slave Women" is, Le Guin says, "a fifth way to forgiveness that didn't get itself written in time to get into the book. It is, however, a bit bleaker than the first four . . . It is a mourning for the horrors of war. Old ways, new wars, Goya's war. Our wars" (Gevers, November/December 2001). The five tales explore many of the same issues about the dangers of character isolation, silence, and stasis in forging a sense of self and home. But the suite that features Yeowe and Werel is different than what we see in either the Orsinia or Klatsand suites regarding character connection.[45] Still, her work in the novel shows, it shouldn't be taken as "progress," necessarily«md»it may well be that her next suite will examine more isolation than connection.

The *Forgiveness* suite covers only five tales, in contrast to the twelve in each of the other two suites. It also differs in the relative unchanging nature of the narrative address: with the exception of the book's second tale, "Forgiveness Day," the tales feature single focalizers. Rather than this being a matter of trying to reinforce isolation—as we see in *Rocannon's World, City of Illusions, The Dispossessed,* and *The Telling*—the stories in this suite seem to employ single focalizers for other reasons. In four of the five tales of the suite, the characters with which the principle focalizer will connect show up late in the story, making the parallel focalization we see in many of the novels difficult to find. In the first tale, "Betrayals," the recognition of a partner comes late in the narrative, but the partner himself is a subject of interest throughout the story. The focalizer spends her time—and ours—revising her notions of a man whose reputation precedes him. It is important for our shared discovery—Yoss's and ours—that Abberkam's consciousness remain inscrutable for a while. We discover when Yoss does at the end of the tale that he is someone with whom she might journey.

The only exception is the second tale in the suite, where we are given only two focalizers. The use of two focalizers in "Forgiveness Day" is useful because both characters have misconceptions of the other, unlike in "Betrayals" where it is only Yoss's impressions of Abberkam that need revision. Le Guin uses dual focalizers to dramatize either a simultaneous revision of ideas in characters (*The Left Hand of Darkness* and *The Beginning Place*) or an ironic and mutual missing of the point ("The Lady of Moge" and "An die Musik"). Otherwise she seems to prefer single perspectives or triangulation.

In "Betrayals," Yoss, the main character, lives alone in order to purify herself through silence, yet she also yearns for contact with the worlds of the Ekumen, about which she constantly reads. The story explains the practice of self-imposed stasis and isolation: "Growing old, the people of Werel and Yeowe might turn to silence, as their religion recommended them to do: when their children had grown, when they had done their work as householder and citizen, when as their body weakened their soul might make itself strong, they left their life behind and came empty-handed to lonely places."[46] This is implied to be the residual practice of escaped slaves: staying quiet and separate from others was a way to keep free after escaping the cities. Yoss doesn't yet see the irony embedded in this slave notion of freedom. She, like Hugh and Irene, fools herself into thinking that cloistered virtue is freedom and that silence is the answer. However, she bemoans her failure to pull herself from the fabric of society: "What a fool, she thought, starting slowly home on the causeway path, what a fool I was to think I could ever drink water and be silent! I'll never, never be able to let anything go, anything at all. I'll never be free, never be worthy of freedom" (4). Yoss ends up reaching out to Abberkam and moving between homes until her own is lost in a fire. By weaving a connection between her home and Abberkam's, Yoss is able to find her way "home" with Abberkam. The story ends with Yoss's promise to try to continue the dialogue that she and Abberkam have begun. In contrast to the characters in Klatsand, Yoss rebels against her isolation through her purposeful movement outward toward and with another. Ironically, Yoss's world imposes isolation through tradition; in Klatsand it becomes tradition through unconscious practice.

All five of the narratives link silence and stasis to the slave-master relationships, which are thousands of years old on Werel and Yeowe. Silence is the equivalent of stasis and must be overcome. Silence is found in other places, too. In "Forgiveness Day," Solly's body guard, Teyeo, a member of a

prestigious military family bound to an estate, is imprisoned in his silence—
due in part to the value placed on that silence by his own people. Teyeo's silence, admired by Solly, has taken years of practice,[47] but it has robbed him
of the expression he needs to free himself from a dead past and misplaced
loyalties for a home now lost. "He was ashamed of his anger, his grief, himself. He wanted to tell [Solly] that she had been a help and hope to him too,
that he honored her, that she was brave beyond belief; but none of the words
would come. He felt empty, worn-out. He felt old" (87). When Teyeo learns
to talk to Solly, he fastens himself to someone who will ultimately help him
rediscover home. Her talk, seemingly nonstop in contrast to his extraordinary
silence, opens him up and wins him over. The two, who begin the tale actually despising one another, depend on each other by the end. They have
learned about each other, and about themselves through each other. He has
broken through the silence and she stops talking long enough to finally listen.

The third and fourth *Forgiveness* stories are linked more closely than they
are to others because they feature the same characters. We've seen this in the
Orsinia suite with the Fabbre stories. In the first of the two, "A Man of the
People," Havzhiva is the focalizer. He tries to find someone with whom he
can be at home in mutual purpose. As a boy in backwoods Hain he finds that
he is interested in becoming a historian, which means leaving Iyan Iyan, the
girl he loves. She stays; he goes. As he flies off for school in Kathad, he sees
the world "fall away";[48] he feels isolated. While training to be a Mobile he
comes to love Tiu, but she also must be in motion, unlike Iyan Iyan, and is
off to another world, Terra, while he finishes his training. She goes; he stays.
He decides that "there was no going back [to Iyan Iyan] and no going forward [to Tiu]. So he must turn aside" (116). When he gets to Yeowe as
subenvoy for the Ekumen, he reflects that in the eighty-light-year journey all
those he has known have died (117). He is alone, silent, waiting for a sense
of home.

He meets Yeron almost thirty pages into the narrative. She, first introduced to us through Hav's consciousness as "an old woman," becomes
someone to whom he can cling and find purpose in after his long journeys
(121). While Hav doubts himself, Yeron is confident. Together they help
Yeowe find a place for women at the table of freedom. Together they move
with this purpose of a people's Liberation.

There is a break in the text, a gap of time near the end of the story that
covers almost twenty years—the time that Hav and Yeron are separated by
their respective journeys. When the story resumes we find Hav a man of 55
years going to see Yeron, now 74. We learn only then that they "had never
made love, but there had always been a desire between them, a yearning to
the other" (142). They share wine and memories, talking about how it was
only after coming to Yotebber to meet Yeron that Hav learned "how to walk
with my people" (144). He has found a partner in the people in Yeowe and a

partner named Araha after learning purpose with Yeron. Orsinians hadn't won freedom until "Unlocking the Air" and the Klatsanders stay isolated by their own choosing. Because he found his voice with the help of a partner, he found purpose with a free people.

"A Woman's Liberation," the story immediately following "A Man of the People," the book's last story, is the story of that gap of nearly twenty years missing in the story that precedes it. It is the story of Rakam, Hav's partner ("Araha," we come to find, is a term of endearment). Hav's story focuses on his partnership with Yeron, but it is clear that he has had another partner for eighteen years helping him with his sense of purpose, helping him keep his sense of home. Rakam's story is not unlike Hav's in that most of it is about her search for a purpose and home. It is at the end of the story that she finds him. As with all of the stories, this is a tale of risk—the risk of breaking out of the silence taught in youth in order to find partner, purpose, and home. She begins her life as a house slave on a large plantation on Werel. She is a "use" slave, which means she serves as a sexual partner. Her life is a series of broken relationships. She is taken from one plantation to a second, freed from that one and taken to the city, put to work in the city, and then smuggled onto a ship headed for Yeowe by Envoy Esdan ("Old Music"). Her "companion" during her rough start on Yeowe is Tualtak, a complaining, self-centered person who is of no help to Rakam in finding a purpose except that it is Tualtak's illness that leads Rakam to see a doctor. In the city she finds Dr. Yeron, whom we have already met in "A Man of the People." As Esdan is responsible for sending both Hav and Rakam to Yeowe, Dr. Yeron is the partner that helps each find a purpose before they each find the other to maintain that purpose. In fact, at the first conversation between Rakam and Hav, Yeron observes, "So, you found her."[49] Connecting with others is vital for slaves and aliens in a hostile world, after all, and Rakam has found that she is only able to find her way toward purpose when she speaks out, which she does in each place after her freedom from the second plantation. Esdan, Yeron, and ultimately Hav are partners in her finding her purpose, her sense of home. With their help she flees her oppressive home world, gets work as a teacher, and becomes serious about her writing, authoring "A Woman's Liberation." Rakam tells us that before meeting Hav her "gate was locked. Now it was open" (207). She ends the tale commenting on discovering purpose through contact with another: "So I wrote this book for my friend, with whom I have lived and will die free" (208).

The last tale in the story-suite is "Old Music and the Slave Women," a tale published four years after *Four Ways to Forgiveness*. Our man in Werel, Esdan, is the principal focalizer. Esdan appears in four of the five tales, but is featured in only the last. He is a means for others to find home in those tales —he connects Solly with Teyeo and sends Hav to Yeowe where he will meet Rakam, whom he as also has sent to Yeowe. Shortly after the events that lead him to send Rakam to Yeowe, Esdan, or "Old Music," decides to leave his embassy to find out what is going on. He is Chief Intelligence Officer of the Ekumenical Embassy to Werel but has been kept in his embassy without contact with the Liberation Command. In order to dispel propaganda that the staff of the Embassy has been co-opted into supporting the Legitimates (or "Jits"), he has been invited to try to cross over to the part of the city held by the Liberation Army, which is "the tricky bit."[50] He is picked up by a faction of the Legitimates and taken to Yaramera, one of the most impressive plantations before the civil war.

The silence that keeps him from achieving a purpose is palpable throughout the story. He begins by being kept silent in the Embassy (not unlike Sutty in *The Telling*). After the civil war has begun, Voe Deo, the largest city of Werel, "still stood, most of its fifteen million people were still there, but its deep complexity was gone. Connections were broken. Interactions did not take place. A brain after a stroke" ("Women," 8). His attempt to cross over, to help heal the stroke, is thwarted, however. After the factionalists, who are eager to use him to their own ends, discover him, he realizes that silence through circumspection is his one chance to stay alive. Even while he is in the car leading him to Yaramera, he avoids eye contact with his captors ("Women," 9). During the ride he is told to "piss himself" by one of his guards, to which he "considered possible replies, good-humored, joking, not offensive, not provocative, and kept his mouth shut" ("Women," 10). Silence is his only protection. He is part of someone else's purpose, on someone else's journey: "During a revolution you don't choose. You are carried in a bubble in a cataract, a spark in a bonfire" ("Women," 10).

Once on the plantation, two of his guards torture Esdan, which is not for the purpose of getting him to talk, but as a means to silence him further through humiliation. His alien presence offends them. After a while a factionalist leader, Rayaye, comes to talk to Esdan. "We can talk," Rayaye assures him, but it is acquiescence rather than dialogue that Rayaye is after ("Women," 16). It isn't until Esdan meets the house slave Gana, who comes to bind one of his feet broken during torture, that he meets someone who might help him discover a new sense of purpose. But at first it is only the silence of a slave that he receives from her. For days after that "no one came into his room but the scared woman, Heo, and the zadyo who came once a day to ask if he had all he needed" ("Women," 19). During his convalescence he thinks about his time on Werel: "His captivity, his treatment here, had displaced, disoriented him . . . He had been at home on Werel, and now was not. Inappropriate comparisons, irrelevant memories. Alienated" ("Women," 22).

He begins, however, to talk with Gana and her daughter Kamsa, mostly about Kamsa's baby, Rekam. "He was cautious of speaking to any of them at first lest he get them into trouble" ("Women," 20). He does decide to reach out when it seems safe, and one scene serves as a metaphor for his reaching out to this small house slave family of three generations. He notes the three sitting far from the house: "The distances at Yaramera, even inside the house, were daunting to a lamed man. When he finally gets there, he says, 'I am lonely. May I sit with you?'" ("Women," 28) His loneliness and self-enforced silence in response to his captors cause him to reach out to this family. Their safety at the hands of one faction, then another, and then in the face of an approaching Liberation Army is Esdan's new purpose; they become home—his new home on Werel. In this most Orsinian tale of the five, Esdan looks for purpose, a sense of home, in the company of others swept up in the turmoil of a land in search of itself. By the end of the tale, the group heads down to the house compound, the slave quarters, to await the Liberation Army. Though he doubts his usefulness as an Envoy over the years, he doesn't doubt his use in relation to this small family, and he seems to have found a purpose, if only for a while.

The novels show us that, with the exception of *Malafrena*, multiple focalization is a way to create character connection. *Malafrena,* however, is more like the first two of Le Guin's suites—it offers multiple focalizers as a way to highlight isolation. Single focalizers were more likely to be isolated in the novels. The suites are an experiment in the use of single and multiple focalizers, and when we compare them to the novels, we learn something more about the way Le Guin connects or isolates characters.

In the first two suites, Le Guin uses the fragmented quality of a story collection to achieve a clear effect: isolation. On the other hand, her novels with single focalizers reinforce isolation by having characters stay alone over the long haul. In the Orsinia suite the majority of individual focalizers presented over the course of twelve stories reinforces isolation and fragmentation in a way even greater than more linear, plot driven novels. The Searoad suite, equal to the Orsinia suite as a collection of twelve stories, divides isolation between single focalizers and overwhelming focalizer numbers, as seen in *Malafrena*. Those suites, thematically about isolation, use the text to reinforce the subtext. They underscore the irony of isolation through the singularity or impossible multiplicities of view over what are simultaneously separate and related stories. *Malafrena*, as a tale of Orsinia, fittingly serves as a sort of crossover text. As her first novel, we see in it the seeds of both the novel and the suite, though what marks it as unsuccessful is how much and how little of each a Le Guin novel and suite we can detect in it.

The Forgiveness suite, however, offers us a view of character connection through mostly single focalizers. And, unlike the first two suites, this one shows that the collection of different stories creates an aggregate of connection rather than reinforcing separation. We see moderation, pacing, and an important difference in theme in the Forgiveness suite. While the first two suites are illustrations of how silence creates stasis, how the failure to connect (through either governmental policy or human shortcomings) is what keeps people from discovering an identity or a purpose, this last suite is about the defeat of silence. While there are single focalizers in most of the suite, something that would indicate isolation in a Le Guin work, the characters manage to fight through the forces of isolation (self-imposed or otherwise) by the end of each long tale in order to connect with others. In this suite the fewer number of stories allows for greater development of that attempt to connect (the suites are all about the same length). In the other suites the juxtaposition of tales that feature the same characters is meant to highlight the ironic separation. In the Forgiveness suite the presence of the same characters fighting through silence reinforces, through their repetition, the idea that the people's individual successes will ultimately build connection. The fewer number of stories that are more carefully developed regarding the process of connection is in sharp contrast to the many brief tales of failure repeated in sharp succession in the first two suites in order to emphasize the continued failure of the communities.

As in the novels, then, the suites operate on a continuum of character connection through narration. The more tales, the shorter the tales, and the more extreme the focalization strategy (one or many viewpoint characters), the more likely we will have isolation. As the stories become longer and fewer, the more developed the single viewpoint becomes, and the more likely the characters will break out of isolation. The more connection the tales have when the tales are fewer, the more likely the single focalizers will work as multiple focalizers do in Le Guin's novels. There are at total of six focalizers in the Forgiveness suite as opposed to the more than twenty in the other suites; the difference between the Forgiveness suite and the novels with multiple focalizers is that the former doesn't require that the focalizers connect to each other—only to other characters. The result is that it doesn't create the burden of multiple and interrelated focalization as seen in *Malafrena*. The Forgiveness suite is the experiment that shows the versatility of the narrative strategies Le Guin uses to reinforce the themes of connection or isolation in what we might call her books that aren't randomly collected by theme or genre.

Children's Picture Books: A Genre of Multiple Connections

Maria Nikolajeva notes that first person is often used in children's chapter books to allow some distance between the telling and the event while also allowing the narrator "to comment on [his or her] own shortcomings and provide educational conclusions for the reader."[51] But in picture books, it is more common for writers to use external narration. Omniscient, external narration allows the writer to provide the child–reader with the thoughts of any and all characters, but more typically it is actually used as a way to stay utterly external to the thoughts of those characters. We see in books for the youngest of readers a distance from the internal lives of characters; Le Guin notes that "all myths and legends and folktales, all young children's stories, almost all fiction until about 1915, and a vast amount of fiction since then, use this voice" (1998, 87). Le Guin argues that external narration that is either entirely omniscient or entirely removed from characters' consciousness is very difficult to write.[52] Characters connect with each other in these forms as well, and it seems that no form of narration limits Le Guin's ability to accomplish this very important condition for her characters. As is the case in her works for adults, characters in Le Guin's children's books find the important links with others to help them in their quests for purpose.

All 12 of her picture books employ external narration; there isn't a first-person tale among them. We see the same proclivity for external narration in her adult work. What varies is the degree to which the narrator allows us insight into the thoughts of characters. While it's true that even in the Catwings quartet there is omniscience—even some of the blurring effect of free indirect discourse—Le Guin almost always stays out of the heads of her children's book characters when she has multiple characters that share thoughts through dialogue. One limitation on the ability of characters to share their hopes and desires through dialogue is the interesting limitation Le Guin puts on interspecies communication. Some creatures can communicate across species, but animals in Le Guin's children's books do not usually communicate with people using spoken language.

The Catwings series (1988–1999) is a good place to consider her different use of narration.[53] The books rely on dialogue to show characters' thoughts for the most part, especially in the first two books. In the first book, the four original catwings travel together from the city to the country. Along the way they speak their thoughts aloud to each other. Le Guin lets their conversation, in the form of direct discourse, speak for itself. As the series continues, however, the group spreads out in location and mission. In the second book, *Catwings Return* (1989), two of the cats fly back to the city to check on their mother. There, too, the direct discourse of dialogue serves as the primary vehicle for thought, though there is one moment when the narrator shares the misgivings each kitten has as the two try to find their way home. Le Guin writes, "Deep in his heart, James was afraid they could not find the way back to Overhill farm. Deep in her heart, Harriet was afraid of the same thing" (*Catwings Return*, 43). This is unusual since the catwings share almost everything else. In the third and fourth books, though, the emphasis shifts to individual characters, one of which is made silent by trauma, so some other techniques are employed. In the third book, *Wonderful Alexander and the Catwings* (1994), Alexander's thoughts are reported by the narrator ("He liked to think of himself as Wonderful Alexander. And he intended to do wonderful things" [*Wonderful*, 2]), but often his thoughts are represented by quoted monologue ("'I'm not afraid of dogs!' Alexander thought. 'I'll scratch their noses!'" [6]) in keeping with the style of the series.[54] So, too, in

Jane On Her Own (1999), the title character, a more troubled kitten, says "to herself" lines like "But I like difficult things"(*Jane*, 3). But we see an occasional internal thought reported indirectly by the narrator: "Did having wings mean she had to be lonely?" (10). Whenever possible, even in the later, more solitary Catwings narratives, direct speech is employed. The internal life of the winged cats is largely left mysterious, as is probably fitting for their exotic design.

There is a continuum of omniscience in her children's books. As we see above, the Catwings books use limited omniscience, as do *The Adventure of Cobbler's Rune* (1982) and *A Ride on the Red Mare's Back* (1992).[55] In *Fish Soup (1992), A Visit from Dr. Katz* (1988), *Solomon Leviathan* (1983), and *Fire and Stone* (1989) there is no omniscience at all.[56] At the other end of the spectrum are the title characters of *The Adventure's of Cobbler's Rune*, *Tom Mouse* (2002) and *Leese Webster* (1979), who are isolated by place or language through their respective stories and serve as clear focalizers for the narration.[57] Leese has one or two words with other spiders, but we are told that "spiders are not sociable people" (*Leese*, n.p.). Tom, however, gets some advice from "an old hobo rat who rode the freight trains," though we never hear Tom's words (*Tom*, n.p.). More important, they cannot communicate with the other most important and enabling characters in the book: the cleaning women in Leese's room who spare her life and tell the world of her web-tapestries and Tom's Ms. Powers who takes Tom under her wing. Tom can only dance his joy to communicate with his human traveling partner. Tom's thoughts are made known as he travels. We are told early on in *Tom* that "when the train gave a little jerk and slid forward, he nearly burst into tears." Later we learn that, "he felt lonely. He felt very lonely. But he ate his crumb and his bit of bacon, and was brave" (*Tom*). And while there is a bit of thought spoken aloud in *Leese Webster*, Leese's thoughts are often shared through the narrator: "she liked her lonely room; she would have been quite content, but for one thing. She was never quite satisfied with the webs she wove" (*Leese*, n.p.). The limits of language isolate them, making omniscience necessary.[58]

The catwings can communicate with dogs and birds but not with Hank and Susan who keep them secret from the human (adult) world. Marianne cannot communicate with her two cats that, together, tend her sickbed as her "Dr. Katz." We either are given dialogue by both humans and critters, inscrutable to each other (*Tom Mouse, Catwings, Leese Webster*) or we are left wondering what the other thinks (*A Visit from Dr. Katz*). This is interesting because in *Tom Mouse, Catwings*, and *Leese Webster*, these are *important* relationships that are established through unspoken understanding. The catwings rely on humans—Hank and Susan, "Poppa," Sarah Wolf—for their well being; only "Poppa" turns out to be a real threat, but even he is well meaning. Tom relies on Ms. Powers to keep him hidden from train porters and other dangers in their travels. And Leese relies on the understanding of the cleaning ladies. In two of the cases, it is important that the human understand, inherently, something about the special needs of each creature: the catwings are endangered by their difference; Tom is in danger as a solitary traveler among humans. The women are moved to let him go rather than kill him—more perhaps to do with old wives' tales about the bad luck in killing spiders than artistic respect, but they clearly make an exception for Leese, perhaps unconsciously moved by a connection they don't understand.

An exception, as there must be, is *Fire and Stone*, in which the townsfolk misunderstand the dragon's roar as only a roar: "RRRAAAHHHX" turns out to be "Rocks," a request to be fed as simple as it is terrifyingly loud (n.pg.). Another exception to the human-animal communication problem appears in *A Ride on the Red Mare's Back*, but there the mare is a toy horse magically turned real and life-sized as a companion to the girl on her trek. Once the journey of one night is complete, the Red Mare becomes a toy again, unable to communicate with the girl. And once the dragon gets through to the two children in *Fire & Stone*, and gets fed his rocks, he buckles under the weight of his meal and turns into a hillock of rock himself, unable to communicate again.

Narration strategies depend on the degree of isolation that characters experience, not unlike her strategy with novels and story-suites. The more characters in union the less omniscience and the more dialogue functions as focalization. The fewer characters the more omniscience is relied upon, but in all cases the limits of human-creature communication is observed. This pattern has implications for communication and connection. The greatest challenges for connection occur in *Leese Webster, Tom Mouse*, and *Fire and Stone* as a result. The most connection happens where there is the opportunity for dialogue, as we see in *Solomon Leviathan* and the first few Catwings books. But, regardless of the degree of isolation a character experiences, the character is not permitted to succeed without the assistance of others in various degrees—whether the aiding characters are of the same species or not. *Despite* the limits of verbal communication, characters help each other find purpose, from the whimsical to the serious. The way Le Guin combines her continua of dialogue, focalization, and species communication all result in connection.

A strong subtext throughout Le Guin's work is the examination of what it means to be connected to others or isolated from them. She experiments with that question across genre, but also—and maybe more importantly—through the use of different strategies of narration and focalization. By alternating types of narration and focalization she creates different degrees and kinds of distance between characters even as it is clear that connection is the prize in her work. Even as there is a continuum of character based on

species, examined in the last essay, there is a continuum of isolation rein-
forced through narration and focalization strategies. Le Guin shows us that
there are as many ways to avoid isolation as there are to be isolated.

What we learn by examining this according to the different genres of
stand-alone fiction is that with each group there are different limits, different
opportunities, but the same issues—connection and isolation—are at stake.
In each genre the characters that connect succeed—and the odds are long for
some, like Tom Mouse and Esden and Genly Ai. Those who fail to connect,
which only happens in adult fiction, can be shown to do so differently in the
novel and in the suite, though *typically* connection occurs through single focalization. And it matters not at all whether we are reading Le Guin's fantasy, science fiction, realism, or imaginary historical fiction. Oddly enough,
these last categories, most often used as contexts in which to discuss Le
Guin's work, offer us no insight into her strategies of narration and focalization that can be used to determine where characters will fall on her most important thematic continuum: the space between isolation and connection.

3
Home as Travel Through Time and Place

Time and distance soften all agony.

Ursula K. Le Guin
"The New Atlantis"

True Journey is Return.

Ursula K. Le Guin
The Dispossessed

Home is the place where you've never been.

Ursula K. Le Guin
The Dispossessed

And we came home: the home where we have never been before, the home we never left.

Ursula K. Le Guin
"The Water Is Wide"

In the last essay, I discussed how Le Guin uses narration and focalization to help characters connect with others or remain isolated. That connection is important in another context—in the development of home. The idea of "home" is pervasive in Le Guin's fiction, but as the collection of epigraphs suggests, it is not simple. Home is never really limited to a place or even to the memory of a place. Rather, home is a condition itself contingent on a set of conditions. Elizabeth Cummins remarks that in Le Guin's fiction, "journeying is an analogy for living; the process of going and returning, of fragmenting and unifying, is regenerating and unending."[1] I would like to extend that by arguing that the sense of home is achieved when one character, journeying with another across time and place, finds a sense of purpose. It is never understood to be secure for all time, it happens by various degrees in different circumstances, and it is always attempted with some risk.

I approach this issue by first dividing the discussion by genre and then by the types of chronotopes Le Guin uses to help characters achieve a sense of home. While it is true that each genre makes use of different chronotopic strategies, the differences are more a matter of degree than kind. I divide by genre, then, in part to show that by itself genre isn't the only context for understanding Le Guin's literary goals. Some chronotopic strategies cross the lines of genre, and some seem more at home within certain genres.

The Novels

Le Guin's novels employ what Bakhtin calls, and what I'll define below as, a threshold chronotope. There are crossings necessary, in other words, and they can be defined in one of two ways regardless of questions of realism, science fiction, or fantasy: they are either deductive or dream chronotopes. First I'll discuss the notion of the chronotope, and then present the two types I believe are in operation. Lastly I'll discuss the continuum that exists between the two types of threshold chronotope.

The Larger Chronotope of Threshold

"Chronotope" is the name that Bakhtin gives "to the intrinsic connectedness of temporal and spatial relationships that are artistically expressed in literature."[2] In other words, time and space cannot be considered separately, and of course, in our real-world rudimentary physics this theory bears out. But as it pertains to art, he wants us to understand that this "connectedness" is a high aesthetic value, not simply a natural law to observe in the service of realism. He goes on to say that "in the literary artistic chronotope, spatial and temporal indicators are fused into one carefully thought-out, concrete whole" (Bakhtin 1981, 84). Pandora in *Always Coming Home* doesn't portray it as thoughtful when she observes that for the Kesh "time and space are so muddled together that one is never sure whether they are talking about an era or an area."[3] However, it is true that for Le Guin the intrinsic connection of time and space is something to be explored and respected. The chronotope is the way home for Le Guin's characters.

While Le Guin claims that "'place' is enormously important in all of [her] work,"[4] at the same time she often denies her characters the actual planting of roots in one soil—or defers it for a time extrapolated beyond the end of the tale. In his observation that in Le Guin's fiction "home is desired, but never attained,"[5] Tschachler points to what is simultaneously "insecurity and liberation" in Le Guin's fiction (1995, 236). Though, in Virginia Wolf's words, a "celebration of place is a celebration of self at one with the world,"[6] Le Guin's text not only resists the stasis of closure—of having protagonists rest without care in a final "home" at tale's end—she examines what it would even mean to rest without care, and where one could ever really do that, even (or *especially,* she might say) in fantasy. She challenges the notion of utopia by never really finishing journeys, to which many critics have already given testimony.

Le Guin tells us that there are people, there is home, "on the other side"[7] —that there is a place other than "here" where home is, presumably outside of the center. Her larger text baits us with binaries of home places and journeys, but at the same time the texts—collectively and individually—resist clearly identifiable "other sides." She accomplishes this by involving complex ways of moving in narrative and more diverse ideological ramifications as a result of those varied and simultaneous movements. "Center" for Bakhtin should "be understood for what it is: a *relative* rather than an absolute term."[8] So too in Le Guin's dynamic, dialogic fiction, the center is dynamic, mediation between sites from a particular perspective: "'we have always known this. This is where we have always been, will always be, at the hearth, at the center. There is nothing to be afraid of, after all."[9] It is important to note that in "The Shobies' Story" the hearth is at the center of their spaceship "Shoby"—hardly a fixed point—and the relativity of their stories is what creates a center and staves off fear. When they find that a new way of traveling—"churtening"—makes it possible that they will each be lost in a personal, isolated, timeless, and placeless state, they come together to tell tales of what is happening to them, of what has happened. The tales they tell form a collective time and place; this is what saves them from dissolution. Home is the shared center that is relative, dynamic, and purposeful.

Leonard Lutwack points out that twentieth century literature is characterized by "a sense of place loss and a sense of placelessness."[10] He goes on to say that "the disappearance of the familiar places and the proliferation of a more and more limited set of uniform places have caused a peculiarly modern malaise called *placelessness*" (182, emphasis in original). This paradox —that a variety of places results in the absence of a sense of place—is certainly present in Le Guin's work. This is not to say that place is unimportant in Le Guin's work: a character can not have a sense of loss without some notion of what is lost, after all. A sense of placelessness—or displacement— motivates her characters to set off on the world roads they travel after having made the disorienting space journey. Scott Sanders wonders how "you can value other places if you do not have a place of your own? If you are not yourself placed, then you wander the world like a sightseer."[11] It is with the help of that important partner discussed previously that characters find home in the purposeful movement through time and place. They aren't simply sightseers. Purposeful movement makes them intimate with, and formed by, time and place rather than reducing them to ships that pass others in the night. They are, rather, passengers traveling together in concert, as on the "Shoby."

But Sanders may be trying to separate the inseparable. Who is more sensitive to the attraction of place than the wanderer? And what fixed soul doesn't wonder about wandering? Le Guin doesn't fall into that binary of good and bad regarding place. As Sanders himself notes, to feel placeless one must have a sense, and a longing, for place. The cows in my father's pasture aren't bored with the field, as near as I can tell, perhaps because they can't conceive of an alternative. They do not see purpose. Perhaps they simply lack the will to revolt, or maybe I'm unable to recognize the paralysis of bovine ennui. To stay or to go aren't simple options for Le Guin's characters, who are more like cats than cows. According to Le Guin, home is the place we've never been because home is the condition of purposeful movement.[12] Almost all of Le Guin's novel characters travel real roads of dirt or asphalt, which lead from city to country, over mountains, and through forests. And almost all of her main characters travel interplanetary and interstellar roads at nearly-as-fast-as-light (NAFAL) speed. Some travel the roads of memory, as I discuss previously; some travel the road of dreams. "There is more than one road to the city," Hugh and Irene are told in *The Beginning Place*, and Le Guin's characters travel them all.[13]

The road is ubiquitous in Le Guin's novels. Her characters *always* travel a dusty world-road, but some cosmic dust is usually kicked up just before that. Each sort of road has its own time. The space journey might be considered only a frame for the more local journey in the novel, but the implications of that space journey—of its distance and time—are crucial to the way the real-time journeys play out. Really, the chronotope of the threshold connecting worlds of different time and space is similar to the chronotope of the portal fantasy—fantasy novels in which characters travel to a secondary world for their adventures. Maria Nikolajeva points out that "the notion of the chronotope enables us to avoid the problem encountered by most researchers of being forced to divide texts into categories such as 'secondary-world fantasy' or 'time-shift fantasy'"—or even science fiction.[14]

It is an interesting fact that no Hainish novel is principally about or set in space travel, though it is the space travel that makes the journey on each world significant.[15] The space journey warps time—it requires NAFAL flight, which will forever displace the characters from both their own worlds and their own generations. They are unable to return to the homes that they leave. Despite Scott Sanders's objection to the contemporary emphasis on placelessness, these characters are necessarily placeless no matter where they go, and timeless no matter when they arrive. They always arrive in an alien environment and always in the Year One.[16] They experience both time and place as outsiders. The space travel warps time, and it establishes the nature of the rather hurried and intense "real" time of the world journey.

Bakhtin tells us that the chronotope of the threshold journey is "highly charged with emotion and value . . . It can be combined with the motif of encounter, but its most fundamental instance is as the chronotope of *crisis* and *break* in a life" (1981, 248). This is the principle chronotope in Le Guin's longer works. Falk, Rocannon, Agat, Lyubov, Genly Ai, Shevek, and Sutty—other than being most of her novels' protagonists—all encounter real-world roads across the threshold of space travel. Each protagonist is affected differently as he or she moves from the frame of space travel across the threshold to the real world road. At one end of the continuum they are, at the least, highly sensitive to their own displacement; at the other end, the protagonist finds himself without even an identity. Each circumstance is an obvious "break in a life," one which makes it highly desirable, if not downright necessary, for the protagonist to find a native companion for the journey.[17]

The Deductive Chronotope

Some protagonists move from the cosmic to the mountain road. Rocannon, Agat, and Luz have, in their respective stories, found themselves on worlds following space flight, and each of them finds his or her most significant journey continued on a road across the mountains of the New World—a world each has adopted and will never leave. In two of the cases the protagonist hasn't him or herself been in space, but is the descendant of space colonists. The residual effect is that even after only a couple of generations (in Luz's case in *The Eye of the Heron*) or many (as in Agat's in *Planet of Exile*) each character feels alien in his native world.[18] They seem to be physiologically unsuited to these worlds, or they have forged a poor relationship with the world culture.[19] In all three cases, however, the space journey is the root of the feeling of displacement, and those initial journeys require that these characters hit the road once again, this time through the mountains. That mountain road journey will enable each of them to discover or make peace with their purpose for being there.

Agat from *Planet of Exile* (1966) and Luz from *The Eye of the Heron* (1978) have different reasons for traveling their world roads, but the time-place relationship as well as the companionable travel remain, and the characters derive a new sense of purpose, identity, and home as a result. In both cases they inherit the New World from their forbears. Both Luz and Agat discover love across the cultural and racial abyss established on their respective worlds, and each walks the road from one world to the other in order to bridge that gap and create a New World from their respective communities. Luz's journey continues as she and a few from the oppressed community set out into the mountains to establish a new place; Agat's journey continues as he fights a third group that would destroy both his community and his wife's. Each relies on the kindness of strangers and the power of the love of a partner to make the world work. Those who resist connection end up perishing the death that comes from blind isolation, after all. Agat's father-in-law and Luz's father turn a blind eye to the road that has to follow the space journey, and each dies in stasis, though each begins to understand the importance of continuing the journey by the end of his respective tale. Isolation leads to stasis, which is death.

After the enemy has killed his colleagues, Rocannon, the protagonist of *Rocannon's World* (1966), is left alone to battle the new rebel outpost on this alien world.[20] He enlists the help of some native hilfers, travels across the world by foot, and ultimately sabotages the invaders' outpost. In the course of his journey he grows to respect the native peoples and becomes one of them in the shared mission to save their planet from the enemy. Rocannon is marooned on the world since the enemy destroyed his ship, and he lives out his days as a respected member of the community of a world that will come to bear his name; eponymy is, perhaps, the ultimate sign of finding home. His mission and sense of purpose is singular—destroy the enemy—but is fortified by his native companions and the memory of his slain colleagues from his previous life. As he travels with his new friends, he combines the motives of revenge for his old colleagues and protection for his new family. He finds a new, combined identity by the end because of the two journeys he takes—one across space in uninterrupted "no" time, the other across land in its quest-time punctuated by smaller forays and encounters along the way. Both legs of the journey are important for Rocannon to find "home"—or, rather, create it: it is the movement across the threshold from space to place, from broad to narrow, over the time of his quest that creates "home."

There are others who are re-formed by their journeys through space and soil. Though they find purpose on the paths they travel, they do not ultimately stay, as do those described above. But their departure from the world isn't treated literally in their respective stories, only implied, and it is the case that each is utterly transformed and finds a sense of home at the ends of the roads into the wilderness. "Home," after all, is the process and not ultimately the place—it is what one identifies with after traveling through space and time with important companions, not where one ultimately stops at the end of a tale.

Lyubov from *The Word for World Is Forest* (1976) arrives on Athshe from Terra and wanders the forest paths with the Athsheans, most notably Selver. With Selver as his native guide he learns the ways of the people of the forest and becomes their spokesperson among the Terran "invaders." Genly Ai from *The Left Hand of Darkness* (1969), another Terran space traveler, is re-formed through his travels with Estraven across the great glacier between Gethen and Orgota. As he travels and talks with his native guide and friend, he refines his purpose and approach as the Ekumen's envoy to Gethen and ultimately helps usher the planet Winter into the Ekumen. In *The Telling* (2000), Sutty, yet another Terran envoy, has to travel by degrees from Terra to the Akan city of Dovza and then into the mountain wilderness.[21] Her trip to the last hold of the Maz, hidden in the mountains, takes her on mountain roads with mountain guides. As it is with Lyubov and Genly Ai, Sutty must leave the city and travel native roads in the wilderness with good and trusted guides in order to begin to understand or even make possible a defining purpose for themselves in the world.[22] They must travel across space in order to lose both place and time and then, once on that new world, find the road into the wilderness with the companions in order to find a sense of self and home.

Shevek from *The Dispossessed* (1974), our only non-Terran traveler in this group, modifies the road from space to sterile city to defining wilderness in that his move from sterile city to wilderness involves finding the wilderness *in* the city. He travels with the help of guides into the underbelly of Nio Essia, capital of A-Io on Urras. From there he defines his purpose that will make him a subversive—as all of these travelers must be. In a sense each travels the broad road of space to the narrow road of purpose in the wilderness, and that purpose always leads one to the realization that to have an individual purpose is to be rebellious. It is the nature of the threshold chronotope of the deductive journey.

But Shevek's journey is a complicated one to chart, and it proves something of an exception to my claims.[23] Though Shevek returns, and his return is important as a unifying act, it is only the logical next step to his newly found mission of making his temporal theories known to the universe, and it transcends the political and geographic boundaries of the two planets. The return to Anarres is a necessary step since it means escape from what has become a potential political prison. He has found on Urras his sense of purpose, though it means leaving Urras, and ultimately Anarres. But, even though the journey of discovery arguably ends on Urras, *The Dispossessed* does feature return as part of the tale, not merely as an implied extrapolation; and it features return doubly. As George Slusser observes, when "Shevek leaves for Urras then, he is both leaving home and going home" because Anarres (Shevek's birth home and satellite of Urras) was settled by Urrasti expatriates.[24] His people began on Urras, settled Anarres; he travels to Urras, then back to Anarres, then, presumably, to other Hainish worlds. Perhaps the novel's failure to completely comply with any either/or category proves that Le Guin refuses easy, systematic readings, thankfully.[25]

Falk in *City of Illusions* (1967) would seem comparable to Shevek and his story. But this novel is different from those described above, though published only a year after *Rocannon's World* and *Planet of Exile*. This character comes from Werel, but his people were from Terra long ago.[26] He returns to Terra—but as an alien. He lands in the wilderness and travels to the city—only then to set out again for Werel. His goal is to return to Werel; if he has a purpose it might be to keep the Shing from finding Werel, which he can do by ending his own life and taking his memory with him. Once he is free of the Shing his purpose is satisfied, and his home world is safe, at least for now. He simply returns. The other novels take the reader and the protagonist on a road that enables the protagonist, with the help of another, to find a self-defining purpose—a sense of identity and mission that isn't limited to or defined by where they are at the moment, or where they aren't.

Itale from *Malafrena* (1979) fails more categorically to follow the deductive journey, and fails to define, ultimately, a purpose for himself as a result. His trek is circular within the tale (rather than simply extrapolated), like Shevek's, but it doesn't allow him to find purpose beyond getting back home for its own sake, as Falk fails in the same way. Egen Brunoy asks Itale, "If you don't know where your home is, how shall you be a pilgrim?"[27] Itale's circular journey finds him neither purpose nor a real geographical sense of home. He's just going in circles. The deductive chronotope is a journey from the broad to the narrow (sometimes so narrow as to be a single room) that may imply return, but doesn't usually (Ah, Shevek!) feature it as important enough to document. I will say more about this following the discussion of Le Guin's children's texts.

The Chronotope of Dream and Memory

Indeed, there is more than one road to the city—or out of it. In the chronotope of dreams and memory one "awakens" to a better place—or rather, to a better self in more than one place. In the dream journey chronotope, the character crosses a threshold as well, but one can cross back to a purposeful and redefined self in the original place. In such a chronotope the protagonists are clearly affected by the journey into the dream or other-time world. This approach differs from many children's tales in which the journey away affects the protagonist only superficially, if at all.[28] In this threshold chronotope, one is in the process of discovering or fashioning home in both places simultaneously and as a result of trafficking between worlds.

Above I address the use of memory, which works in the respective cases of Rocannon, Shevek and Sutty to help them connect to another on their respective world journeys. Shevek's and Sutty's tales feel "simultaneous" because they, as discussed above, place two times together for our consideration. Perhaps it is this quality that marks *The Dispossessed* and *The Telling* as transitional tales that have qualities of both the deductive and dream chronotopes. *The Dispossessed* is closer to the dream chronotope for its importance of return within the tale itself; *The Telling* is closer to the deductive chronotope for its quality of linearity. Both memory and dream are violations of time, after all. Memory is anachronistic because it takes us back; dream because it happens outside of regular world time. The dream chronotope is also different, though, because the journey necessarily features return —for who can ultimately live only in the dream except the insane? We can relocate across the cosmos, but we must return from our dreams. The deductive chronotopes may imply return, but it is the narrowing journey out that is the focus of the purposeful journey in most cases. For Shevek, Sutty, and Rocannon, memory is the anachronistic tool used by these isolated travelers to gain them help on the road in world time.

The look of the dream and its chronotope in Le Guin's work is less uniform than what we find above in her deductive chronotope, though its nature is consistent. In the cases of Selver, Hugh and Irene, Owen, and George Orr, the dream world is manifested somewhat differently. In each case it is both the dream world and the real world that help the protagonist understand himself or herself better, making that person a fit partner and, therefore, eligible for a purpose and the feeling of home.

While I describe Lyubov's journey above in terms of the deductive chronotope, his partner in subversion lives in the dream world chronotope. Here we see Le Guin having two threshold chronotopes exist simultaneously in one book, which makes the novel all the more fascinating and important. But it isn't unique as a literary mixture of chronotopes: "chronotopes are mutually inclusive, they co-exist, they may be interwoven with, replace or oppose one another, contradict one another or find themselves in ever more complex interrelationships" (Bakhtin 1981, 252). In Selver's threshold chronotope there isn't the narrowing exchange of one set of time and place for another, as in Lyubov's deductive chronotope. Instead, Selver drifts through and back across the threshold of real and dream-time—though for him the dream-time is more real. While Lyubov negotiates the road between outpost and wilderness, Selver uses the forest as setting for the dream journey.

A principle difference between Lyubov's and Selver's journeys is that for the dreamer, Selver, the worlds traveled between are for him inseparable: together they make a whole. The deductive chronotope shows us necessarily separate worlds in separate times. While the dream journey shows us different use of time in most cases, the dream and "real" worlds exist on a scale from more to less separate, but they are seldom completely separate. What Selver and the other Athsheans see as the Terrans' madness, or lack of humanity, is a seeming denial of the dream world. In the Terrans' case, living exclusively in the dream world does not cause insanity; it's the failure to live there at all that causes madness. Home is a purposeful journey across dream and world times, as fellow Athshean and dreamer Coro Mena says to Selver: "before this day the thing we had to do was the right thing to do; the way we had to go was the right way and led us home. Where is our home now?"[29]

Figuratively speaking, home is the purposeful journey. The dream journey tells the Athsheans the way to go in both worlds. That has failed them with the introduction of the Terran threat because they have had to deal with insane people who deny their dreams. How do you deal with a creature you aren't sure is human? Selver needs to be a "god, a changer, a bridge between realities" (35). He helps the Athsheans find a new road to travel, find a new way to be in the world. He introduces a new solution: killing what *might* be human—the Terrans. He does that by consulting his dreams. Lyubov notes that the Athsheans "balance [their] sanity not on the razor's edge of reason but on the double support, the fine balance, of reason and dream . . . " (99). It is a trait of the dream threshold chronotope that the two worlds balance each other. The journey is back and forth—reverberative, not straight on. The successful dream or memory journey reconciles worlds, instead of narrowing in on one, which again is a reason why *The Dispossessed* is itself straddled across chronotopes.

The dream chronotope has an effect on the presence of the companion as well. In Selver's case there is a partner in each world to help: in the real world there is Lyubov, and in the dream world there is Selver's dead wife. In most other cases, however, the partner is singular, though not usually a presence in both worlds.

While Selver chooses his dreams, George Orr in *The Lathe of Heaven* (1971) tries desperately to keep them at bay.[30] His dream journeys are like Selver's in that the real and the dream are inextricable: the two worlds cannot, ultimately, be distinguished. Each of George's dreams becomes his replacement reality, and each erases any distinction between real and dream. As with Selver, dreaming for George means changing the "real" world. As Selver has the guidance of his dead wife in the dream world, George's partner, Heather Lelache, is "dead" or simply nonexistent in some of the worlds he dreams up, though he remembers all past world versions. This memory enables him to seek Heather—or reconstruct her—in subsequent dreams according to the rules of that new world. Until Heather crosses George's path the first time, George is the jellyfish that is the book's opening metaphor: he is current borne and not in control. He has no purpose. As Selver's wife gives him guidance in his dreams, Heather gives George a sense of purpose in his.[31] George wants a world with Heather in it, and until that realization he simply "took it as it came. He was living almost like a young child, among actualities only" (125). The aliens George dreams up (or discovers?) in one dream also show him that he is not alone as an "effective dreamer." They show him how he can tap into a collective dream unconscious to determine when a dream should be "effective" or transformative of the world. Changing the world, after all, depends on real need. Orr's psychiatrist Dr. Haber wants to use George's dreams to change the world into Utopia. He ultimately attempts to do it himself with the help of his Augmentor, a machine that he uses to impose George's dream-state brain wave patterns onto his own dreams. He fails in his dream journey because he is intentionally alone and arrogant in both worlds. He isn't out to use dreams to help make sense of the world: he simply wants to dream in order to make the world fit his singular vision. He descends into madness as he is lost in the dream world; the journey into madness must, like the journey into death, be a solitary journey.

The Word for World Is Forest and *The Lathe of Heaven* don't end with a false promise of stasis—of having "made it home"—but with the promise of further purposeful journeying. But in *The Lathe of Heaven*, as in *The Beginning Place*, the purposeful journey continues outside of dream world and in the real world with the discovered partner who will help with the project of self-discovery. George loses the ability to dream effectively by the end, but he has found and clings to the partner that gives his new and final (though incomplete) world meaning.

Hugh and Irene, like George, don't seek the dream world journey. But, like Selver, they embrace it. While they think their respective journeys into Tembreabrezi are a sort of escape from the real world, they will discover only with their joining together that it is a way to improve themselves through each other, and hence their real world. The two worlds can't be separate. As the novel progresses, each discovers a special ability with regard to the threshold: Hugh is able to enter at will but can't always get out; Irene can always get out but can't count on getting in. Together they are able to navigate the two worlds. Their association with each other progresses from one of begrudging convenience to one of mutual discovery. They help each other not only navigate the portal but keep each other from being "stuck" in their respectively inadequate real worlds. In the real world and separate from each other, Hugh and Irene, "lacking the individual strength to overcome the dearth of collective resources [to pursue self-affirmation], are unable to do what they want to do, or what they need to do."[32] As they move from the resentment of their mutual dependence to the freedom of equality in true couplehood, they leave Tembreabrezi behind and start a new life together in the real world away from Hugh's possessive single mother and Irene's abusive family. The two young adults, like the adults Heather and George, begin a journey back into the city with a renewed sense of purpose. They also have no further need for solitary dreaming; they have a purposeful dialogic reality. They are coming home.

Owen's experience with the dream world in *Very Far Away from Anywhere Else* (1976) is different from the others'.[33] His dream world is of his own making, though not in the same sense as the world George creates. Thorn is Owen's secondary literary world. He is its creator, and he uses it as a refuge from a world that doesn't understand him. He doesn't "go" there physically or in sleep, but as a reader entering a fictional world to deal with his life. Should he spend much time there he would become the reverse but no less "mad" counterpart to the Terrans on Athshe who pay no attention to their dream lives—the "escapist" reader rather than the reader who reads in order to make sense of the real world. What saves Owen is a companion in the real world who makes any ultimate retreat into Thorn untenable. Natalie gives Owen a reason to stay in touch with his world. He concludes, "I don't want to play king of the castle any more. I want to live with other people, Nat. I used to think that other people didn't matter, but they do. You can't hack it all by yourself" (82). The castle in Thorn is a false dream, and he crosses back over that threshold, like George and Heather, like Hugh and Irene, for the last time—but not because his journeying is over. Natalie's

passion for her music and her life makes Owen understand that he has a purpose to pursue, and he will go off to MIT to study his passion for cognitive
psychology. While Natalie doesn't accompany him there (she has her own
real dreams to follow) they vow to keep in touch and ground each other
along the way. It's pretty certain that this is not the typical delusion written
in many high school yearbooks: "we'll always keep in touch." They have
found in each other a partner to help with the work of purposeful journey
through music and science. They have found home.

When we are allowed insight into multiple minds, when those minds
achieve a connection with the characters' partners in travel—companions
who travel with purpose across thresholds—we see Le Guin's strong novels.
They are strong because there is a clear and achievable sense of home. In
those novels, characters travel with the help of the other through the deductive or dream chronotope that leads to the condition of "home." As Le Guin
resists binary in genre, we see it in her chronotopes. And we see that genre
within the novel isn't the dividing tool here—portal fantasy and science fiction exist in each chronotope. The chronotopes present us with a continuum
rather than a binary. Within the threshold chronotope there are two spec-
trums—at one end the deductive chronotope and at the other end the dream
chronotope. That line runs from the threshold novels in the deductive
chronotope (*Planet of Exile, The Eye of the Heron, The Left Hand of
Darkness,* and *Rocannon's World*) to the transitional novels (*The Telling* and
The Dispossessed) to the dual chronotope of *The Word for World Is Forest,*
and ultimately to the threshold novels of the dream chronotope (*The Lathe of
Heaven, The Beginning Place,* and, loosely, *Very Far Away from Anywhere
Else*). As *The Word for World Is Forest* contains both the deductive and
dream chronotopes, *Rocannon's World* is dual in the sense that it portrays
Rocannon as reliant on companions present to him and those in memory,
both of which give him purpose. Indeed, the gradations on the continuum are
subtle, which points to the difficulty in coming up with any satisfying classi-
fication of Le Guin novels that rely on discrete categories—generic, chronotopic, or otherwise. *Malafrena* is without a real home in Le Guin's novel
chronotopes, which may be one reason why it is not discussed very often. It
doesn't work. It hasn't a home. *City of Illusions* is, unlike *The Telling, The
Dispossessed,* and *The Word for World is Forest,* a less satisfying mixture of
the two chronotopes. All three of the transitional or dual chronotopic novels
are, interestingly, award-winning novels.

The Suites

"Suite" is, as I explain in the previous essay, Le Guin's term for her collections of stories that are connected by character and place. The chronotope of

the threshold is seen here as well, connecting it to the novel genre, though two of the three suites employ different chronotopic strategies. I'll begin with those two new chronotopes.

The Chronotope of Singular Place in Anachrony

Tales of Orsinia The trio of tales about the family Fabbre—"Brothers and Sisters," "A Week in the Country," and "Unlocking the Air"—are an oddity in the tales of Orsinia because they are presented in chronological order.[34] The tales are otherwise characterized by an anachronous organization that parallels the lack of coherence in Orsinia itself. The stories in *Orsinian Tales* (1976) are presented in order by the following years, all AD: 1960, 1150, 1920, 1920 again, 1956, 1910, 1962, 1938, 1965, 1640, and 1935. "Unlocking the Air," the last Fabbre family tale and Orsinia story, published separately from those found in *Orsinian Tales*, is set in 1990. The anachrony of presentation creates the sense of simultaneity that typifies Cetian physics, dialogism, and the structure of *The Dispossessed* and *The Telling*. While there is a controlled simultaneity in those two novels —a twin linearity of the present and past, the tales of Orsinia, are arranged such that all moments are equally present, which has the ultimate effect of removing us from time. The anachrony becomes achrony. The place is constant, and we see the world as a place for which time is rather unimportant since it seems the same problems are played out time and again. There are no thresholds crossed, just lines of vision shifted. There is neither linear movement out nor circular journey in the collected experience of the tales. We are told by the narrator in Le Guin's "Winter's King" that "time stretches and shrinks; changes with the eye, with the age, with the star; does all except reverse itself—or repeat."[35] This is the sense of time in the collected tales of Orsinia.[36]

Different tales of Orsinia employ different plot movements, though the isolated character on a journey is the most prevalent. Le Guin likes to match subtext with text in her work. The subtext of a nation lost is mirrored in the chronotope employed. Unlike the novels—those tales that are threshold chronotopes—the tales of Orsinia feature disorientation. There is no master narrative that provides even the illusion of progress or definition over time— there is no control of the helm. We read of a place, and of its people, adrift in random historical moments, and this forces us to feel a bit adrift ourselves as readers. While the novels of the threshold chronotope present us with chronological time, the order of the tales of Orsinia scrambles time. While individual characters in individual tales of Orsinia often return to a place— Freyga, Kereth, Maler, Mariya, Ladislas, even the second Stefan Fabbre with Bruna—they return to a place still roiling with conflict in which few have hope for the journey of purpose. The return is a signal that the larger journey is not theirs alone, however, nor even simply shared with a single partner, but a national journey that requires that nobody leaves.

They are little different from the solitary, linear journeyfolk—Sanzo and Lisha, Stefan and Ekata, and Dom Andre—who find conflict in different parts of Orsinia suffering "the long chance."[37] To move about Orsinia is to stand still. It is to wander and wait, with luck with the important partner that helps one find some purpose despite the land through which they travel. The couples that find both purpose and a promise for a future bury the needs of Orsinia beneath their own. The Fabbres, Sanzo and Lisha, Mariya and Pier have the most hope despite returning or leaving the original place (what difference does it make in Orsinia?), though nobody has much. Dr. Kereth shows in the book's opening tale, "The Fountains," that he knew not, "perhaps not himself, . . . where he wandered in [Versailles] while defecting."[38] He walks past all of the embassies, potential asylums, on his return to Paris. He realizes that safety or even autonomy isn't something he can have, and "knowing now that he was both a king and a thief" he was "at home anywhere" (5). He recognizes that he is a part of a land in search of purpose, and he chooses to be a part of that search; that's the limit of his ability to act purposefully. The journey home for an Orsinian is undertaken in the form of a thief stealing and a king ruling the land.

Searoad The story-suite *Searoad* is divided into 12 sections (as the tales of Orsinia are 12 short tales in total). The first 11 tales deal with the same span of time in the town of Klatsand. The 12th tale, "Hernes," accounts for the last 65 pages (one third of the book) and whose first-person narration is divided among four generations of Klatsand women.[39] As it is in *Orsinian Tales*, the tales in "Hernes" are presented anachronistically. There are fully 36 fragments in "Hernes," each of which features the character narration of one of the four women, each in a different year of her life. The time covered is 77 years. Neither date nor character provides any pattern to the presentation of the 36 fragments, though the last two are the earliest and latest, respectively. We see here, as in tales of Orsinia, that in certain chronotopes, "time is essentially instantaneous; it is as if it has no duration and falls out of the normal course of biographical time" (Bakhtin 1981, 248). *Searoad* and the tales of Orsinia are stories that take us out of time and leave us in a place that is static.

This last story in *Searoad*, "Hernes," employs the same chronotopic strategy as the tales of Orsinia. As the occasional Orsinian tale will show us action outside of Orsinia, in "Hernes" we get a glimpse of San Francisco—but really the primary setting is Klatsand. As Kereth decides that defection to Paris is untenable in "The Fountains," Jane Hernes is drawn back to Klatsand because the land is a more stable partner than her husband is—as her granddaughter Virginia also discovers. The four generations (five including Virginia's daughter Jaye who has no voice in the tale) show us the development of both the land and their family over time, but only if we do the work of rearranging the tale chronologically, and even then we don't see so much a development as difference.

A major partner to help the character find some purpose in such a chronotope is the land itself—either Orsinia or Klatsand. In the threshold chronotopes, the land is not the focal point—the movement with a partner is the process for purpose. In the chronotope of singular place in anachrony, however, the strongest partner is the stable land itself—though as we see in both Orsinia and Klatsand, that land defines without much comfort. In "Hernes," speakers and their ages (and hence the years) shift in a patternless way. The land, however, remains stable, even over time and with some small urban development. As place increases in importance in Le Guin's work, character pairings become less likely, though they would be just as important if she chose to use them. Le Guin seems to be saying that as one thing becomes a constant in a particular chronotope, it frees up other things as variables.

The chronotope seen in the tales of Orsinia encourages a sense of isolation; and so it does in "Hernes" and the rest of *Searoad*. The land offers them connection, but woman, daughter, granddaughter, and great-granddaughter never really connect with each other in "Hernes." Their narratives are disjointed enough to see the same needs but a lack of connection in their personal relationships. Any similarity among the first-person musings of each woman in a random time and place is purely the product of the attentive reader; the characters never share empathy with each other.

Unlike *Orsinian Tales*, the first eleven stories of *Searoad* are not identified by year. It is clear, however, that they take place in the same span of time (the contemporary moment, it seems) since characters allude to each other and recent events from story to story. The absence of date, combined with the juxtaposition of tales sharing the same place, creates a strong sense of a single place in a single time. In one case, this achrony is translated into a location: "the days after Barbara's death had not been a period of time but a place of a certain shape, a place where Shirley had to crouch down and hold still because it was the only thing to do."[40] All of the characters in this volume crouch down and hold still in the shape called Klatsand because it is the only thing to do.

The reader of this book and of *Orsinia* seems to be invited, like the reader of *Always Coming Home* (1985), to read the sections in the order that makes most sense to her, and this might prove the way toward alleviating stasis by imposing some other rationale on the presentation of stories. One might read the vignettes in "Hernes" in the order that Le Guin presents them, or by character (they each have seven or eight vignettes), or by chronology (in order from 1898 to 1975), or even by a cross section by character. The first 11 tales are not reliant upon one another by chronology or character, and may be read in any order at all. For that matter, they may be read as a group before or after "Hernes." To be extreme, there's no reason to keep "Hernes" from being divided in installments between each of the other stories and at either end of the other 11 stories in *Searoad*—no reason, that is, beyond Le Guin's desire not to confuse a reader more than necessary. While *Always Coming Home* directly invites this, the other books with this chronotope imply this organizational possibility. In this chronotope, the land organizes, coheres, gathers people in a holistic, nonlinear way; you choose any direction you can think of, and you may decide you need a different way with each reading. Really, this chronotope rewards the reader's return with a new way to experience the place outside of time.

Five Ways to Forgive in the Threshold Chronotope: Four Ways to
Forgiveness *and "Old Music and the Slave Women"*

What marks this story-suite as different from the other two is that it shows suite-like tendencies regarding form but has employed the threshold chronotope. While place seems fairly static here, as in other suites, it only seems so because they all feature either Werel or Yeowe—but Le Guin has her characters come from far afield and move between the two planets, not unlike Shevek between the two Cetian worlds. There is the feel of anachrony here because the tales are contemporary, simultaneous with each other, but there is a definite pattern of shifting time in and across the long stories. Because there are fewer tales that are longer in the telling we are able to see time develop, in contrast to the brief and many tales found in the Orsinia and Klatsand story-suites.

For the most part the individual stories employ the deductive chronotope, discussed above. The two clearest examples of this are, not surprisingly, stories that feature Envoys as single focalizers. In the first of these, "A Man of the People," Havzhiva follows a common pattern in a Le Guin novel of the Ekumen, which follows the philosophy that home is the place you've never been rather than the philosophy that true journey is return.[41] The pattern is typical: he begins on Hain (or another long-time planet of the Ekumen), and then he makes the space flight that will effectively warp time by being a time out; when he arrives, time will seem to speed up as he acclimates back to real time. Havzhiva is sent to Yeowe and does much of his work in the city of Yotebber where he and Dr. Yeron work at helping the Liberation Movement discover a voice for women. But from there he moves to the North, to live in the province of the old Capital, moving farther into the country as time passes and seems to slow—as he "goes native." The 18-year span between visits with Yeron is documented but not discussed, as if to say it is important but not very dramatic. Its pattern mirrors the linear, deductive chronotopes found in novels of the Ekumen.

Like "A Man of the People," "Old Music and the Slave Women" is the story of an envoy who finds himself moving out into the wilderness, so to speak. Esdan, also Hainish, makes the space journey and finds himself on Werel.[42] After many years in the city of Voe Deo, the capital city of the largest nation on the planet, he finds his adopted home torn by civil war. In an attempt to cross the divided city to visit with the Liberation Army he is captured by the "Legitimates" and finds himself in the wilderness—a war-ravaged plantation on Werel. His journey is also from city to "wilderness"—and before that from the disorienting time of space flight to hectic city life before he arrives at the slow life as a prisoner on a plantation. As in Hav's case, though, it is this journey that helps Esdan cleave to people who give him a sense of purpose—a sense of being home after having home called into doubt earlier in the narrative.

Two stories that also have deductive chronotopes are two that feature not envoys but ex-slaves. Instead of experiencing the disorienting, nearly-no-time feel of NAFAL flight, the slaves are what Rakam calls "enslaved by the present time."[43] As Mobiles of the Ekumen are temporarily enslaved by the nearly timeless and disorienting feeling of NAFAL flight, slaves are kept from getting a bearing on time because to them a life span is all the same day. Rakam notes that as slaves, "nobody knew anything about any time when things had been different" (172). It is for this reason she decides to study history once she is free. Time is both what she studies and what changes in her life. Like an envoy coming out of NAFAL, Rakam's life hits overdrive as she tries to acclimate to a way of life truly alien to her. It feels like a blur. The narrative speeds up as she escapes to the city, finds work, has to escape yet again at a moment's notice (this time to Yeowe) and bounce around in unfulfilling work until Dr. Yeron gets her connected to a school. Once at the school, and after she has been connected with Yeron and Hav, time in the narrative slows a bit—months and years go by in a line or two to indicate comfortable, calm routine rather than speed. She is coming, through purpose and connection to significant others, home.

"Betrayals" works in exactly the same way.[44] Yoss is an ex-slave as well. Although she has been on Yeowe all along, she has made the "NAFAL flight of slavery," moved to a city to work (also as a teacher, though of physics), but then has moved out into the old marsh land to be alone, which we learn above is not her ultimate fate. Her life is marked by different kinds of time, like Rakam's, and she learns in her new home, and with Abberkam, to live slowly and deliberately.

The tale that seems to be the exception is "Forgiveness Day." While it too has an envoy, Solly, who is a focalizer and, for the course of the story has lived in a deductive chronotope, the story is as much the tale of Teyeo. Teyeo complements his new companion by living an inductive chronotope. His story is unique in the five. While he grew up on a plantation, as Yoss and

Rakam have, he was an owner. For him time isn't timeless, but comfortable and easy with the full knowledge of the outside world, its history, and its rapid speeds. He moves from the slowness of a life spent on a plantation to the city for military duty, to war, back to the city for guard duty. Following that, however—following the enforced slowed down time of captivity with Solly at the hands of rebels—he lives life on the interstellar road with his wife. Solly and Teyeo share a small cell for days and days with no sense of time; this forces them to connect. Fortunately for them both it is a significant and positive connection. Without this enforced "timeout," or at least a slowing down, the inductive chronotope doesn't likely to provide a character either the time or the specific place in order to find purpose. It is interesting that while we sometimes get the story of an envoy only from space flight to planetary mission, Le Guin never *only* tells the story of an envoy's early life before heading out on a mission. When she gives us the first part of an envoy's life (the countryside to city for training) it is *always* followed by the rest of the curve—space flight and the reverse, deductive, slowing chronotope.[45] It is as if the story of the inductive chronotope isn't one conducive to finding partners and purposes—homes. "Relations," the most vital quality of dialogism and in building home, "can only be established in terms of temporal and spatial parameters" (Holquist 1990, 150). The inductive chronotope doesn't do as good a job of setting those parameters, it seems.

As the story-suite with the threshold chronotope, the *Forgiveness* suite breaks out of the ironic mode that typifies life in Orsinia and Klatsand. These five stories provide romance, individually and collectively. They provide romance because of the way purposeful movement with companion creates home.[46] As Le Guin's novel genre varies in terms of threshold chronotopes, and the suites show us more than one way to handle time and place, the children's stories also employ multiple chronotopic ways to find home.

Children's Picture Books: A Genre of Multiple Chronotopes

In the sixth chapter, I discuss the implications for Le Guin's approach to age-based genres in relationship to the traditional genres of fantasy and realism. I argue there that she uses the genre of fantasy as her ethical guide for defining the boundary between children's and adult literature. While it is true that Le Guin relies on fantasy as a generic context for children's picture books, the works vary in the ways chronotopes are used, which would suggest that her approaches are more varied than it would at first appear.

While the novels and suites have fairly consistent chronotopic patterns, though they vary by degree, the children's books are much less consistent despite their surface level similarities. While they are almost exclusively fantastic, they are not at all consistent in terms of the way time and space operate. Some of the 12 operate in a dream chronotope, others use the deductive chronotope, others still an inductive model (as described in *Four Ways to Forgiveness*), and one is an example of the chronotope of singular time and place as seen in two of the three suites. In short, the short books are long on chronotopic variety. Even within fantasy there is some variety among the 11 purely fantastic picture books. Le Guin uses portal fantasy (where primary and secondary worlds exist), fantasy that features a world that mixes the real and the fantastic, and outright secondary world fantasy, but the chronotopes don't correspond to those fantasy subgenre lines. How characters attempt to find home in Le Guin's picture books doesn't seem to be a matter of genre but a matter of chronotope, and some characters are more successful than others.[47]

The dream chronotope (which isn't restricted to stories about dreams) accounts for the largest group within Le Guin's children's picture books. In the dream chronotope we have the reverberating movement back and forth—the repeated cycle. The Catwings books (1988–99), which mix the real and the fantastic by featuring anthropomorphic cats with wings in our real world, participates in the dream chronotope. The series chronicles the four, then five, cats' journeys from the city (where their wingless mother resides still) to Overhill Farm and back again. The fact that the kittens are so unearthly helps Le Guin create the need for their constant movement and accounts for its difference from other dream stories. This is also true of the children in *Fish Soup* (1992), as we'll see below.[48] The cats are trapped in a constant dream world that has horrifying possibilities and would almost necessarily lead to madness in an adult story, which is itself interesting. Consider that what makes much horror fiction horrific is that the unworldly is found in or brought here to our world. It is for this reason that the kits—ironically the "monsters" in this story—are in a sense doomed to keep on the move. These cats are the product of a dream: their mother theorizes that they have wings because she "dreamed, before they were born, that [she] could fly away from this neighborhood" (*Catwings*, 3). As children from the dream world they can never be completely at home in any one place, and so they are to find home on the wing. The series, on to its fourth book now, keeps moving them about between places—it's too dangerous for them to be still in the waking world.

Home isn't settled upon when the kittens find Overhill Farm in the first book: home would be purchased at the high and ultimately certain price of discovery. Safety here comes only with the conditions of silence and secrecy at the price of true freedom. The kittens are hidden from the world as well as they can be. Their discovery would mean their likely capture, and their human child "caretakers," Susan and Hank, are only so powerful in terms of ensuring safety because they are themselves children. At the end of series' first book, *Catwings* (1988), the children promise each other that they will "never ever tell anybody else" because, as Hank observes, "you know how people are" (38). That fear is reiterated in the beginning of *Catwings Return*

(1989): "the children had known that they must keep [the catwings] a secret. They feared people would want to put them in cages, in circuses or pet shows or laboratories, to make money by owning them or selling them" (5). Indeed, by the end of the third book the farm is becoming dangerously busy. The kittens end up visiting their mother and valiantly trying to avoid the deleterious effects of staying both still and quiet. Small creatures are always in more danger when they are denied the option of movement; silence and stasis can often lead to more danger, to which any farmer who searches his or her fields for, and always finds, fawns at haying time can attest.

On the very last page of the third book in the series, Wonderful Alexander and the Catwings (1994), James decides that they've "got to pay another visit to Mother. It will make her so happy when you talk to her, Jane" (*Wonderful*, 42). The danger is finally realized when, in the fourth and last book of the series, *Jane on Her Own* (1999), Jane takes off on her own without out a partner with whom to confer along the way. She is off "adventuring" because she is bored by life on the farm; they've stayed still too long, she thinks (*Jane*, 6). She may be right, but their sense of purpose stays clear when they travel together. Upon arriving in the city, Jane flies into the window and life of a man who presents himself as "Poppa" but who mysteriously promises that he "has plans for [her]" (*Jane*, 15). Her solitary flight almost ends tragically, except she has the good luck to escape. It is pretty clear that any of her siblings would have advised Jane to avoid flying into open windows, windows that can easily be closed. With "Poppa," Jane finds a model of home that is prison, where windows stay closed, where a bad "parent" keeps her trapped at home because "it's dangerous out there" (*Jane*, 23), and where she has to perform in order to be of any worth.

The movement from, to, and back home in this series shows the degree to which neither any one place nor caretaker can be settled upon, and implies the danger of hasty, or in fact any settlement, as we see above in *Jane on Her Own*. Early in *Catwings Return*, James and Harriet decide to head back to the city in order to see how their mother is and to "see the old alley just one more time" (7). The two leave the farm despite Roger's serious objection: "It's dangerous. Mother told us to use our wings to escape, and we did. We should stay where it's safe" (6). But where is it safe? Is being with Mother safe? Not in the first book. Both places offer their own dangers and conditions of safety, after all.

To make the return trip even more provocative, Harriet, in the series' second book, lays claim to a "Homing Instinct," while her brother James's instinct "doesn't say anything" (10). "The Homing Instinct," Harriet tells us, will lead the kittens "straight back to the place where [they] were born" (9). Harriet's instinct, it turns out, is questionable at best. She decides it is "out of practice" and abandons it for sight and smell as the city lights and the aroma of refuse guide them "home" (10). While Le Guin says, "it is the animal that knows the way, the way home" ("The Child and the Shadow," 63), it seems that some of them have a little trouble. On their return from their return, the cats "cheerfully [hoped] that their Homing Instinct knew what it was doing" (*Catwings Return*, 43). "Home" is, as illustrated by instinct, neither of the two places—and both; home is found in the reverberation between two sites by sets of characters. Jane, upon her escape from "Poppa" in the last book, decides to find Mother, and she does. Mother is with a human named Sarah Wolf. Jane and her mother look on, more than a little concerned, as this "wolf" approaches the window through which Jane has just entered: "Sarah opened the window wider. 'I expect that's how you'd like it,' she said to Jane" (*Jane*, 39). She turns out to be a civilized wolf.

These are risky circular journeys, illustrating that neither one safe place nor one special person necessarily makes for a sense of security and identity. *Lutwack* contrasts the circular with the linear journey: the circular journey, consisting of a trip out to a number of places and a return to the starting place, suggests a closed universe of limited possibilities. The linear journey, on the other hand, originates in the hope that some foreign place harbors a truth that the familiar place cannot supply (60). Le Guin's Catwings series couples the insecurity of reverberating between each contingent home with the liberation of multiple truths found in different sites.

Le Guin has claimed that most of her stories are excuses for journeys, though "in the most circuitous ways" ("Introduction," *City of Illusions*, 140–42). She observes, however, that "if all novels achieved or even attempted circularity, novel readers would rightly rebel" ("Introduction," *Rocannon's World,* 129)—including children, presumably. While Perry Nodelman observes that the plot of the "generic" children's story follows a circular narrative pattern (*The Pleasures of Children's Literature*, 148), Jon Stott observes that "the most common pattern in stories enjoyed by younger children is that of the linear journey of wish fulfillment" (473). In this series, Le Guin gives us linear tales that double back continuously making it difficult to say whether they are linear or circular—interestingly we have in this children's picture book series the same complication that gives critics fits when dealing with Shevek. It is less important to return or leave than it is to stay in motion with a companion in the search for purpose. The wingless ones may stay put in this series: Alexander (a neighborhood farm cat) and the human children, Hank and Susan, always keep home base on Overhill Farm; Mother and Sarah Wolf hold down the fort in the city. But then they aren't the main characters. The winged ones need to stay on the move.

The Catwings books show that home is left unfixed—both in the individual ends and beginnings and in their extrapolative, collective ending; *Fish Soup* has an open ending as well. The protagonists, the Writing Woman of Maho and the Thinking Man of Moha, lead contented and neatly separate lives that are in binary opposition (she is neat, he sloppy; she writes, he thinks). While the text at first limits itself to a study in opposites, it moves beyond a simple binary opposition as the main story develops. What results is a tale that ends with movement and community, leaving readers unsure of what single place home might be and with whom.

One day, as the two protagonists sit in the Man of Moha's spotless kitchen eating custard, the man gets a thought—a thought shared between the two that will serve as the literal "conception" of the children: "'I've been thinking,' he said, 'that it would be nice if we had a child.' 'Whatever for?' the woman asked. The man thought for some time and then said, 'It could run back and forth between our houses and carry messages for us when we're busy'" (6–7). From this moment of the children's conception their movement between places seems to be identified as purposeful—as a way and a reason for them to exist; however, this vision of isolated and limited movement won't ultimately work.

The man dreams up a girl, and the woman, a boy. After the parents find their respective dream children inadequate for various reasons, they re-conceive their plan and, therefore, their children: 'I've thought of something,' said the man. 'Let's trade. You take him and I'll take her' (16). These parents continue to keep the children separated from each other and restricted to one site, divided up like tradable property. When, near the end of the book, the two adults confer regarding their dissatisfaction with the children (interestingly, in the children's presence, reinforcing their status as objects), the woman observes, "Perhaps it depends on what we expect of them" (26). After the children are given voice and tell the grown-ups what it is that they like to do, they become free to move between homes, serving as agents of mediation between the two extreme sites of behavior on their own terms and for their own purposes.

Once the adults and children seem happier about the expectations for the children there is produced a version of "home" that is unclear and dynamic regarding the notions of parents, purpose, location, and affiliation. One result is that the binaries break down, and relationship is no longer a simple matter of opposition: we are told near the end of the tale that "she could think, and the man could write, too" (26). With the breakdown of opposition at the end of the tale we seem to get a formulaic "happily-ever-after" trajectory. "So they all lived at Maho and Moha, in and out and back and forth across the hills. The woman's house got a little neater, and the man's house got a lot messier. The boy made a Trained Mouse Circus, which the cats took a great interest in; and the girl climbed every tree in the woods between Moha and Maho. And they all learned how to cook excellent fish soup" (30–32). They all become less extreme and, therefore, less one-dimensional, though the children hardly become fleshed out in a satisfactory way. As characters, they do not become unified in or bound to a single home with a common vision of where and how one should spend ever after—or with whom. The boy will spend a lot of time at the river fishing for dinner, and we might assume he takes the catch to both home sites; the girl will spend some of her time in the woods on either side of the bridge between the houses; the man and the woman will spend time in both homes and also in moving between sites with their children. All will spend time with others and alone. Le Guin has elsewhere criticized the simplistic vision of Tolstoy's happy family; happy families are more complicated, and their happiness is always tentative ("All Happy Families," 46). Home and identity, it seems, exist not only somewhere in the middle, but also in all points between in the journey and at each end with a variety of people.

The close of *Fish Soup* is at once promising and tentative in its open-endedness. Like the Catwings series, *Fish Soup* defers settlement in favor of establishing a home of process. To keep the sense of home(s) that they have opened up through dialogue, the children in both tales need to keep moving with purpose and according to some expectation. Standing still will result in a return to the problems found earlier in *Fish Soup* or the dangers present in any one home site in the Catwings books. As dream children in the waking world, these characters need to keep on the move.

I would argue that one reason that the children fail to ever become real to the reader isn't due to their dream origin (the catwings are endearing, after all), or to any lack of movement, but because they remain rather isolated from each other. They each move between houses, but they don't seem to move together; they remain rather silent and ephemeral to the very end, despite ultimately gaining a normal appearance. But then the children arguably aren't really as important as the Man of Moha and the Woman of Maho, who remain the protagonists and who do manage to help each other grow through their association. I think one could make a convincing case that this isn't a children's book as much as it is a picture book/cautionary tale for adults who are planning to have children.

Another dream chronotope, *A Ride on the Red Mare's Back* (1992), also features a journey through mediating forests that ends in a return home.[49] In this story, a nameless girl searches for her brother, who has been wrested from his father in the forest and kidnapped by trolls. When it is apparent that her parents have given the boy up for lost, she takes the wooden red mare figurine that her father had carved her, which comes to life and assists her in her quest, and goes after her brother. The red mare keeps the trolls at bay as the girl rescues her brother from the troll's nightmarish lair. The companions return triumphant from the nightmare world to their happy parents in the real, waking world.

As we see in the above children's books in the dream chronotope, each tale ends happily enough with the hint that more movement is to come, and the protagonists are better equipped for those journeys. Central to each of these tales is the threshold: the bridge in *Red Mare*, as in *Fish Soup*, spans a river at a central point in the narrative geography just before a forest. The forests through which the protagonist must travel serve as opportunities for confronting the dangers of silence, isolation, and the resulting stasis or homelessness that would come from giving in or staying put.

The forest between homes is a construction Le Guin uses in several books: the catwings must fly over and through the woods in their visits to and from home(s); Tenar and Therru travel through the woods between the farmer's and wizard's houses several times in the course of *Tehanu* (1990);[50] and Davidson must try to navigate the forests of Athshe in order to stay alive in *The Word for World is Forest*.[51] The forest is the threshold to a completely different kind of place: the dream world. The respective forests offer the characters the opportunity for mediation, action, and meditation—time to process and become. Ironically, however, the forest simultaneously threatens the sojourner with more dangerous and oppressive manifestations of the things they left behind: silence, darkness, loss of self though isolation, and paralysis. Characters must tether themselves to each other as they travel in order to avoid aimlessness, which is one reason why we see so much weaving and threading imagery in Le Guin's work. The metaphor of weaving explains the necessary connectedness one must have among places and people in those spaces between homes.

In Le Guin's fiction, weaving is a powerful means of both connecting people and shaping the world, helping the reader to understand the importance of connectedness and purposeful movement. Threads pulled from the fabric of one reality can be used for finding one's way through the labyrinth of another—and offer material for this purpose more trustworthy in a forest than breadcrumbs! When her mother tells her not to go far, the girl in *Red Mare* finds that "her mother's voice was like a fine, thin thread of silk or silver that lay behind her as she walked across the snowy fields and into the forest, looking for her brother who had been taken by trolls" (16).[52] Such a thread reaches out to the other side without cutting oneself off from "this side." The girl uses it as a lifeline as she walks on and sees "nothing but the tall dark trees" (*Red Mare*, 16). Once she secures her little brother from the trolls, the girl knows that "down the slopes of the mountain, across the snowy plain, reaching into the forest, lay a thin, fine, silvery thread, delicate as a spiderweb. 'This way,' the girl said. And they set off, following the silvery thread" (*Red Mare*, 41). The thread gives them the power to move and offers the reader a vision of the multiple sites of the home, the forest, and the troll castle through the link. The thread helps the children defeat the immobilizing panic of both the forest and the truly alien others with whom they have made contact.

Le Guin's treatment of the question of whether protagonists may stay in the places to which they've traveled connects *The Beginning Place* and *Red Mare* with the Catwings books and *Fish Soup*.[53] Le Guin makes it clear to the reader that neither Hugh nor Irene can stay in Tembreabrezi—nor can the little brother stay with the trolls, as he seems determined to do when his sister first finds him. The other worlds in these narratives are seductive fantasies that must be resisted with the help of another.[54] These alternative homes offer only escapism rather than the reflection of solitude. Alone, Hugh, Irene, and the little brother think they've found "home" on the other side of their respective forests in the dream world, but Le Guin reminds us that "the point about Elfland is that you are not at home there."[55] Hugh, we understand, is kidding himself when he claims, "I got here. I finally got somewhere. I made it" (*Beginning*, 10)—a sentiment the deluded Jane seems to echo when she finds Poppa's open window in *Jane on Her Own*, or Cob—another "spider" who believes he has cheated death in *The Farthest Shore*.[56] Hugh and Irene, separately and in isolation, share the same false vision of Tembreabrezi. Slowly, though, the adolescents come to realize that complete separation between the two worlds is unnatural: "You did not talk of one place in the other place. You did not tell them where you came from, unless they asked. No one, in either country, ever asked" (*Beginning*, 48).

The home that the girl and her little brother return to in *Red Mare* is silent without being expectant. The silent, still parents listen in disbelief to the story of the rescue (45). After the thread of their narrative has spun itself out, the parents embrace their children. But the father's gift to his brave daughter challenges the "resolution" at story's end. As *Jane on Her Own* ends with the promise of action, the father's gift of the carved yet unpainted colt indicates an unfinished state in the guise of the traditional closed ending. There is a continued story implied in the young colt: there will be a use for that colt as there was for its "mother"—the red mare. While Elfland isn't a place in which we can stay, we will travel there from time to time and will need means of keeping a healthy purpose and a link to other places and people.

In *The Adventure of Cobbler's Rune* (1982), Le Guin's first children's story, the dream chronotope is also used. The protagonist, the horse Cobbler, wanders "into the jungle which covered the western side of Kroy. He soon lost his way, but he did not care, and went on."[57] His meandering comes to a purpose, however. He dives into a pool of water, guided by a magical fish, only to find the world of the Milts—absurd and nasty creatures that are unfortunately designed amalgamations of various other creatures. Cobbler discovers that the Milts are planning to cross over into Kroy to conquer Cobbler's people through a door that opens once every five hundred years. Cobbler returns just ahead of them to sound the warning and leads the nightmare of horror behind him across the threshold of the alternative or dream world. Thanks to the advance warning, the Kroy folk repel the invaders and Cobbler is rightly celebrated as a hero. In this first of Le Guin's books, written when she was still a teenager, she shows us a traditional circular movement from which her later children's and adult works would break. Home is simply where one began and, like Dorothy's Kansas farm, is where one should be. We could argue that because Cobbler's nature is what made him wander in the unfamiliar jungle in the first place that he will go journeying again, but the narrative doesn't offer this open ending.

The second book of Kroy, *Solomon Leviathan's Nine Hundred and Thirty-First Trip Around the World* (1983), employs the inductive chronotope that we see in *Four Ways to Forgiveness*'s "Forgiveness Day," however. As Teyeo's journey is inductive, so is the journey of the three travelers in *Solomon Leviathan*. This is perhaps the rarest chronotope in her fiction and is actually most often seen in her children's fiction, an irony given the common assumption that children's fiction usually celebrates a return to a particular home, as discussed above. In this tale characters move from the specific and narrow place to the more general and limitless expanses enjoyed by the wanderer.

Damon[58] the giraffe and Ophidia the boa constrictor, last seen as the first of Cobbler's helpers in Kroy, embark on a journey to find the horizon. In their little rowboat they meet up with Solomon Leviathan, "the second son of the first whale."[59] By book's end they "have already been around the world; they have not caught up with the horizon yet, but they are having such a good time trying that they intend to go right on" (32). It is a whimsical book on all levels, and Le Guin has the three unlikely companions join in a purpose for what they are told—by the eldest elephant—"is not a place. It does not exist" (29). Solomon decides, however, that "the horizon must exist . . . if we want to get to it" and off they go (29). The journey begins on Damon and Ophidia's home island of Kroy—but home, it seems, is really continuous (in this case endless) and purposeful journeying with companions who are necessary to the trek.

The other inductive journey can be found in Le Guin's latest children's picture book, *Tom Mouse* (2002).[60] As in *Solomon Leviathan*, *Tom Mouse* features an animal on a journey. What is different is that Tom, like the catwings, lives in a mixed fantasy and has to deal with humans in our world. As the catwings find friends in Hank, Susan, and Ms. Wolf, Tom Mouse finds Ms. Powers.[61] However, the human is the partner in the journey.

Tom's story begins in a diner in a train station somewhere between Chicago and San Francisco. There "his family was content with their cozy nest," a "hole in the wall," but Tom "watched the great trains come into the station and leave again [and] wished he could go with them" (*Tom*, n.p.). Emboldened by the tales of the old hobo rat that visits his family, Tom makes the break and stows away on a train heading to Chicago. Only through Ms. Powers' friendly intervention and well-intentioned chiding does Tom gain some safety as a traveler. He hasn't the wings that the catwings have to help him on his way, and so he must rely on the kindness of this stranger who is soon to be friend and traveling companion. Ms. Powers serves the same purpose Solomon serves in *Solomon Leviathan* in that without her help the traveler's physical limitations would keep his journey to a few miles—and very likely a gruesome end. Even though they are unable to speak to each other, they each sense the need of the other—she of Tom's for travel and he of Ms. Powers' for companionship. Tom gains that much needed help to achieve his purpose. The principle characters from *Solomon Leviathan* and *Tom Mouse*—Damon and Ophidia and Tom, respectively—move from a specific place, their homes, to the wide open spaces of constant travel in a way few of Le Guin's travelers do.

The eponymous spider Leese Webster (1979) and the children in *Fire and Stone* (1989) undertake the deductive journeys most evident in Le Guin's novels.[62] In these narratives the journey is from the site of civilization to the wilderness, but narrowed to a place of peace with the help of a companion. It is characteristic of all of Le Guin's deductive chronotopes that the move to the more and more narrow actually takes one into the wild, but the wild in Le Guin's work is not part of a binary of order and chaos. It is a different kind of order.

Leese moves from the central part of the deserted palace—the throne room, and the throne itself—to a more deserted room upstairs in order to find a place in which to practice her web art. After doing a great deal of work and improving her art, she is still unsatisfied. She remembers the beautiful jewels of the throne and is frustrated that she cannot "catch the colors of the light, as those stones caught it" (*Leese,* n.p.).

The cleaning ladies find her art and alert the authorities, which begin to encase the beautiful webs behind glass. "Stop that!" Leese calls to the workers. "'If you cover my webs with glass, how can they catch flies?' Leese shouted. 'I'll starve!'" We are told, "the workmen paid no attention" (*Leese,* n.pg.).

The ladies find Leese during their room cleaning. Instead of stepping on her, as one of them suggests, they shake her out the window into the garden. Leese lands on a "broad, sunlight-speckled leaf" and at first thinks herself killed. She opens her eyes to see the stars reflected in the water of the lily pool and believes them to be jewels. Heartened by the sight, she decides to try to "decorate" this new "room" she finds herself in and begins a simple web to catch a meal. The next morning comes and Leese is excited to find that the dew on her web has caught the light of the morning sun. The beads of water "shone brighter than the jewels of the throne, brighter even than the stars." We learn then that "breakfast came buzzing by. Leese ate it thankfully, while she watched her web glittering with diamond water beads. 'That's the most beautiful web I ever wove,' she thought" (*Leese,* n.pg.).

Leese, like E.B. White's Charlotte, knows that a web is functional art. While Charlotte is a wordsmith, Leese is a visual artist, and each finds new purpose with the exercise. The branch of roses on which Leese weaves is the place where she finds her latest home; though we can be sure others will follow. But home isn't the plant, after all, it is the purpose she pursues on that or any plant, initially achieved through both her own sense of need and the help of others offered in a journey up and out. And the web is "the most beautiful" not because of her own design, but because of the help of other elements that, as George Orr finds in his "creations," contribute to success. Leese, too, has found "home" with a little help from her friends.

Fire and Stone also features the movement out toward peace with the help of another; the story begins with the problem clearly laid out: "there was a country that lived in fear of a dragon" (n.pg.). The visits were mysterious— "no one knew when the dragon would come, or why, or what it was seeking. The visits were as destructive as they were mysterious. As a result, when villagers heard the cry "RRRAAAHHHX!" they would drop everything and jump in Rocky Pond.

On one occasion the children Podo and Min find themselves side-by-side in the pond, each having trouble: Podo is sinking too deep and Min is floating too high. They cling to each other and balance out, sinking just right. Together they begin to talk about the dragon, something that apparently didn't happen very often. Fear silences, after all, but the comfort of a companion helps to loosen the tongue. Min observes, "It sounds like it's saying *rocks! rocks!*" Podo wonders aloud to her, "If it wants to eat us . . . why is it saying *rocks! rocks!*" Min offers up a wild theory: "Do you think it wants rocks to *eat*?" They decide to feed the dragon rocks. As the mayor continues to hiss at them to be still and silent, exactly what a Le Guin character must never be, the children toss the rocks they find at the bottom of the pond up into the air. The dragon swoops to catch and gulp them down.

The dragon finally alights, heavy with stones. Min and Podo, along with some of the pluckier villagers, continue to offer it rocks until it is full. "When Min walked right up to it and put a nice flint into its mouth, the dragon slowly, slowly chewed the rock, as if it were a piece of toffee." The dragon, now full, "closed its mouth and closed its eyes. It slept. All its fire and hunger had been filled up, and it was only stone."

Together Min and Podo do what those alone in their fear and stuck in the mud of Rock Pond never consider. Le Guin does not move from this scene to one in which the people return to the village to complete the circle and resume happy home life and, perhaps, a celebration. Rather, Le Guin shows the children atop the grassy hill that once was the dragon. They are looking at the sunrise. From there they can "see far" and "sit there and talk about things." They continue to search for meaning, as children must. They have come this far together, through their own collaboration of wits and courage, and go out beyond the threshold of the village to a "wild place" called home. As children they go home each day to the village, but as these two look outward toward the sunrise we are given a sense that some unknown journeys await them. As a reminder of their accomplishment, "sometimes they hear the dragon singing with them, very softly, deep down inside."

Another of the only three Le Guin picture books to feature an actual child as the main character is *A Visit from Dr. Katz* (1988). Like *A Ride on the Red Mare's Back* and *Fire and Stone*, this book's main character is for now tethered to home, but unlike those books the bond is stronger because it is also Le Guin's only picture book that employs realism, and it features a sick child. It is the picture book most like the story suite chronotope of singular place in anachrony.

Marianne has the flu and is made to stay in bed. Her mother, whose face we never see, tells her that she'll "see if Dr. Katz will come in and see you" (n.pg.). The illustrations clarify the odd information the words provide: "Dr. Katz comes in on eight white paws, and goes two different directions." Her two cats, Philip and Lorenzo, "who is called The Bean," are pictured entering the room. The entire action of the book takes place over the course of about an hour and never leaves the little girl's bedroom. The book marks an exception in so many ways, but none more important than being the only children's book by Le Guin that really isn't a narrative. The book is a delightful description of two cats and their activities with and around Marianne over a brief span of time. Events are not sequential and easily interchangeable. The activities of "Dr. Katz" are randomly described, much as the activities of characters in *Orsinian Tales* and *Searoad*. But for all of that, the book shows us someone being helped toward a goal—in this case comfort, and ultimately sleep—by friends. The book does show cause and effect (cat comforting leads to sleep), so it isn't without chronology, but the interior action is not guided by cause and effect. The sense of "purpose" is small in scale, though Marianne might disagree. It isn't enough, though, that she is in the house she lives in; she still has to be helped home.

Margaret Higonnet argues that "children's literature creates clear expectations about how narratives will proceed and particularly about how they will conclude"[63] (37). She argues that "it is by now a cliché that authors of children's literature rely on the 'return home' to round an adventure and restore a sense of security and world order" (47). But there really isn't that much agreement. Christopher Clausen speculates, "when home is where we ought, on the whole, to stay—we are probably dealing with a story for children. When home is the chief place from which we must escape . . . then we are involved in a story for adolescents or adults."[64] In contrast, Jon Stott observes that "the most common pattern in stories enjoyed by younger children is that of the linear journey of wish fulfillment."[65] And Perry Nodelman explains that "a child or childlike creature, bored by home, wants the excitement of adventure; but since the excitement is dangerous, the child wants the safety of home—which is boring, and so the child wants the excitement of danger—and so on."[66] He acknowledges recursivity. We see linearity, circularity, and recursivity all within Le Guin's 12 picture books. So, in a sense Le Guin isn't doing anything that isn't ever done in children's literature, instead she does it all. This suggests that while the idea of home is important to her, it isn't manifested in a single pattern.

Whether the move is toward the broad or narrow, across thresholds in one direction or back and forth, it needs to be made with a purpose clarified and fortified by a friend, which is itself the movement to/of home. This is true across all of her fiction to varying degrees, regardless of genre, the age of the implied audience, or even chronotope. It is the chronotope, however, that best reveals how this phenomenon is manifested. Characters fail and succeed in the process of finding home, and they can be said to do that based on the ways they connect with each other and the way they move across time and place. We see healthy characters in all of these tales and books negotiating among places through space, tethered to places and people, risking place-lessness and isolation in search for purpose and home. Le Guin's narratives —whether "simple" chronological tales for children or fragmented narra-tives for the adult—are "creation unfinished."[67] In all of her books, home is that space in which we are all always moving, with whomever we're with, and with the great risk of actually arriving.

An examination of Le Guin's chronotopes reveals some things not other-wise clear simply by grouping her stand-alone stories by genre—whether that might be by novel, suite, children's tale, or fantasy, realism, or science fiction. Genre separations are useful in many ways, but, in examining Le Guin's work as a series of variations in the same project, how surprising to see just how similar her children's picture book *A Visit from Dr. Katz* is to the suite *Orsinian Tales*, and how interesting that the science fiction novel *The Word for World is Forest* and the picture book folktale *A Ride on the Red Mare's Back* should be so similar in topic! These are stories that might be considered incomparable as specimens from different genres or as experiences meant for different age readers. It is certain that genre is no limitation for using one of the four chronotopic variations for the same goal of getting characters home. The deductive, inductive, dream, and single site/time chronotopes cross all of the genres listed above, and provide us with lines of connection, lines of vi-sion, lines of thought that are typically ignored because of the often hierarchi-cal effects of generic divisions. We can, starting from a point at the beginning of each tale, consider in what direction characters move over time and to what degree they are assisted as they pursue a purpose. Here we see the subtle vari-ations of her work because we consider all of her projects to be attempting the same thing—finding home through time and place.

By examining this chronotopic variety, we are able to consider the de-grees of movement and time (as well as the directions) that Le Guin draws on in her mission to help characters find their way home. This helps us un-derstand that her work is related by degree as well as by kind. Any format (novel, suite, picture book) and any context (fantasy, realism, science fic-tion) can be the vehicle for a search for home. Home is found—and lost —in all genres and can be sought in many directions and over, in, and out of time by various degrees.

4

Earthsea: Crossover Series of Multiple Continua

> The epic world is an utterly finished thing, not only as an authentic event of
> the distant past but also on its own terms and by its own standards; it is im-
> possible to change, to re-think, to re-evaluate anything in it.
>
> **Mikhail Bakhtin**
> *The Dialogic Imagination*

With the recent publication of *The Other Wind* (2001), Le Guin makes it clear
that neither past nor present Earthsea can be considered "known" even to her
most careful readers.[1] The islands shake under our feet, and the stars in the
sky change before our eyes. *Tehanu* (1990)—the fourth of what is now six
books in the series—was subtitled *The Last Book of Earthsea*, but as James
Bond actor Sean Connery learned, one should never say "never again."[2]

That Earthsea has been continued and revised shouldn't surprise us anymore. That Earthsea has undergone gender, culture, and even species re-
alignment is obvious. What may surprise, other than the time that it takes a
new Earthsea vision to bubble up from the depths of Le Guin's imagination,
is the development (rather than evolution) of both the place and the telling of
the place by genre. The Earthsea series is Le Guin's crossover series; it's
where she creates connections between genres, readers of different genres,
as well as readers defined by age. From *A Wizard of Earthsea* (1968)[3] to *The
Other Wind,* we have an expansive movement from younger reader to more
mature, from epic to novel, from a binary world to a world of continua and
blurred distinctions—therefore, from solitary and more archetypal characters to novelized characters multiple in identity and communal in their approach to the world. The journey from 1968 to 2001 is one traveled along
multiple lines.

From Epic to Novel

The first two Earthsea tales appeared in *Fantastic* in 1964. In January of that
year "The Word of Unbinding" was published,[4] which introduced us to our
first Earthsea wizard, Festin, stuck beneath the earth in a spell trap by the

corrupt wizard Voll. Festin becomes free of Voll's trap when he "whisper[s] the word of unbinding, which is spoken only once."[5] He goes to the land of death in order to chase the evil wizard and conquer him there. This is Le Guin's first statement on making one's peace with death in Earthsea. The echoes of this idea of the wizard's relationship to death and to the nature of magic are to be heard 37 years through all six books. The second story, "The Rule of Names," came out in April of that same year and introduced us to our first Earthsea dragon, Yevaud, whose name, unlike Festin's or Voll's, will appear throughout the series and in the latest volume.[6] Ideas and characters will remain constant throughout the series, albeit revised.

A Wizard of Earthsea appeared in 1968 after Herman Schein of Parnassus Press convinced Le Guin to write something for young adult readers.[7] This is the story of young Duny whose aunt, a village witch, sees in him the power of wizardry. Ogion, mage of Duny's home, Gont Island, gives the boy his true name—Ged—and begins to train the boy. But Ged, known as Sparrowhawk (for to know one's true name is to have power over him or her), goes to Roke to train at the wizard school. There, full of pride, he releases a spirit from the dead as part of a schoolboy dare, and with it comes a shadow that tries to kill Ged. The Archmage Nemmerle, who dies in the attempt, chases off the shadow. After healing from his wounds, Ged travels Earthsea, a vast archipelago. At first he is pursued by the shadow, but soon acts as pursuer himself. At the end Ged, with the help of his old schoolmate Vetch, learns that he must embrace his shadow and, after a long chase, finds the shadow and names it with his own name, freeing himself from torment.

The series, then, begins with what Le Guin understood to be an important kind of story for adolescents: the tale of a young person's coming of age.[8] From the very beginning, the series was to target (and be adopted by) the young adult reader, though as is the case with all of Le Guin's work, readers came from all directions. Closely following this first novel came, in two-year increments, *The Tombs of Atuan* (1970) and *The Farthest Shore* (1972).[9] The second book of the series, *The Tombs of Atuan*, is the story of Ged's pursuit of the other half of a sacred ring, The Ring of Erreth-Akbe. To claim it, he must travel to the Tombs of Atuan at the eastern edge of Earthsea and steal it from the tombs themselves, guarded by the Old Powers. The tombs are the province of a child–priestess, once named Tenar before she was taken from her parents as a toddler and put in her office. Tenar traps Ged in the tombs, but instead of killing him, as she had other raiders, she listens to his tale of the ring, a ring which, he tells her, is necessary for a king to rule over Earthsea, for "no king could rule well if he did not rule beneath that sign" (*Tombs*, 110). The two become friends as Tenar begins to desire a new life away from the barren place, and they plot to take the ring from Atuan before the priestess Kossil, Tenar's corrupt mentor, can stop them. Ged and Tenar escape, and in the process the tombs, and Kossil with them, are destroyed. The two ring bearers return to Earthsea's capital city, Havnor, in triumph.

The concluding book of the initial trilogy, *The Farthest Shore*, pairs now Archmage Ged with yet another young adult—Prince Arren of Havnor. Magic has begun to fail in Earthsea, and wizards forget their spells, so Ged and Arren begin their journey over Earthsea to find out what is happening. They discover that a wizard, Cob, has devised a spell from ancient lore that has opened the door between the land of the dead and of the living, a door through which magic is draining. Ged and Arren journey to the land of the dead, called the Dry Land, and confront Cob, a character trapped in life by his own spell. In their confrontation, Ged helps Cob die and seals the doorway between the two lands, though it drains his power. While Arren ascends his throne as King Lebannen, Ged—bereft of power and "done with doing" (196)—flies off astride the great dragon Kallesin toward his boyhood home on Gont. He is secure in the knowledge that prophecy has been fulfilled with Arren's ascension, and he has finished sealing the great breach in the world.

This first Earthsea trilogy garnered praise from those in a position to reward excellence in children's literature, yet it was not commented upon by critics of fiction for adults. As Ged flew off into the north astride a dragon, Le Guin picked up the American Library Association's Newbery Honor citation, the Boston Globe Horn Book Award for Excellence, and the National Book Award for children's literature. Twenty years after *The Tombs of Atuan* was published it was runner-up for the International Children's Literature Association's Phoenix Award, given to a book that didn't win a major award when it first came out but which has stood the test of time. Interestingly, her next Earthsea book after the initial trilogy, *Tehanu*, came out about the time Le Guin was given a Phoenix honor citation for *Tombs,* which seems to indicate that 18 years is enough of an increment for a book in this series to win an award for adult literature—the Nebula.

By the end of *The Farthest Shore*, Le Guin, while leaving us with so many possibilities unseen until *Tehanu*, seems to have her myth-teller narrator re-establish order through Ged's and Lebannen's heroic journey to the dry land to reaffirm the boundaries of death. [10] The dry land, so reminiscent of the ancient Greeks' Hades, is walled back up and we hope for a return to equilibrium in life, death, and magic—all with the additional bonus of fulfilled prophecy: the establishment of a king in Havnor. It is to be believed that the Summoner, and those with special summoning powers like Ged himself, will still be able to engage in traffic between the land of living and dead, though a wall will mark the clear difference between two poles of existence. [11] Le Guin will rethink the nature of that traffic in subsequent volumes, however. We have, by the end of the third volume of the first series, the hero's life story as far as it is necessary to tell, and he flies off into the ether with the eldest of all dragons in what amounts to the ascension of the hero, body and soul, onto "The Other Wind." His return will differ greatly from that of Christ and Arthur, however, as he returns to earth in the novels to come, more carpenter than king.[12] It is the fourth book, published almost two decades later, that marks a change in Earthsea.

The fourth book of Earthsea, *Tehanu*, begins shortly before Ged arrives on Gont following his trials in the third book. On Gont we are reintroduced to Tenar, who has lived her life as a farmwife and mother following her decision not to study magic with Ogion. Returning from a visit to her daughter, Tenar finds a badly burned and physically abused girl left for dead. She names the child Therru and cares for her. During this time Ged returns, a shell of his former self and embarrassed at his loss of power. He, Tenar, and Therru form a family and Ged tries to learn to live as an ordinary man, but not without difficulty. On Gont a disciple of Cob's, the wizard Aspen, holds contempt for all three in the new family—Ged for his defeat of Cob, Tenar for her presumptuousness as a woman, and Therru for her "monstrosity"—and attempts to destroy the them all. Shortly before he prepares to cast Ged and Tenar off a cliff into the sea, Therru calls to the great and eldest dragon Kalessin, who carries Ged back to Gont. Kalessin arrives in time to destroy Aspen and claim that Therru is really Tehanu, and is also somehow both dragon and human. Kalessin promises to return for her someday, and the book ends with the promise of more change in Earthsea. For now, though, the family makes plans to live in Ogion's house and be at peace.

Tales from Earthsea (2001) is a collection of five tales that span hundreds of years of Earthsea history. It concludes with "A Description of Earthsea," almost thirty pages of Earthsea lore and history.[13] The first tale, "The Finder," is the story of Medra and the founding of the wizard's school on Roke.[14] With the help of Anieb, Medra escapes from Tinaral, who traps her as a slave. Aided by others, he finds his way to Roke, where those with wizardly power hide from Tinaral and an Earthsea that has grown distrustful and fearful of wizards, where corrupt wizards help warlords rule the Archipelago. When he is accepted on Roke, hidden from the world in a fog of wizardry, he volunteers his services to recruit powerful young people to attend a school on Roke, where they will be trained in responsible uses of power, in an effort to restore wizardry to respectability in Earthsea. The story explains how the school was formed as a place for both men and women, but it also shows the seeds of prejudice. By the time of *A Wizard of Earthsea* takes place hundreds of years later, the school strays from its egalitarian origins and develops a culture of misogyny that keeps women out of the school and away from the discipline, reducing them to ill-trained witches in years to come. "The Finder" ends before this time, however, and in the conclusion we see Medra become the ninth Master of Roke School—the Master Doorkeeper.

"Darkrose and Diamond" is a love story in which Diamond, a budding musician and son of a wealthy merchant on Gont, is found to have a wizard's power.[15] This is set in a time after women have been shut out of Roke and wizards must take a vow of celibacy in order to keep their power "pure." Diamond is forced to choose between wizardry and his love, Darkrose, a witch's daughter in his village. He initially chooses to study to be a wizard, pleasing his father in his choice to forgo a future as a "lowly" musician, and loses Darkrose in the process through a misunderstanding. Unhappy with his training, Diamond returns to his father's house and helps him run his business, forsaking his music and submerging his broken heart in business. At the celebration of his birthday, Diamond meets with Darkrose, who plays in a band at the celebration. He and she decide to run off together in order to foster both music and their love, shunning wizardry and wealth.

The third story, "The Bones of Earth," is the tale of how Ogion and his master, the wizard Dulse, still an earthquake that threatens to destroy much of Gont.[16] It is the true account of the event that contradicts Ogion's renown in *A Wizard of Earthsea* as the one who silenced the earth single-handedly. Dulse senses the impending disaster and has his apprentice Ogion help him stop the quake. Ogion is to go down to Gont port, stand for all to see on the signal tower of the city, and work to keep the Armed Cliffs from closing in on the port city. Dulse enters the earth at the top of the island and, working a spell that will have him become eternally one with the rock, quiets the rage of the earth. The Gontish folk see only Ogion's actions and attribute the act to him, which he denies to no avail. He returns to Dulse's house, weeps for his master, and begins his life in Dulse's old home—a home which will ultimately house Ged and Tenar at the series' end.

The penultimate tale is one that takes place during Ged's time as Archmage. "On the High Marsh" tells of Irioth, a renegade wizard who misused his power in summoning the dead, and then in summoning the Master Summoner and Ged to him in a power struggle. After being resisted, Irioth runs off into the wild. The story is one of his learning humility after great defeat as a sorcerer and animal healer among the common folk. There, in remote Semel, "a bit, desolate, waterland with a far horizon, few trees, not many people,"[17] he begins his self-healing. He becomes attached to Emer, a local widow woman, and their trust and love grow. When Ged tracks him down at the end of the story, he sees Irioth's change of heart and asks him to return to Roke with him. Irioth declines. He tells Ged that the people of the village "show me what I should do, and who I am" (194). He believes he has good, honest, and valued work to do there as a village sorcerer. Ged replies that he will tell them back on Roke "that the changes in a man's life may be beyond all the arts we know, and all our wisdom," ironic given Ged's future (194). As Ged will stay with Tenar despite calls for him to return to Roke, Irioth stays with Emer in domestic solace and humility and forgoes great power.

The volume's last story, "Dragonfly," brings us to the time of *Tehanu* and looks forward to *The Other Wind*.[18] Dragonfly is born to a landed family on the island of Way in their domain of Iria. After her mother dies, Dragonfly, a mysterious woman not originally from the island, is left alone with her father, a drunken and bitter man who resides in the old manor house of Iria but whose land has been divided among his rivalrous brothers. Dragonfly is, in effect, left to grow on her own—as undisciplined but as strong as a weed. At the age of 13, upset that nobody prepares a visit by a wizard for her to be given her true name, she seeks out the witch Rose to do it for her in secret. The witch reveals to her that her true name is "Irian," which enrages Dragonfly who sees the name as her father's rather than her own. The witch is uneasy about the name that has come to her, feels it is unfinished, but understands no more. Shortly after, a young wizard named Ivory arrives from Roke to be court wizard to Irian's uncle, owner of the richest land in Iria. Ivory tells them that he hasn't his wizard's staff because his Masters on Roke want him to have experience first, but assures the Master of Iria of Westpool that it will happen soon, to trust him. After Ivory meets Irian, who is fascinated by Roke and would love to be able to go, he devises a plan. Because it turns out Ivory has actually been expelled from Roke, he wants revenge. He also wants to sleep with Irian for the conquest of it. He works it out that he will tell his Master that he must return to Roke; he will take Irian with him, disguised as a boy, get her admitted to the school, and make a mockery of them all—a woman at Roke school! On the way, he tells her that he needs her true name to make a spell to make her seem a boy—all so that he can use the name to force her to sleep with him. He loses his nerve, and it seems that Irian only really used him to get to Roke. He still tries to help her to enter. Once at the gates of the school she is allowed inside by the Master Doorkeeper, who is not fooled, but senses that she is more than she seems, as the witch Rose sensed. She stays with the Master Patterner, who studies the patterns in the world, while the Masters of Roke discuss this curiosity—a woman who is more than she seems asking entrance into Roke. Thorion, Master Summoner and one who wishes to be Archmage, is adamantly opposed to the idea. A schism develops at Roke between those who want the Rule of Roke upheld (no women allowed), lead by Thorion, and those who want Irian to stay so they can understand what she signifies in the changing pattern of Earthsea. When Thorion confronts Irian, with intent to destroy her, Irian reveals the reason she is named only partly right: she transforms into a huge dragon and destroys Thorion. She hadn't herself suspected this transformation until this confrontation. She flies West, to the dragons, to find her other name, but promises to return to the Master Patterner if he should ever call. As Tehanu is at the same time being revealed on Gont as girl who is both girl and dragon, Irian is revealed on Roke.

The latest volume of Earthsea (though tempted, I cannot say "last") is *The Other Wind*. In this book, we learn about important Earthsea history and are given explanations for what the mysterious Tehanu and Irian actually are. Alder, whom we meet at story's outset, is a sorcerer and a mender—he is gifted in mending things that are broken. He begins to have dreams in which his dead wife, Lily, calls to him from the other side of the wall that divides the Dry Land from the world of the living; Ged himself spent his powers in the attempt to mend that division. The dreams come more and more insistently to Alder, however, and he senses that they aren't merely dreams but summons. It appears that Lily, and increasingly more spirits from the other side, calls to him for release. On Gont, he seeks Ged's help. Ged tells him to go to Havnor where Tenar, Tehanu, Lebannen, Irian, and others confer about what to do about the madness that has taken over many young dragons in the West Reach—they have encroached on the lands of people and have burned many farms. While on Havnor, in council, the dragon Kalessin (the Eldest), arrives to explain to them the history of the current imbalance in Earthsea, briefly described as vague lore in the appendix to *Tales from Earthsea* as *Vedurnan*—"The Division" ("Description," 270).[19] Once all dragons and humanity were one race. Over time some valued possessions, and others the liberty of flight. Kalessin explains that "Long ago we chose. We chose freedom. Men chose the yoke. We chose fire and wind. They chose water and earth. We chose the west, and they the east" (*Wind*, 151–152). He goes on to say that since then "in every generation of men, one or two are born who are dragons also. And . . . one of us is born who is also human" (*Wind*, 152). Irian is a dragon who is also human; Tehanu is a human who is also dragon. They will be the last to choose, Kalessin says, before the division that has been broken is re-established. Soon a party representative of all on Earthsea is established—Earthsea King Lebannen, Tenar (once priestess of Atuan), Tehanu, Irian, the sorcerer Alder, Roke wizard Onyx, Pelnish wizard Seppel, and Princess Seserakh of the Kargs of the far East of Earthsea—and they journey to Roke to the Immanent Grove of the Patterner, Azver, friend to Irian. There, at "the center of things" (155), they hope to be able to understand the pattern of a changing Earthsea. Over the course of the novel we learn more from different sources about the situation. It turns out that after the division when humans were to give up the Old Speech (and the Kargs did), men in Earthsea devised runes and began recovering it. Greedy wizards who wanted immortality, then, Irian relates, "by spells and wizardries of those oath-breakers, . . . stole half [of the dragons'] realm . . . and walled it away from life and light, so that [they] could live there forever" (227). The land, walled up to keep the Earthsea dead in and the Earthsea living and dragons out, was therefore cut off from the wind and water and light and became a dark, dry land where the dead of Earthsea humanity lived as shadows. So the task before the entourage is to tear down the wall and let the

spirits return to the cycle of things, as the Kargs in the far east and all animals have always done. Together, they—dragon, Karg, wizard, woman, and
child—succeed in tearing down the wall and releasing the spirits back into
the cycle of life. Breaking the wall will mend the world. Once this is accomplished, Tehanu chooses to fly on the Other Wind as dragon and joins Irian
and Kalessin. Tenar returns to Ged on Gont. The mad and marauding dragons leave Earthsea. The Kargish princess Seserakh marries Lebannen, unit-
ing all of Earthsea. There is, then, a strong monarchy joining all on Earthsea,
no Archmage on Roke, and we are left uncertain about the fate of wizardry
and magic in Earthsea.

And so ends, for now, the thirteen-hundred-page story of Earthsea, all the
more difficult to summarize in the second series for the mysteries and com-
plexities it offers as novelistic rather than epic discourse. I want to argue that
what we have in the companion trilogies, if it is acceptable to view them this
way, is the movement from epic to novel and on to an implied readership, as
Michael Levy argues, that grows more inclusive rather than being traded.[20]
Some have noted the epic quality of the Earthsea series, usually comparing it
to Tolkien's epic adventures in Middle Earth. George Slusser called the first
three books a "genuine epic vision" and the "purest epic fantasy."[21] David
Rees observes that the deeds of characters "have an epic quality."[22] It's easy
to assign the first trilogy to the category "epic" as its presentation of history
and its chronology in the story form, as well as its narrative voice, are quite
in line with the oral and mythic pattern of the great man's life story seen
within a people's tradition. As we'll see, though, the second trilogy revises
all of that through strategies of novelization. The Patterner Azver complains
that they "are ruled by the dead" ("Dragonfly," 246) before Irian comes into
her own and the subsequent events of *The Other Wind*. Le Guin changes both
the epic nature of the series and the way death functions in Earthsea. When
Irian shows herself as dragon and jumps upon the startled Summoner she
stamps out one possible manifestation of death as well as one dominating
genre in Earthsea.[23] But for now I wish to focus on that epic nature of the
first series.

The history of Earthsea as told around the implied campfire is epic. The
epic can be about traditions outside of the "real" history of the world, as seen
in Homer, Dante, Milton, Tolkien, and Pullman. Bakhtin tells us that "the
world of the epic is the national heroic past: it is a world of 'beginnings' and
'peak times' in the national history, a world of fathers and of founders of
families, a world of 'firsts' and 'bests.' The important point here is not that
the past constitutes the content of the epic. The formally constitutive feature
of the epic as a genre is rather the transferal of a represented world into the
past and the degree to which this world participates in the past."[24] Ged is
Earthsea's national hero who brings order back in each of the first three volumes. The narrator tells us of Ged's place in history from the outset in *A*

Wizard of Earthsea. That the narrator is proleptic (or one engaged in moments of "flash forward") is not unusual, for the epic's early stages assure us of the grandeur of our subject matter and the place in history of the hero. While the fabula itself (the true and unexcised version of all moments in a story from beginning to end) requires us to know all things in their due time, a story teller arranges the chronology at the story level to best suit his needs and the demands of his genre. Bahktin claims that in epic "the dead are loved in a different way" than the sorts of very visceral, messy, and rounded characters in the novel, as we shall see in the second trilogy (1981, 20). Margaret Esmonde is one critic who sees in that first trilogy the "heroic epic mythos" as it portrays death.[25] In myth and epic, "a thing that could and in fact must only be realized exclusively in the *future* is here portrayed as something out of the *past*" (Bakhtin 1981, 147), and our narrator presents us with *The Tale of Ged* as a relic of history, as a tale of a character who is long dead and loved as larger than life and part of legend.

In the first book, *A Wizard of Earthsea*, the tale begins with the singing of "The Creation of Éa." The song is presented before the beginning of the first chapter and presents us with what amounts to a ritualistic beginning to an epic of the land. Those gathered sing this most ancient and most basic of Earthsea songs as a prelude to the arrival of the storyteller on center stage. Our teller of this embedded narrative tells us in the very first paragraph that of the wizards of Gont, famous throughout all Earthsea, "some say the greatest, and surely the greatest voyager, was the man called Sparrowhawk, who in his day became both dragonlord and Archmage" (*Wizard*, 1). The listener (rather than reader) is important here as "one more or less essential, more or less irreplaceable as a narratee" because it is this storytelling context of one Earthsea citizen to others about the legends and history of his world that creates the epic quality of the text."[26] This teller reminds the listeners, the implied narratees who are surely citizens of Earthsea and familiar with its lore, that Ged's famous life is "told of in the *Deed of Ged* and in many songs," but that "this is a tale of the time before his fame, before the songs were made" (*Wizard*, 1). In this first paragraph both the narrative and epic contexts are established.

The storyteller makes other passing allusions to the vast history and cultural nuances of the archipelago. It is clear that the listeners know of the Kargard Empire (*Wizard*, 6), that they appreciate the beauties of pellawi fur (26), that they understand the Serpent of Andrad reference (27), that casual references to Earthsea geography are no problem (28), and that they know of the Great Taonian Harp (157). The fact that the implied narratees are of this world makes it easy for Le Guin to be less expository. Too much exposition can crush a fantasy, science fiction, or historical tale under its descriptive weight, after all. At the same time Le Guin shares some things with the reader, including the content of the *Deed of Erreth-Akbe* (*Wizard,* 55) and the implications for traveling and naming children during the Fallows (*Wizard*, 170) which, presumably, are important for the reader, not the narratee, to understand. In the third book of the original trilogy, *The Farthest Shore*, we are brought up to date on his exploits since *The Tombs of Atuan*: he "capped the Black Well of Fundaur" and built "the deep-founded sea wall of Nepp" (*Farthest*, 6). These exploits are shorthand for the implied narratee, the Archipelagan, who already appreciates these accomplishments. In any case, this largely imperceptible narrator is no mere conduit for the story since it is important that he is addressing his country folk about their own familiar tradition and world. His tone invites the reader to sit around the fire with the narratee and listen as an Archipelagan. The relationship between teller and audience is further established when this teller tells that "even now [Spevy] is an isle of ruins" in the aftermath of Kargish expansion (*Wizard*, 7). From this telling point he weaves an epic vision "so back into the times of myth" (*Wizard*, 22), which is now and always in the telling. It is "always" in the sense that it is clear that he can again be proleptic by claiming early that "this was Duny's first step on the way he was to follow all his life, the way of magery, the way that led him at last to hunt a shadow over land and sea to the lightless coasts of death's kingdom" (*Wizard*, 5). The listeners have heard this before and aren't bothered (nor are we) by this constant looking ahead and behind (prolepsis and analepsis, respectively), for in epic and myth all time is eternal and distant—even if the relationship between teller and told is close. This first novel, as representative of the first trilogy, includes many instances of analepsis and prolepsis as befits the context of this tale as national epic.[27]

It is interesting to consider the place in time of this telling, for either it is being told before the events of *Tehanu* take place or the teller isn't aware that Ged will not follow magery all of his life, that its pleasure won't stay with him (*Wizard*, 6). It isn't inconceivable to envision this as told in the courts of Havnor shortly after Ged's flight into the ether since a great future seems the logical inheritance of the Archipelago. It is likely that through the events of "Dragonfly" in *Tales from Earthsea*, and even through much of the beginning of *The Other Wind*, such a teller would be ignorant of the events taking place and of Ged's actual whereabouts. In fact, it is in *The Other Wind* that the Patterner Azver tells Alder "what not many know"—which is that Ged is alive and living on Gont (*Wind*, 8). Azver thinks that Alder "will keep his secret" (8).

The best case to be made for the teller sharing this story from mythic distance is the afterword: "So of the song of the Shadow there remain only a few scraps of legend, carried like driftwood from isle to isle over the long years" (*Wizard*, 183). Again, "long years" is subjective; but the feeling of that half page is that this is ancient lore, which makes the "mistakes" that the speaker makes regarding Ged's future problematic. It's clear, though, that an epic feeling is sought. The epic, as Bakhtin describes it, is "the environment of a man speaking about a past that is to him inaccessible, the reverent point of view of a descendent. In its style, tone and manner of expression, epic discourse is infinitely far removed from discourse of a contemporary about a contemporary addressed to contemporaries . . . To portray an event on the same time-and-value plane as oneself and one's contemporaries . . . is to undertake a radical revolution, and to step out of the world of the epic and into the world of the novel" (1981, 13–14). It seems clear that while a contemporary tells the tale to contemporaries, the subject of the tale is mythically distant. It is also presented as ancient glory rather than documented historical artifact.

One last possibility is that the time distance is great, and it turns out that the events of the first trilogy are what the people choose to sing, the rest either forgotten (unlikely) or lacking the more grandiose epic qualities of heroic adventure. The singer, not historian, simply chooses to sing the most heroic of tales. In any case, these "mistakes" exist because of Le Guin's revision, but otherwise this is a narrator telling a tale within a tale that is either limited by human knowledge within the context of the story or he intentionally omits subsequent events as a revisionist himself. In either case, the telling creates an epic distance. Bakhtin reminds us that "the destruction of epic distance and the transferal of the image of the individual from the distanced plane to the zone of contact with the inconclusive events of the present (and consequently of the future) result in a radical restructuring of the image of the individual in the novel—and consequently in all literature" (1981, 35). The fact that the storytelling quality of epic is more about celebration than true historical documentation is made overt in "The Finder" from *Tales from Earthsea* when the narrator tells us that on Mt. Onn on Havnor "nothing ever changes much. There a song worth singing is likely to be sung again" ("Finder," 3). The subsequent "radical restructuring of the image of the individual in the novel" will be addressed later on in this chapter.

A most interesting shift from the first book in the second trilogy to *Tales from Earthsea* is the presentation of the text—as a whole and as individual stories—from a new perspective by genre. The foreword introduces the voice of history to the series, history outside of epic. Le Guin tells us that "in order to understand current events, [she] needed to do some historical research, to spend some time in the Archives of the Archipelago."[28] From this point onward, we are to understand that the overriding authority of this collection is not the epic storyteller around the campfire but the historian who is researching the stories in the library. It is the anthropologist Pandora returned from *Always Coming Home* (1985).[29] The novels not only become less epic in their telling, but more self-conscious about the hero tale as a genre. The narrator of "The Bones of the Earth" in *Tales from Earthsea* tells of how the people refuse Ogion's claim that he had a partner in holding the earthquake at bay: "they praised his modesty and did not listen to him. Listening is a rare gift, and men will have their heroes" ("Bones," 161–62). In the latest Earthsea novel, *The Other Wind*, the narrator contrasts the people's relationship to their king to the King's Council: "There were a thousand lays and ballads about the son of Morred, the prince who rode the dragon back from death to the shores of the day, the hero of Sorra, wielder of the Sword of Serriadh: the Rowan Tree, the Tall Ash of Enlad, the well-loved king who ruled in the Sign of Peace. But it was hard going to make songs about councilors delegating shipping taxes" (*Wind*, 138). Le Guin contrasts the song of the epic to the nitty-gritty of both history and the novel, and shows that because the principle interest of this story is what the councilors and "ragbag" (199) group on the *Tern* have to say (rather than do), it is novel we have in the second trilogy, not epic. We can sing of "Tenar of the Ring" from the first series, but we are given Goha, farmwife and mother, to consider in the second. This isn't myth; it's history—told now and through the eyes of the novelist, the anthropologist, and the historian. The back of the book is exactly the sort of "report" about language, custom, and institutions given at the back of *Always Coming Home*, the sort of thing that epic doesn't bother with because its audience is intimate with the culture. Of course, Tolkien seems to have changed all that with *The Lord of the Rings*, but such paratextual information—that which is beyond the story and the voice of reason—is really the work of fictional scholarship, not epic. The historian that begins "The Finder," the first tale in *Tales from Earthsea*, gives us "the first page of the *Book of the Dark*, written some six hundred years ago in Berila, on Enlad" (1) in quoted form, not as mythic story received from a line of tellers. It is quotation and footnote, not fireside and mystery. Unlike epic, a unified national story told to inspire and deify, this is a story "pieced together from such scraps and fragments"—the work of the novelist, anthropologist, and historian ("Finder," 5).

The narrator of "The Finder," the first story in the collection, tells us that this story is "a compilation of self-contradicting histories, partial histories, and garbled legends" (2). "This is a tale of those [dark] times. Some of it is taken from the *Book of the Dark*, and some comes from Havnor, from the upland farms of Onn and the woodlands of Faliern" ("Finder," 5). The first sentence in this last quote could be the start of epic, but from there it is brought down to earth(sea). The historian becomes perceptible in her scholarly aggression when she challenges her detractors to "tell us how it happened otherwise" ("Finder," 5). The narrator doesn't try to fill in with fancy, only to report what has been told before. Educated conjecture is fair game for the historian, however, and she lets us consider that "most likely he left Havnor as soon as he could" ("Finder," 49). This conscientious historian tells us that where Medra "went then, the songs don't tell" ("Finder," 49) and "there's no knowing if" certain stories about a man similar to Medra on

Havnor are actually about him, though it would be convenient story-telling to forge that connection (49). The text remains self-conscious as report first rather than entertainment at the expense of historical accuracy. With *Tales from Earthsea* Le Guin introduces another layer of narration—the historian or cultural anthropologist sharing found shards of narrative of which the novels from the first trilogy are part.

Tales from Earthsea ends with "A Description of Earthsea," a text that is neither story nor afterword. While the foreword is clearly in Le Guin's voice as author, this end piece is less clear. "The Back of the Book" in *Always Coming Home* is true to the voice of the anthropologist examining the ways of the Kesh. "A Description of Earthsea" is told from outside the world of Earthsea rather than by the historian from within. We learn that "the Hardic people of the Archipelago live by farming, herding, fishing, trading, and the usual crafts and arts of a non-industrial society" and that "ordinary life in the Archipelago seems to resemble that of non-industrial peoples elsewhere" ("Description," 267–278). To know something is "non-industrial" one must know what "industrial" is—and just where is "elsewhere?" In fact, *A Wizard of Earthsea* and *Tehanu* are named as novels themselves rather than in-world lore like "The Deed of Ged" ("Description," 276). Yet the teller ducks back into Earthsea to explain that from "tales of ancient times come stories of recent days about dragons who take human form, humans who take dragon form, beings who are in fact both human and dragon" (270). The teller qualifies like the historian from within the world of Earthsea with phrases like "may be" or "it appears that" and will allude to stories that have "come" recently, as if not from the author herself. In this end piece Le Guin blurs the boundaries of narration across frames and the lines that weave in and out of worlds.

A Shift in Narrative Strategy

For all of the ways *A Wizard of Earthsea* is epic, it seems from the outset to be preparing for the more involved novelization of the second trilogy. It is a convincing *bildungsroman* to a reader as young and possibly as headstrong as Ged, and therefore sympathetic to him. Back in 1976 George Slusser noted that in *A Wizard of Earthsea* "we seem to fluctuate between objective reality and the hero's mind" (36). Len Hatfield disscusses the ways Le Guin moves from the mimetic (representations of character speech in the story) to the diegetic level (the level of narration).[30] What we have in Earthsea specifically, and indeed in much of Le Guin's stories, is a steady use of free indirect discourse. Gerald Prince defines free indirect discourse as "a type of discourse representing a character's utterances or thoughts" that "does not involve a tag clause ('he said that,' 'she thought that') introducing and qualifying the represented utterances and thoughts."[31] This sort of discourse removes the distance between the narrator and the narratee so that the two states of consciousness are difficult to distinguish. This technique can make the reader feel as though the narrator is sympathetic to the characters' thought or at least echoes it. In the case of character thoughts that might be inappropriate, naïve, or unconsidered (and young Ged is full of these thoughts) free indirect discourse removes the feeling that "this is only what the character thinks and should be read guardedly." This narrative strategy takes the distance of epic and moves it a good deal nearer the reader (as opposed to the narratee) for the purpose, especially, of its being effective as young adult literature. It is this strategy that enables the smooth transition from epic to novel in the first and second trilogies.

A Wizard of Earthsea confuses the issue of narrative assignment early on when it isn't entirely clear whose impressions we are given in some relatively minor situations. That it appears "as if another voice sang through" the old witch or that "it seemed a broad, bright road" may be true enough, but to whom does it seem this way (*Wizard*, 4, 5)? That "nothing happened" during Ged's apprenticeship is also given as narrative report, but is it Ged's impression (16)? These, again, aren't major moments of confusion, but they do establish the reliance upon free indirect discourse from the work's outset. While the strategy isn't dominant in the tale—indeed we mostly have clearly indirect discourse or even character speech (direct discourse)—it is occasional enough and in such important places that it achieves that sympathetic closeness to the adolescent character's consciousness typical of young adult literature. Focalizing through the character is pervasive in the novel, however, and makes the move to free indirect discourse less noticeable as a strategy—and therefore more effective. The strategy is most usefully employed in the first half of the novel when we need to accept the veracity of what might otherwise be represented as a naïve set of worldviews.[32]

An important juncture in the story occurs when Ged feels beset upon by Jasper, a student on Roke two years ahead of Ged. This section of the novel is presented through Ged's adolescent male consciousness. He clearly feels that he is a Great Dane thought to be a toy poodle, and he will bark, which the Great Dane should know is beneath him if he is secure in his dominance. He is angry and worried about others' potential misunderstanding of his own greatness, especially as compared to Jasper's. Earlier he believes that even Ogion is mocking him: "He did not like to be made to feel a fool" (*Wizard*, 18). It's clear that he believes Ogion is toying with him. The narrator does not tell us otherwise. We have to wait for Ged's own confession of Ogion's mastery later in the novel for verification (128). Jasper, too, "had made Ged into a fool," and the narrator defers comment (42). Though in retrospect we understand Ged's preoccupation with his own coming-of-age, it is important for the young adult reader—the reader most likely to empathize with Ged's particular feelings of being misunderstood of having his true worth misperceived—

to see Ged as justified in his feeling the way he does. This, I think, is one great difference in reading this novel at different points in one's life. Le Guin's narrator allows the young adult reader to find for the plaintiff early in the tale, though the adult jury almost surely arrives at a different verdict. We are provided with a certainty on Ged's part when, just before the tragic loosing of the shadow, Ged/narrator assures the reader that "he knew that his power, this night, on this dark enchanted ground, was greater than it had ever been, filling him till he trembled with the sense of strength barely kept in check. He knew now that Jasper was far beneath him, had been sent perhaps only to bring him here tonight, no rival but a mere servant of Ged's destiny" (59). But he doesn't feel so secure in this knowledge that he won't bark after all. The twice repeated "he knew" without a narrator's comment, indeed with the confusion between the narrator and Ged's surety, allows the reader to be swept up in the ultimately wrong-headed relationship to power. The narrator, unlike C. S. Lewis's avuncular yet moralizing alter-ego in the Narnia books, doesn't give the reader any "mature" view from the outside of the telling. In *The Lion, the Witch and the Wardrobe*, which is clearly a children's book, the extraordinarily perceptible external narrator is constantly cautioning the reader not to go into wardrobes or to judge Edmund too harshly for his actions. We are not given this "protection" in Le Guin's novel. As prelude to the moment of Ged's foolishness in the previous chapter, Ged/narrator tells us that "surely a wizard, one who had gone past these childish tricks of illusion to the true arts of Summoning and Change, was powerful enough to do what he pleased, and balance the world as seemed best to him, and drive back darkness with his own light" (*Wizard,* 44). We are unsurprised, but also unwarned, that this machismo will lead Ged to loose the shadow in the next chapter. And the young adult reader may not be unhappy with Ged's actions until both he or she and Ged realize the price of that action, the price the mature reader fears and knows will have to be paid.

But then there are some places where the narrator allows himself to be seen—makes his role as narrator clear as he argues his case. In such cases, the perceptible narrator makes us understand that the thought is Ged's alone, as in this moment of reflection: "these moments of fear and darkness, he said to himself, were the shadows merely of his ignorance" (*Wizard,* 54). Again, however, no opinion is offered on the matter. He becomes perceptible when he says that stories of the Immanent Grove are all "hearsay; wizards will not speak of it" (*Wizard,* 72), as if to show the limitations of his knowledge as a teller, or to keep a suitable amount of mystery alive for his listeners.[33] For the most part, though, when it is important that the reader—or the young narratee in his audience—should stay caught up in Ged's immature emotion, the narrator slips not only into Ged's consciousness through focalization but blurs the boundary between himself and Ged through free indirect discourse and reinforces the legitimacy of even the most unwise thought. Ged will set himself aright as the story unfolds, making it unnecessary for the narrator to comment. Le Guin, we could argue, trusts her readers more than Lewis does his.

I argue elsewhere that the young adult writer can abuse this strategy if he or she uses it to keep important truths from the less experienced reader.[34] One way to ensure a responsible portrayal is to provide contextual evidence that makes the narrator, perhaps in retrospect, dubious or unreliable, thereby freeing the reader to draw responsible conclusions without the feeling of a narrator's coercion. Le Guin does this well in her fiction. In her other two young adult novels apart from the Earthsea stories, *Very Far Away from Anywhere Else* (1976) and *The Beginning Place* (1980),[35] Le Guin uses other techniques for establishing closeness for the young adult reader while simultaneously asking the reader to question the represented discourse of the adolescents without authorial discourse interceding; in *Very Far Away from Anywhere Else* we have traditional young adult first person narration with a doubtable narrator, and in *The Beginning Place* we have the two young adult protagonists' starkly different consciousnesses represented in alternating chapters.

As Ged grows in this first novel, the use of free indirect discourse is less necessary as a strategy of novelization, of marking a link between the epic and the young adult novel of development. As the trilogy progresses and we are given the adolescents Arha/Tenar and Lebannen in turn, we see the same use of free indirect discourse as a strategy of young adult empathy.

In *The Tombs of Atuan* there are some instances of this strategy as well. Though the first two chapters rely on indirect and external narration (the narrator's description and argument), the narrator tells us of the "truth" of the Nameless Ones as rulers before the time of men and gives a vista of the place through what seems to be Tenar's eyes (*Tombs,* 15). Tenar's despair is echoed through the narrator when we are told, through free indirect discourse that "nothing had changed . . . Were all the years of her life to pass so?" (*Tombs,* 24). Tenar's own fears of being lost in the Undertomb are given to us through free indirect discourse. This creates empathy for the girl through language that keeps us from attributing it only to her thought and possibly disregarding it. As in *A Wizard of Earthsea*, this strategy is used to help us believe the truth of what could be argued is "only" a young person's fears. It is necessary for us to believe that "any other, man or woman, who ventured [into the Undertomb of the Temple] would certainly be struck dead by the wrath of the Nameless ones" so that the shock of seeing Ged there later will be palpable (*Tombs,* 55). That Tenar had visited the Undertomb "in all the generations of her priesthood" is given as both her belief and the narrator's report, entirely without attribution, so that we might feel her comfort for only a short while. She will come to the conclusion that she isn't endlessly reborn, but it is important to feel assured at this point in the novel if we are to believe as firmly as she does that what she thinks is true.

The Farthest Shore uses free indirect discourse in the presentation of our third principle adolescent in the series: Lebannen. Late in the novel it is important that we not only experience the prince's despair but also have it legitimated by having it blur with the narrator's speech. We are told that he "saw now what a fool he had been to entrust himself body and soul to this restless and secretive man . . . ," (*Farthest*, 98) and that this man, Ged, is to be blamed for Lebannen's being doomed to die and be lost forever like all of the others being lost in an Earthsea gone wrong (108). The young reader can be convinced of the soundness of these assertions because of the authority of free indirect discourse—and will be as relieved as Lebannen when they are shown to be wrong.

Tehanu, Le Guin claims, is "seen through a woman's eyes."[36] It is important to have the reader believe that Ged is a lost cause, selfish and, so unlike his Great Dane days, "a whipped dog" that would care only for his wounds of body and pride (*Tehanu*, 182). As the paragraph progresses without attribution to Tenar as thinker, the reader is convinced of the verdict. Again, it allows us the relief and perhaps surprise that this sensible report is ultimately wrong and that Ged will "pitch in" with all his might later in the novel.

In contrast, the stories in *Tales from Earthsea* contain very few false confidences created by free indirect discourse. One rare case of free indirect discourse happens when the difference between the wizard Early's thoughts and the narrator's are blurred to give weight to his plans of dominating the Archipelago ("Finder," 50). These plans prove unfounded, but told through free indirect discourse the reader is almost convinced. The plans worry us for a time. The collection of stories certainly employs Le Guin's characteristic use of focalization through characters' eyes, but as she uses adult characters more principally, she seems to feel less inclined to feed the sense of naiveté in her readers. When we do have a young adult character, Le Guin returns to that strategy. The sorcerer Ivory in "Dragonfly" is a young man recently expelled from Roke. His delusions of grandeur are similar to a young Ged's. In order to build a sense of reality that will later be debunked, the text portrays Ivory's confidence through free indirect discourse. We are told that "he kept himself to himself, as a man of craft and learning should" ("Dragonfly," 206). This justifies his actions, to himself and to us, which in one circumstance lead to the death of his host's daughter through his neglect. We need to believe that he is a dangerously and surprisingly powerful person. Later we see him "trusting to chance and his own wits, which seldom let him down if he was given a fair chance to use them" (218). While this also proves untrue, the use of free indirect discourse makes it possible for us to believe that it *is* true and that his plans of manipulating Irian in order to embarrass his old masters on Roke might come to fruition. We are told that "he

knew now that coaxing [Irian] was no good. To have her he must master her
... " (224). It proves the case that he has been foolish; Irian would have slept
with Ivory, though rather disinterestedly, if he had only asked. We are convinced earlier, through free indirect discourse, that his is really the only
strategy to employ because we are never given a phrase like "he thought" or
"he believed" in the course of the explanation of his plans so that we might
challenge the claim. In addition, we aren't given Irian as a focalizer until she
leaves him for good at the door to Roke School. It is only then that we learn
that she had herself used Ivory to get there and was, in her belief and ours, in
control all the while. Irian isn't entirely to be compared to adolescents in the
previous books because, simply, she is as much dragon as young woman.
While she is in doubt about her identity, she does not as either woman or
dragon operate under naïve delusions about her power or grandeur—that's
for young men with some promise of institutionalized power.

The series shifts from reliance on free indirect discourse—from a narrator
who wants us to believe the fears of the young in the service of suspense—to
narration about young adults both dragon and woman. The series drops the
use of free indirect discourse in *The Other Wind*. Since the world is inexpli-
cable to all in *The Other Wind*—adult and young adult both—the novel does-
n't need to rely on creating a deferred sense of knowledge about the way of
the world through the eyes of the young for the young. From start to finish
the book is about trying to understand the New World order, physically and
metaphysically, through dialogue among peers of all ages, races, genders,
and species. Readers of all ages are put in the same boat, literally, with the
passengers of the ship *Tern* on its way to Roke.

From Young Adult Literature to *Bildungsroman* for All Ages

This first book of the trilogy, *Tehanu*, shows us the same Earthsea, but now it
is entirely new. We've come home to a place we've been before. Home gets
even less familiar through *Tales from Earthsea* (2001) and *The Other Wind*
(2001). As Earthsea develops (or is recovered, if we consider the history re-
claimed in *The Other Wind*), the world not only shakes beneath the archipelago, but beneath genre, implied readership, and our understanding of
"equilibrium" itself.

As early as 1976 George Slusser decried the "silly publication classifica-
tion designating the original series as 'children's literature.'"[37] In contrast,
though, Barbara Bucknall points out that "Le Guin was not writing for
young children when she wrote these fantasies, nor yet for adults. She was
writing for 'older kids.' But in fact she can be read, like Tolkien, by ten-year-
olds and by adults. These stories are ageless because they deal with problems that confront us at any age."[38] We see here the contrast between a
hierarchy of arts and her readers' access to the mythic and fantastic— the

good myths and fantasies are always accessible. Philip Pullman, Milton's revisionist, doesn't see epic as anything antithetical to children's literature—in fact, he seems to believe it is more appropriate for children than for adults. Pullman's *The Golden Compass*, the first of the His Dark Materials series, was the 1996 winner of the prestigious Carnegie Medal, England's highest honor for children's literature; the third book of that series was awarded Britain's Booker Prize, that nation's highest honor for (adult) fiction. Pullman claims that "there are some themes, some subjects, too large for adult fiction; they can only be dealt with adequately in a children's book." He complains that in adult literary fiction, style is considered more important than story. "Adult writers who deal in straightforward stories find themselves sidelined in genres like crime or science fiction, where no one expects literary craftsmanship."[39] It seems, as I discuss in this volume's last essay, that the implied audience of epic fantasy is a complicated matter.

Perry Nodelman notes that Earthsea isn't characteristic of children's fantasy, however, which is more likely to "include fantasy elements in real settings . . . which tends more toward Peter Pans and Treasure Seekers than it does to Earthseas."[40] He also believes that *Tehanu* is a revisionist act in terms of genre "by the fact that it is not the kind of story one expects in a novel supposedly for young adults. Although it does tell how a child grows into knowledge of her power, that is not the central issue."[41] Len Hatfield seems to share Nodelman's doubt about *Tehanu*'s status as children's book: "In fact, because Tenar, the girl we met in *Tombs of Atuan*, is the protagonist, now an older woman, it might be argued for a moment that this last book is not part of the series in the same way that the earlier tales are: this seems hardly to be a children's story at all" (Hatfield, 54). But, as Hatfield goes on to say, it does continue the series' theme of patriarchal ignorance of women as well as children. While he claims that they are thematically related, he doesn't ever claim that *Tehanu* is a children's or young adult book in the same (or any) way as the first three books. Hatfield is a scholar of science fiction, which may account for his avoidance of the question; recently, however, Michael Levy, president of the Science Fiction Research Association as well as a seasoned children's literature scholar, argued on the Child_Lit discussion list that there isn't "anything in *Tehanu, Tales from Earthsea,* or *The Other Wind* that is specifically not for children, though they do deal fairly explicitly with some grim subjects . . . It's just that they're written on a higher reading level and contain more difficult ideas or at least ideas that are more clearly of interest to adults," by which he means "old age and impending death."

Levy goes on to say that he "wouldn't hesitate to give these books to any child who'd read and enjoyed the original trilogy," though "the child might find them somewhat heavy going." The arguments seem to focus on the contrast between text and subtext, style, and message. I don't think that we can so neatly separate these things. It is the dialogue between style and subject that makes Earthsea so interesting and a remarkable example of a crossover series.

Others have observed that the original trilogy as a whole, and the individual books in that trilogy, are the stories of young adults who try to find (or are forced to find) their place in the world.[42] Each tale in the first trilogy that focuses on a young adult is testimony to the fact that this whole series is largely an investigation of the adolescent of whatever age. While Elizabeth Cummins notes that Ged's story through the first half of the series is more like epic than *bildungsroman* in that it tells the hero's whole life, each book's focus is squarely on the story of growth or change in the life of one young adult (1990, 58). The Earthsea series continues this focus through the publication of *The Other Wind*. Although Nodelman says that *Tehanu* isn't typical as an adolescent novel because it doesn't feature an adolescent, we might consider *Tehanu* the transition from the stories of one set of grown adolescents in the original trilogy to the establishment of the new generation whose adolescence is of utmost importance. The girl Tehanu is introduced in this story, and it is her coming-of-age, as well as Irian's (a contemporary whose story is told in "Dragonfly" in *Tales from Earthsea*) that will be the main concern in the last half of the series.

Arguably, *Tehanu* is about a second adolescence for Ged, a man who has to go through a sexual awakening after his loss of wizardly power and its attendant spells that suppress sexuality. The witch Moss remarks, "It's a queer thing for an old man to be a boy of fifteen, no doubt!" (*Tehanu*, 106) Ged becomes a man in the more normal sense in *Tehanu* as he explores his own sexuality for the first time. True journey is return, and it is back on Gont that Ged continues the true adolescence he denied himself when he left for Roke to become a celibate wizard. Even in *The Farthest Shore* Lebannen wonders about Ged's achievement of maturity: "How could such a man . . . be in doubt as to who and what he was? He had believed such doubts were reserved for the young, who had not done anything yet" (35). It is Tenar who guides Ged in *Tehanu* rather than the reverse in *Tombs of Atuan* (Sobat, 28).[43] After they make love for the first time, Tenar teases Ged by telling him that "now [he is] a man indeed" (*Tehanu*, 212). In a larger sense, Hollindale argues that "guided by such complex and radical rather than simple and conservative ideas [as are found in the initial trilogy], *Tehanu* is a splendid completion of the series, but it is an adolescent novel, not a children's book."[44]

Roberta Trites notes that "YA [young adult] novels evolved historically from the Bildungsroman,"[45] which explains the natural dialogue between the epic and the coming-of-age story in this series set in a mythological and epic world aimed at a young adult audience yet of interest to readers of all ages. She goes on to say, "young adult literature shares many characteristics with books marketed to adults about adolescents. The major intersections between

these two sets involve various types of novels about the maturation process
. . . " (9). In this way all six books of the Earthsea series satisfy qualities of
epic, *bildungsroman*, and young adult fiction through dialogue. The series
has become a wonderful example of Le Guin blurring boundaries among the
qualities of seemingly different types of fiction.[46] Trites claims that "the YA
novel, with its questioning of social institutions and how they construct individuals, was not possible until the postmodern era influenced authors to explore what it means if we define people as socially constructed subjects
rather than as self-contained individuals bound by their identities" (16). The
series becomes not only more postmodern in its sensibilities, but from the
outset has shown that through its anthropological tactics that it is actually
"young adult" in the ways that it prepares readers to come of age. But it
would be wrong to claim that the books from *Tehanu* onward are young
adult books. No longer is writing that restricted. Indeed, the books are
coming-of-age for characters—and readers—of all ages.

Jeanne Walker noted in 1979 that "Ursula Le Guin's fantasy, *A Wizard of
Earthsea*, performs certain tasks for modern adolescents, which in other societies are dramatized by rites of passage."[47] The rite of passage at the end of
chapter one, Ged's naming, is "in all its brevity, . . . in miniature the whole
action of *A Wizard of Earthsea*" (Walker, 182). In *A Wizard of Earthsea*
Ged's rite of passage is an analogue to the whole plot, and the plot itself
functions as a rite of passage for the reader" (Walker, 183). Indeed, it is a
rich series of anthropological exchanges, as W. A. Senior notes.[48] The series
has always had this agenda, though *Tehanu* onward makes it more explicit
and personal and less epic. While the society is fixed in the original series,
the hero, and the reader, is being initiated into that world and into the symbolic world of adulthood. The shifting of the order in subsequent books
makes the portrayal of coming-of-age less certain, and the novels, truly novels now, have to work out that process for themselves and for a reader already used to the old order. Trites makes it clear that "the Young Adult novel
. . . is less concerned with depicting growth reverently than it is with investi-
gating how the individual exists within society" (18–19), and while that was
always the case in Earthsea, the second trilogy invents the new process as it
goes rather than simply depicting an age-old way of representing finding
one's place in the order of things. "The entire action of *A Wizard of Earthsea*
. . . portrays the hero's slow realization of what it means to be an individual
in society and a self in relation to higher powers" (Walker, 181). *Tehanu* onward asks us to consider a self in relation to equals, previously thought either
to be higher or lower, which, while more egalitarian, is a strange model for
western youths and their parents to understand. What is said of Lebannen is
true of the whole cast of characters from *Tehanu* onward: "So the first step
out of childhood is made all at once, without looking before or behind, without caution, and nothing held in reserve" (*Farthest*, 8). Even though the

characters are mostly adults in *The Other Wind*, they realize that they are in a world that is magically new and must figure out who they all are and will be. As Le Guin puts it, "Enchantment alters with age, and with the age;"[49] the sense of discovery of self doesn't stop at 19, and that discovery takes on a sense of great importance in a new age in Earthsea.

Instead of creating characters who come of age independently and through a hierarchy, as is traditional in the *bildungsroman* of the Modernist tradition, the characters in a new Earthsea, a world in which there is no longer a clear doorway from uninitiated to initiated, have to work through error and carve a world together—initiation by committee. As the Shobies do in "The Shobies' Story" in *A Fisherman of the Inland Sea* (1994), the people of Earthsea have to engage in "entrainment" as equals, even the children. In "The Shobies' Story," the crew of the Shoby has to go from point A to point B by telling the story of their journey, and it is the telling that saves them from dissolution through the dangerous churtening process, a process that removes time from travel between worlds separated by light years.

"Entrainment" occurs when a group of people shares the story of what has happened when nobody is very sure individually, and that story isn't written hierarchically. It's what neo-historicism is concerned with, after all, and anthropology—the story of all, not just the "great men" and their wars. The narrator of "The Shobies' Story" points out that "a chain of command is easy to describe; a network of response isn't."[50] They have to fumble through an answer together without a clear order. As "instantaneous" and simultaneous as that new physics in the Hainish novels is, the shift in Earthsea is no less simultaneous for all characters. To construct a world and to come of age in it there has to be either totalitarianism or anarchy; it's clear which Le Guin prefers. The character Forest in "Dancing to Ganam" puts it best: "we make sense of the world intentionally. Faced with chaos, we seek or make the familiar, and build up the world with it."[51] As is the case in the world-altering events taking place in Earthsea in the second trilogy, "one man can't destroy them and one man can't save them! They have their own story, and *they're* telling it!" ("Ganam," 141). "History is no longer about great men," Le Guin tells us; though it will be about great people all working together (*Revisioned*, 13). And Le Guin's own preference these days for Earthsea is for the sort of characters who are more novelistic. She says, "the novel is a fundamentally unheroic kind of story, ... That is why I like novels: instead of heroes they have people in them."[52]

Both trilogies in the series entertain the irony of the wizard as an independent being who is guardian of equilibrium and balance in the world. This irony goes largely unnoticed in the first trilogy, I think; in the second it becomes a focus for what is wrong. Rather than being paradox, it is revealed as irony. While Ged points out to Tenar in the series' second novel that "alone, no one wins freedom" (*Tombs*, 115), he later in that novel drops her off in safety and tells her "I go alone" even after she asks him to stay (135). In *The Farthest Shore,* the Summoner Thorion notes that Ged's solitary methods change with the plan for Lebannen to accompany him on his quest: "always before you were alone; you have always gone alone. Why now companioned?" Ged responds, "I never needed help before" (*Tombs,* 25), which any reader of *The Tombs of Atuan* knows to be untrue. Ged seems to have forgotten that he ever needed help, which is what a wizard has to believe, it seems. Ged seems to embrace the irony of the phrase, "lifting himself up by his own bootstraps"—a phrase that shows the impossibility of the belief itself. The series won't let him retain this fiction.

Glory, the glory of the hero tale, is partly what feeds this need to believe that one has done it alone. It enables Ged to forget Ogion, Tenar, Lebannen, and even his Otak as beings who have saved him over and over. Near the end of *The Farthest Shore,* Ged glories in the songs that will be sung of him after he places Lebannen on his throne even though he claims to look forward to a life of being rather than doing (*Farthest,* 156). Even when he arrives on Gont without his wizard's powers he wants to relive with Tenar his arrival in Havnor with the ring (*Tehanu* 69). He does for a while grieve for his loss, one he never fully understands until late in the fourth novel. Tenar chides him with the mercilessness of love: "Why do you think only of yourself? Always of yourself?" (81). But Ged will reach out after pain, and be reached to: "Was he burned?" Tehanu asks of Ged, seeing his scars (52). He will learn to be scarred and to depend on others, though it takes four novels for that to happen. He becomes a man not by having sex, but by making love, and by learning to love, which is never possible for the solipsist. Freedom is gained, paradoxically, by losing power. An earlier Summoner tells Ged a wizard does what must be done, but a free person makes choices (*Wizard,* 71). The biggest choice is to love—to forge a self by being selfless. "Only I exist," Cob says to Ged near the end of *The Farthest Shore;* Ged tells him "But you have no self" (180). It is the right thing to say, but Ged himself doesn't understand the link between pride and isolation until later in the next novel.

The series is rife with similar wizards, after all. It is an occupational hazard. Ged notes of Hare in *The Farthest Shore,* "For all his craft in sorcery he has never seen the way before him, seeing only himself" (65). It is an ironic statement, for it isn't in spite of his wizard's staff that he does this but because of it. Wizards have built this secrecy, power, and solipsism into their job descriptions so as to make it seem both natural and necessary. In the second trilogy this is still argued, but it becomes weightless and even mocked. Unlike in the first trilogy, the second always shows that the choice to be isolated (which for the wizard is said to be no choice at all) is unhealthy. Hemlock tells Diamond in "Darkrose and Diamond" that "the entanglement of family, friends, and so on is precisely what you need to be free of. Now, and henceforth" ("Darkrose," 124). It is that "freedom" from entanglement that shuts him out from the loves of his life—music and Darkrose. The malady extends to other men of power. Diamond's father Golden, a rich merchant, tells him that he "must make [his] choice alone, as a man" ("Darkrose," 115). Diamond feels "a little dead" both in the spell-protected home of Hemlock and the ledger room of his father's house ("Darkrose," 121). Hemlock's parting note to Diamond is that "True art requires a single heart" ("Darkrose," 131); this is countered by the women in his life. Tuly, Diamond's mother, argues that all things mix: "They do, they do . . . Everything is hooked together, tangled up!" ("Darkrose," 134)

Wizards aren't much for dialogue. It is because they engage entirely in monologue that they are, by themselves, unfit guardians of the Archipelago. They've never grown up. They are the lost boys in the Neverland of Roke, and they don't trust others. As the King's council debates what is to be done in Earthsea late in *The Other Wind*, the wizard Onyx tells Lebannen that he doesn't believe "that this is the place to discuss such matters—before all men—until we know what we are talking about, and what we must do." Irian responds with derision: "Roke keeps its secrets" (154–155). Irian is the cause for the wizard's desire for secrecy, for monologue. In the earlier "Dragonfly" the Summoner Thorion claims that she "can bring only confusion, dissension, and further weakness among us. I will speak no longer and say nothing else in her presence. The only answer to conscious error is silence" (234). On the contrary, the only answer to error, conscious or not, is dialogue. The witch Rose is correct in her observation, "It's a poor cart that only goes one way" ("Dragonfly," 211). Knowledge and a sense of self come from interaction. The narrator of "The Finder" observes that a mage is someone who has "clear in his mind . . . the wholeness of knowledge" (50), which is not the same thing as *having* all knowledge. That is to be gained through dialogue and working through errors with those who, from the outside, can identify and help rectify them.

Everyone goes through the coming-of-age process in the second trilogy, though the ages are different. Nobody knows his or her place in the order, and so it must be that everyone must go through the process of finding one's place in a world that is both becoming and returning. "Only error individualizes," Bakhtin tells us. Rather than having only one or two protagonists in the second series being individualized by error, we have a host of characters, almost all seen in previous stories, becoming more clearly individuals through the process of trial-and-error.[53] Trial and error is a theme in the second trilogy, and while Ged can be said to have gone through that process himself, the product of his journey was solitary and more of an epiphany than a truth arrived at through dialogue with others. Ged is one of many in the series who is formed from the creative anarchy of informal foster parenthood. This is one way that Le Guin removes the question of "becoming" from the natural order of biological family and puts it in the context of the society taking responsibility for the formation of individuals. Ged comes to Ogion; Tenar and Lebannen, to Ged; Tehanu and Lebannen, to Tenar; and the foster parent—not the step-parent so stereotyped by fairy tale—takes the child that has come to him or her and raises it.[54] Tenar tells Tehanu that Ogion was a father to her, "the way I'm your mother now" (*Tehanu*, 8), and that "way" is a special quality of Le Guin's fiction. At least one of these relationships is key to each of the novels in the series.

From Monologue to Dialogue

In *The Other Wind* the focus is on communication for understanding others and the world. Much of the communication among the characters in the novel revolves around dreams. When they discuss their first set of dreams in the garden of Havnor's palace they do no more than share them before Lebannen suggests that they "put dreams aside for a while" so they can get caught up on current events and why each is at the court (*Wind*, 94). Perhaps he is sympathetic to Tosla, captain of the *Tern*, the ship they will take to Roke, who observes that "many heads make light thinking" (94), or perhaps he thinks that news and strategy are more important. Ultimately, many heads make right thinking in this story, as was the case for the crew of the Shoby. However, their own "entrainment" will have to include their dream visions of what is happening to the world. The crew, representative of all the world of Earthsea, will ultimately share their shipboard dreams when they arrive at Roke and in the Immanent Grove. It is then that Lebannen sees the dialogic importance of sharing "the dragons and the dreams," and tells those gathered that they "must join together to learn what that change is, its causes, its course, and how [they] may hope to turn it from conflict and ruin to harmony and peace" (221). The dreams are part of the experience and need to be shared if any understanding is to be achieved about what is happening, what will happen, and what the crew should do.[55] The dreams, individually and collectively, are short glimpses of the different experiences that these people from different cultures and with different life experiences have had with death and dragons. These dreams help the characters feel the rightness of what their fates in the face of what reason and tradition might tell them is wrong: tear down the wall of stones that separates life from the Dry Land.[56] And as important as that "information" is in helping them act, their talking and meeting is an important act itself. It unifies them in purpose, though they do not clearly know that purpose. They "entrain" in order to know where they are and what is happening. Alone they would each be of little use.

And many hands at work are keys to the story's outcome. Kalessin, the Summoner, Alder, Irian, Tehanu . . . they all bear down in order to raze the wall before the Dry Land and free the people who have been trapped for centuries in the false afterlife created by wizardly greed. No one person makes

Earthsea, or frees anyone by himself or herself. "Truth is not born nor is it to be found inside the head of an individual person; it is born between people collectively searching for the truth, in the process of their dialogic interaction" (Bakhtin 1984, 110). As foster families or shipmates, individuals are formed through their interdependence with each other, through choice, and with the knowledge that that choice necessitates responsibility. "'Not many of us know who or what we are,' said the Doorkeeper. 'A glimpse is all we get'"—and we glimpse it through our interactions with others (*Wind*, 29).

The wizards as conceived in the original trilogy, and much of them in the second trilogy, stand alone and are largely bankrupt as a result. Apart from the foster family or large collective, Le Guin establishes character formation in pairs. "What can anyone do alone?" Mead asks in "The Finder," and we understand through the characters that the answer is "nothing" (45). Nothing worthwhile, anyway. "The idea begins to live, that is, to take shape, to develop . . . only when it enters into genuine dialogic relationships with other ideas, with the ideas of *others*" (Bakhtin 1984, 88). Most important characters have an "other" with whom to build an identity, because, as Mead has it, "nobody can be wise alone" ("The Finder," 46). Not only what, but who are these people without their "other?" Who is Ged without Vetch in the end to push him to the end of the world? Who is Ged without Tenar, or Tehanu without Tenar? What can Irian come to be without Azver, or Medra without Anieb? For even though there is a sidekick quality to Tenar and Lebannen in *The Tombs of Atuan* and *The Farthest Shore*, respectively, Ged—though he forgets—is lost in two kinds of underworlds without them. In the second trilogy, the power sharing is more obvious, even in the case of Tenar and Tehanu. People share different kinds of power in order to make more than the sum of their parts.

Consider the special case of Medra, the eponymous character of "The Finder." He becomes one of the principle founders of Roke not only because of his alliance with others at different points, but specifically because of his deference to them. What enables Medra to defeat the wizard Tinaral is Anieb, slave woman with a wizard's power. Medra "saw himself through her eyes" ("Finder," 26) and "saw through her eyes" what needed to be done to defeat the wizard (33). "Tell him what he sees," Anieb whispered in [Medra's] mind" ("Finder," 35), and Medra parrots back to Tinaral the false vision that wizard has of an underground treasure, which will enable Medra and Anieb to trap him under the earth. "Oblivious to all this," the wizard "talked on, following the endless spell of his own enchanting voice" ("Finder," 33). The wizard cannot see or hear anything other than what he wishes, not uncommon to wizards, after all. He cannot hear what he doesn't expect to hear and cannot see what he doesn't expect to see. But since Medra and Anieb operate as a shared vision, they can work together to get Tinaral to fail himself, which is what we do when we try to lift ourselves by our own bootstraps, reducing ourselves to the absurdity of hunched-over hopping. Tinaral was "used to being listened to, not to listening" ("Finder," 34), and when he sees Medra he only sees a part of his plans and extension of himself" (34). After Tinaral is defeated, Medra takes Anieb from her tower prison and escapes, only to have her die in his arms as they approach her village. But she will come back to him in dream vision later because he has forged his identity with "the stranger who was himself" ("Finder," 39).[57] This is the model for how people become in this second trilogy—always through the stranger, the other, that one person admitted into our consciousness and with whom there is creative collaboration with equality. While wizards force people to speak their true names, free people are given the names of the other by free will, and they work to be worthy of that trust.

The latest novel has the most rounded cast of characters of any of the previous volumes, and they speak their own truths to themselves and to others so that they and the reader might begin to see how the world is to be for the individual and the collective. The weight of the epic is upon them, however, and though Le Guin relieves that by recasting the narrative as history, as anthropology, as Ekumen-like report, it would be easy for characters, as Bakhtin says, to "fall silent, close up, and congeal into finished, objectivized images" (1984, 65). The characters remain both "The elusive individual, upon whom all the givens act, but who simply is," and a dialogic host that together can construct a reality.[58] While individuals are configured into pairs and groups, each has his own multiplicity. More and more Le Guin relies on the double or even multiple identities of characters who have to make sense of who and what they are in Earthsea. Characters have to become "double hearted," as it is claimed in "Darkrose and Diamond" in *Tales from Earthsea*. They have double vision, as Tehanu and Irian show in their respective debuts.[59] Myra in "Buffalo Gals" (1990)[60] also shares a split identity, spreading the vision of both human and beast, and seems to be another working through of the issue for Le Guin. This is different from the way a person holds a true name as well as a use name; it is more a shared, multiple, and equal sense of identity than a hierarchical system of false use name and true essence. It is akin to what Reid points out about Falk-Ramarren in *Planet of Exile* (1966),[61] that he is truly double. There is no "real" Falk-Ramarren; only two versions, neither of which is less important to whom he is.

Tenar as Earthsea's New Model Citizen

Tenar is Le Guin's finest and most complicated multiple character in the Earthsea series, and maybe in all of her fiction. Warren Rochelle says that "*Tehanu* is . . . the story of what is happening while the hero is gone: it is the story of what the heroine does, . . . "[62] I'd say, rather, that *Tehanu* is the story that challenges what a hero is in this series when it moves from epic to novel. Tenar is too complicated to be simply one thing, and while she might have been a "heroine" in *The Tombs of Atuan*, she not only breaks out of that gender-specific (and secondary) designation but also breaks down a simplified notion of "hero." The new series distributes hero status to all principal characters. Tenar wears her true name out in the open because, like the dragons, it is not her only name. She, like Ged and Lebannen, is a crossover character from one trilogy to the next. Le Guin has claimed for Tenar that "All her former selves are alive in her: the child Tenar, the girl–priestess Arha, who still thinks in Kargish, and Goha the farmwife, mother of two children. Tenar is whole, but not single. She is not pure" (*Revisioned*, 18). "I have my name back. I am Tenar!" she cries at an important moment in *The Tombs of Atuan* (96). Later Ged cautions her with the limited wisdom of wizardry: "You must be Arha, or you must be Tenar. You cannot be both" (113). But this isn't true. In *The Other Wind* she even expands herself to be foster mother to King Lebannen. It is in this role that she works to expand his vision of the Kargish princess, sent to him as a peace-offering bride. "She resented Lebannen's failure or inability to take the girl's point of view" (*Wind*, 84), which from Tenar's multiple and dialogic character is thus: "People whom she knew of only as irreligious and blood thirsty monsters who dwelt at the far edge of the world, not truly human at all because they were wizards who could turn into animals and birds—and she was to marry one of them!" (84)[63] It is made clear that Tenar "and Seserakh were indeed in league against [Lebannen] and ready to betray him, if he truly was nothing unless he was independent" (*Wind*, 174). She has learned that independence is a false value, and can't bring about growth. She observes at the beginning of *Tehanu* that, with her farmer husband dead and her grown children gone into the world, she 'used to live in a silent house, alone,' she thought. 'I will do so again.' (2), but this is not her fate, for each isolation is to be followed by an intense time of connection, and that isolation makes her appreciate the value of community.

Tenar, like most of the players in the second trilogy, is not a psychological type placed in a fixed role as in epic. Bakhtin sees this aspect of character in the novel as central to the genre. Characters can't simply be ideas or psychological types. "In both cases it is quite obvious that artistic problems as such are either avoided entirely, or are treated superficially, almost by accident" (1984, 8–9). We cannot reduce Tenar, or any of the crew of the *Tern*, to one role or as a simple vehicle for archetype. The dialogic character is expansive, empathetic without being vacuous and unpredictable without being inconsistent. The monological hero, Bakhtin explains, "cannot cease to be himself, that is, he cannot exceed the limits of his own character . . . without violating the author's monologic design concerning him" (1984, 52). Tenar is capable of considering how the other sees, which is partly what makes her unique. She learns early in the second novel "how very different people were, how differently they saw life" when, amazed, she first runs into irreverence in the person of her childhood friend, Penthe (*Tombs*, 41). She forces others, like Lebannen, to see that difference in people throughout the second trilogy.

Le Guin explains that for Tenar, "'private' acts and choices [are] made in terms of immediate, actual relationships" (*Revisioned*, 13). This, as noted above, is not the case for wizards who can't hear people from whom they don't expect to hear anything; they don't have "actual relationships." Even the Master Windkey, a positive character in the latest novel and someone who has no reason to dislike Tenar, can't hear her simply because she is a woman. Tenar notes the "utter unconsciousness of his disrespect" (*Wind*, 160), and notes that Lebannen "was not deaf" (161). Yet Tenar herself isn't trained to hear what the witch Ivy has to say about Tehanu's gifts (*Wind*, 181), which illustrates that there are, even for the most empathetic of worldly characters, and for any truly realistically portrayed character, gaps in knowledge and hearing.

Tenar is Goha, the little web-spinning spider of Gont, without whom the collectivization and novelization of the second trilogy fail. She is at the center of a web of interdependency that would take a long time to document. Consider what Ged, Tehanu, Lebannen, Ogion, Seserakh, or even Alder would be without her. But also consider what or where she would be without most of those characters. She spins webs of relationships, yes, but that web holds her up as well. She is the epicenter of the second series in a way that Ged is not equipped to be. As Ged holds the action of the first epic trilogy together, Tenar connects the characters of the novelized second trilogy, and it is character, not action, that drives the novel as opposed to the epic. If the wizard Cob is the evil spider and unmaker of the last book of the first trilogy, Tenar is the good spider, the maker and binder, of the second trilogy.

The Continuum of Character in Earthsea

By the end of the second trilogy, a continuum of existence is established. It is apparent in the ways peoples exist with each other and in the way the series expands into the past and present. Rather than sticking with pairs or even with only characters that exist as individuals, Le Guin has made a clearer link among all persons of different cultures, races, and species. Le Guin has argued that "if you deny any affinity with another person or kind of person, if you declare it to be wholly different from yourself . . . you may hate it or deify it; but in either case you have denied its spiritual equality and its human reality. You have made it into a thing, to which the only possible relationship is a power relationship. And thus you have fatally impoverished your own reality. You have, in fact, alienated yourself."[64] Instead of "things" that are made other in Earthsea—the dragons, Kargs, women, children—the second trilogy succeeds in portraying all beings as related by degree rather by kind. In the first trilogy we saw alienation, even more than we find, ironically, in the Hainish cycle of stories. In the Hainish series we have, from the beginning, an argument for the blood link among all of the worlds of the Ekumen. Lord Mobile Axt tells King Argaven XVII of Karhide on the planet Gethen the story:

> "Once you said, Lord Axt, that different as I am from you, and different as my people are from yours, yet we are blood kind. Was that a moral fact, or a material one?"
>
> Axt smiled at the very Karhidish distinction. "Both, my lord. As far as we know, which is a tiny corner of dusty space under the rafters of the Universe, all the people we've run into are in fact human. But the kinship goes back a million years and more, to the Fore-Eras of Hain. The ancient Hainish settled a hundred worlds."[65]

There wasn't, until the beginning of the second trilogy of Earthsea, any reason to expect that there was any relationship between even the Kargish and the Archipelagans, but from the Woman of Kemay on Gont in *Tehanu* we know that people can be both dragon and person (*Tehanu*, 11).[66]

Alienation now can only occur based on culture, and even that has been broken down with the arrival of princess Seserakh to Havnor; she and Lebannen are betrothed by book's end and will wed sometime after the events of the novel, Tenar tells Ged (*Wind*, 244). Le Guin makes the case that "alienation isn't the final human condition, since there is a vast common ground on which we can meet, not only rationally, but aesthetically, intuitively, emotionally."[67] In this second trilogy she has engineered that common ground for all in Earthsea. The "ragbag" that Tenar describes as the crew of the *Tern* is in its wholeness all of Earthsea: dragons, Archipelagans, Kargs, wizards (of Roke and Peln)—and not singly, but in the persons of Tenar, Irian, and Tehanu, those things in combination. The continuum of peoples is strengthened by particular individuals who, like those women, create an imbrication of types in that horizontal rather than vertical chain of being. "It is impossible to represent an alien ideological world adequately without first permitting it to sound, without having first revealed the special discourse peculiar to it."[68] All in Earthsea speak for themselves in the latest trilogy, which helps us finally to understand their relationships with each other, which is best understood as a continuum rather than as a division.

Because of the richness and overlap of that continuum, it is difficult to lay the path out in a neat little line. On the western edge is the dragon, those who have chosen freedom over possession as explained by the *Vedurnan*—the agreement that some would fly west and be dragons free of good and evil and possession, and others, stay in the east and live with possession and the choice between good and evil. To its right are those dragons, like Yevaud, which are still dragons but covet possessions like people. This acceptance of land and riches explains why his name would hold him, as we see in *A Wizard of Earthsea*; it doesn't physically control other dragons like Kalessin or Orm Embar.[69] To the right of Yevaud come those mixed people, The Woman of Kemay, Tehanu, and Irian, whose essences participate in both dragon and human kind. Arguably all women and the men who are dragonlords are placed to the right of the mixed women because they speak to dragons; and women, we are to understand, aren't in risk when they look into the eyes of dragons as men are. This places women even closer to dragons. To the right of the dragonlords are ordinary men and women of the Archipelago whose souls go to the Dry Land as dark payment for ancient wizards' attempts to cordon off part of the Western lands for human habitation. Women, as we see, are complicated and resist placement, which isn't surprising for a Le Guin universe. Next to the right live the Kargs, who T. A. Shippey has claimed "are most like Americans than the inhabitants of the islands Ged considers home. The Kargs do not believe in magic, they have an organized religion and an organized state, and they live under a class system" (White, 22). They have kept to the *Vedurnan*. By keeping it they do not go to the Dry Land when they die, as the Archipelagans do: they are reborn into the cycle of life as any living thing.[70] To their right live the animals that are born back into the cycle of life. Among those animals are the dragons of the Kargish lands, small and dumb beasts that eat fire and seem to retain some of their dragon nature. Also there are the harrekki, the small, hand-sized "dragons" of the East Reach. These two types of dragon wrap us back around to the other side of the continuum to the True dragons, which creates a sense of circularity to this model, and the circle is the ultimate continuum. They are animals and dragons both, as Irian, Tehanu, and The Woman of Kemay are both dragons and people. Before the beginning of the second trilogy we had more clear separations between dragon, Archipelagan, Kargish, and animal; now all are intimately linked in that horizontal chain of being. Seserakh tells Tenar that she knows that "they are all gone . . . On the Dragon's Way" (*Wind*, 237). The Dragon's Way is where the Kargish dragons travel by land; when the dragons disappear from Earthsea to fly on The Other Wind in the West, we assume that Seserakh is given knowledge that it includes the Kargish dragons, though perhaps not the harrekki. Alienation was the source of that first separation; coming together—as symbolized by the crew of the *Tern*—is what will save Earthsea from its own evil doings. They are all, as the taverner says of the wizards' staying at Emer's farmhouse, "all foreigners in one basket" ("Marsh," 186). In that same story, the wizard Irioth confesses to Ged that Le Guin wants us to understand about not only residents of Earthsea and the Hainish but any other: "I didn't understand . . . about the others. That they are other. We all are other. We must be" (195).

Continuity among people on a much lesser scale is achieved through the lineage of wizards. From *Tales from Earthsea* to *The Other Wind* we learn that Ged's line is more "ragbag" than what we might expect of the Last Archmage. This, in microcosm, shows how as wizardry reaches back into the past it was more inclusive by person and by tradition. Ged, a Roke-trained wizard, was trained by Ogion who was not trained on Roke, which we come to learn in "The Bones of the Earth." He was sent there only to return to Gont to be trained by the wizard Heleth. There is no doubt, however, that Ogion is considered a mage. Heleth was himself a Roke-trained wizard, though his first teacher was Ard, whom, it turns out, was a woman from Perregal where the Pelnish Lore (a tradition that draws more on the Old Powers of the earth than Roke wizardry) was in use. We can only imagine who trained Ard, but it is certainly unlikely that any Roke-trained wizard did. It is true that Ogion was willing to train Tenar, but he himself wasn't of Roke. This line, made known in the second trilogy, would have been unthinkable in the first trilogy in which women's magic is "weak" and "wicked" and in which Old Powers are almost exclusively negative.

While it is true that the second trilogy ultimately reestablishes a division rather than a link with the reaffirmation of the *Vedurnan*, the trilogy establishes a shared heritage in the first place that more firmly links all people than the reaffirmation of the *Vedurnan* divides. There is a separation made more clearly, but it comes from the knowledge that they were all one and share a heritage. Despite the reparation of boundaries, "people" are in a greater state of linkage than they were before. The Patterner says, as the dead go free from the Dry Land to enter the cycle of life, that "what was built is broken. What was broken is made whole" (*Wind*, 240). It is, I think, right to put it in that order: Earthsea has experienced a division, but it is possible only because of the larger union, which is now understood.

The Inheritance of Place and Time

Another way that inheritance links the two series is related to place. What we think of as Ogion's house is a three-generation anchor in the series. While it begins in *A Wizard of Earthsea* as Ogion the Silent's house, we learn in "The Bones of the Earth" that Ogion's master, Heleth, lived there before him. We learn in *Tehanu* that Ged and Tenar, two of Ogion's pupils, will inherit the house from Ogion. Both Ogion and Heleth are buried near that house, and it is almost certain that the aging couple will find rest nearby. But it is home not because of its place, but because of the people who share it and each other. Heleth makes that clear when he muses, "what matters, it seems to me, is whose house we live in. And who we let enter the house" ("Bones," 159). The place becomes identified with safety and simplicity, but as the series moves into the second trilogy it becomes richer and less an archetypal wizard's safe haven and more a home found in a novel: colorful, detailed, lived in—and at risk. Ogion's house is emblematic of the changes between series regarding the focus on people and the details of their ordinary lives.

There is also overlap in time between the two trilogies that helps connect the series as a whole. While there are years separating each of the first three novels in the series, in fact as many as eighteen years between *The Tombs of Atuan* and *The Farthest Shore*, there is an overlap—not simply a continuation—between *The Farthest Shore* and *Tehanu*. In fact it is fully 41 pages into *Tehanu* that Ged arrives in Gont atop Kalessin. He has come directly from Roke where he had returned with Lebannen from Selidor at the end of *The Farthest Shore*. In story time, the events of *Tehanu* begin before the time of *The Farthest Shore*, for the girl Tehanu is with Tenar "more than a year" before Ogion asks Tenar to be by his side as he prepares to die (*Tehanu*, 6). The extreme textual overlap provides continuity where we might otherwise only see a sub-textual division between the two series. We might say that Kalessin flies back to Gont bearing the Earthsea novel on his back, leaving epic on Roke among the wizards. Le Guin observes that over time, "archetypes turn into millstones, large simplicities get complicated, chaos becomes elegant, and what everybody knows is true turns out to be what some people used to think" ("Foreword," xiii). *Tehanu* is the place where the millstone is dropped. Even while the telling of an epic featuring wizards, dragons, princes, and the dead is going on at the edge of the world, the novel is already underway in a small village on Gont in the farmhouse of a widow. It is almost as if Le Guin is not asking us to replace one with the other, but showing that they can occur simultaneously in the same world about the same events, but with a different focus. Tenar might be talking about the Earthsea novel as well as Tehanu when she tells the girl, "you're a cocoon. In the morning you'll be a butterfly and hatch out" (*Tehanu*, 7). Here early in the first book of the second trilogy we have a metaphor for what will happen at the end of the latest book of the series. Tehanu asks Kalessin at the end of the novel that bears her name, "Shall we go there now . . . where the others are, on the other wind?" (249). Kalessin tells her that there is yet "work to do here" (249). But the promise is made when Kalessin tells Tenar, "I give you my child, as you will give me yours" (249). A promise is made that makes us wonder how we could ever have thought that Le Guin could stop thinking about, and writing about, that promise.

While in the course of *Tehanu*, Tenar thinks back over the 25 years since she first arrived at Re Albi on Gont. That is represented as analepsis or flashback in the novel. In contrast, *Tales from Earthsea*, the collection of stories that is the next book in the series, covers in real story time over 300 years of Earthsea history. By using stories that range from a few centuries ago to only a few years ago in conjunction with historical apparatus that explains Earthsea traditions and beliefs, Le Guin fleshes out the world of Earthsea for the reader between the novel that introduces the idea of change and the novel that fulfills it. By the time the reader has made his or her way through *Tales from Earthsea*, he or she actually knows more about Earthsea than do most of the characters of the next novel. While this helps the reader of *The Other Wind* feel a bit superior to the characters in the novel, the feeling can only be about background; everyone is in the dark regarding what will ultimately happen.

In both narrative and expository form, the second trilogy expands the series in two directions: the horizontal axis of time is extended into the past and present, and the vertical axis of character and place is made rich and complicated. As the continuum of people is made more intimate and non-hierarchical, the series extends not only up to a more recent "now," but further back into its rich history. What Ogion tells Ged regarding his flight from the shadow is true of the series as well: "A man would know the end he goes to, but he cannot know it if he does not turn, and return to his beginning, and hold that beginning in his being" (*Wizard*, 128). The series' second trilogy brings us closer to the end, but also turns and returns closer to its beginning. Closer, but as there is the possibility for more time to pass in Earthsea, so there is the chance that we will return, perhaps only through myth, to the First Cause.

"There is a way to go now," Kalessin tells us at the end of *The Other Wind* (241). But where, Eldest? At the end of *Tehanu*, "Kalessin's great head bowed very slightly, and the long, sword-toothed mouth curled up at the corner" (249). This knowing smile tells us that something's afoot, and we learn the extent of that in the two subsequent books. The end of the first trilogy provides us ambiguity as well: two endings, one of which is verified in *Tehanu*. Le Guin seems to enjoy ambiguity as a way to leave an Earthsea story. Consider Azver's interchange with Kalessin near the end of the latest novel: "'Eldest, will [Irian] follow the way back through the forest, sometimes?' Kalessin's long, fathomless, yellow eye regarded him. The enormous mouth seemed, like the mouth of lizards, closed upon a smile. It did not speak" (240–241). Kalessin, like Le Guin, knows when it is time to say no more, but smiles as if to say, there may well be more to say later. Tenar tells Ged at the end of the tale that "the Patterner believes Irian will come to the Grove if he calls to her" (246). We will have to wait to hear whether he does.

The Earthsea series, Le Guin's crossover series, is revised halfway through in important ways. Le Guin creates epic using narrative strategies similar to other young adult novels and refashions it into a novel form that puts all readers in the position of the young adult as those naïve and hopeful

—it charts the line connecting, not dividing, epic and novel. In that move, tantamount to stopping a fugue halfway through and continuing it as waltz, Le Guin creates characters that are multiple, nonhierarchical, and more novelistic than epic. The series extends the world of Earthsea into both the past and into the present and gives readers a feeling that while the Archipelago isn't new, it is being rediscovered. The series also charts the line that unites young adult with adult literature through the *bildungsroman*, it propels us from monologue to dialogue, and it shows the continuum of place and character and of the inheritance of time and place. The Earthsea sextet is Le Guin's masterpiece in multiple continua.

Bakhtin tells us that "to create does not mean to invent . . . Every creative act is determined by its object and by the structure of the object, and therefore permits no arbitrariness; in essence it invents nothing, but only reveals what is already present in the object itself" (1984, 65). While Le Guin has said all along that she found Earthsea rather than creating it ("Dreams," 44), she finds that she must discover it all over again: "What I thought was going to happen isn't what's happening, people aren't who—or what—I thought they were, and I lose my way on islands I thought I knew by heart" ("Foreword," xv). She reaches into the past of Earthsea to make a new future, shows the continuity rather than the separation of the two series through characters and places familiar but changed, and along the way revises that series by genre, tradition, and implied audience.

5
Always Coming Home
Childhood, Children's Stories, and the Child Reader

> Things from here on will be just as fictional, though more factual, although equally true.
>
> **Ursula K. Le Guin**
> *Always Coming Home*

Bernard Selinger notes that "one main project of [*Always Coming Home*] is to blur boundaries."[1] While that is true of just about all of Le Guin's work, *Always Coming Home* is a special project in erasing divisions. By 1985 Le Guin had made a conscious effort to rethink narrative as a linear, masculine exercise. She expressed this concern after *Tehanu* came out in 1990: "our refusal to accept rules we don't make and boundaries that make no sense to us is a direct expression of our being women writers in the ninth decade of the twentieth century."[2] The refusal she speaks of is manifest in *Always Coming Home*.[3] In fact, the second trilogy in the Earthsea series would scarcely be imaginable without both *Always Coming Home* and "Buffalo Gals" preceding it.[4] The development of voice, narrative strategy, and subtexts regarding multiple identity and coming of age are all apparent from 1985, with the publication of *Always Coming Home,* to 1990, when *Tehanu* appeared. Le Guin has always discussed her relationship to each genre in which she plays, but it could be argued that, though she hasn't talked about it, her experience with *Always Coming Home* was a prelude to writing more for younger children. *Always Coming Home* was published during a stage in Le Guin's work when she was beginning to turn her attention to those younger readers for a while. She didn't publish much for adult readers between 1979 (*Malafrena*) and 1994 (*A Fisherman of the Inland Sea*).[5] In that time, she published *Always Coming Home* (1985) and *Buffalo Gals* (1987), which feature child protagonists, *Wild Oats and Fire Weed* (1989),[6] a collection of poetry, and *Tehanu* (1990), the continuation of her fantasy series originally intended for young adults. In that same time period, she published 11 children's picture books and two adolescent novels. Between 1979 and 1994, then, she was focused on young adult and child readers. Though I won't argue that *Always Coming Home* is a children's book, in it she offers us what is arguably the most impressive set of narrative strategies to make what is a novel "for adults" invite the whole span of readers on the continuum of age.

The Novel

Many of us who are challenged in home repair come to believe we can do every job in the house with a hammer and screwdriver. Le Guin illustrates with *Always Coming Home* that a tool meant for one job isn't necessarily right for every task: "because the literary traditions and models and forms of my own language were not fully suited to what I was trying to do—weren't made, as it were, out of adobe and madrone—I went to the people who did make their words and their art out of our native ground."[7] This resulted in something readers of novels in the western tradition found unusual for its versatility of form. With *Always Coming Home* Le Guin gives us a new definition of "novel" as toolbox.

In this, her great experiment, she had to move beyond the fact that "the principle mode of our thinking is binary" (*ACH*, 536). *Always Coming Home* is anything but binary, and that includes the dichotomy of child/adult. Not only is the book a departure from her more tried and true narrative strategies for exploding binary, it is a departure from the limits of the novel itself[8] It is, as a novel, "a medicine bundle, holding things in a particular, powerful relationship to one another and to us."[9] The book contains four sections of poems; sketches of the local flora, fauna, and cultural artifacts, some editorial commentaries, myths, philosophies, old sayings, insults, histories, romances, oral tales, "life stories" or autobiographies, dramas, and several sections of anthropological descriptions. These elements regard things like time in the Valley, dances, rituals for dying, naturalist notes, and even a CD-ROM filled with the Kesh texts shared orally. And, as others have pointed out, the three sections focused on the character, Stone Telling, are in their aggregate a novella within this novel—though in the book it is described as an autobiography (*ACH*, 279). There is even a fragment of a Valley novel, *Dangerous People*, "written" by Wordriver of Telina-na. Mention is made by the editor of other novels of the Valley: "novels of the writers Marsh, Cowardly Dog, and Mote, which are alas far too long to include in this book" (541). In case we believe ourselves to be uneasy regarding how a Valley novel is a novel, the "editor" is careful to assure us that the "Valley novel was a novel, not a romance; it was concerned with the daily lives of ordinary people in real places at some time not too far from the readers' present" (337). As we have been pleasantly surprised by Le Guin's return to

Earthsea, I wouldn't be surprised to see a full Valley novel appear someday
—perhaps Windriver's full text or a wholly new story, a new novel, that is set
in Sinshan.

Despite our editor's reassurances, the status of *Always Coming Home* as
novel is problematic for some of us outside the Valley. This is the entire
point. As a "novel" it is ambiguous, as *The Dispossessed* is an "ambiguous
utopia." Richard Erlich is also uneasy: "I'm not sure I'll call *Always Coming
Home* a novel, although it says right on the cover, '*Always Coming Home*: a
novel'; but perhaps *Always Coming Home* is best seen as one of Le Guin's
major contributions toward the redefinition of the novel: a step toward the
nonmasculinist novel."[10] Erlich even goes so far as to categorize *Always
Coming Home* as Le Guin's "anti-Bible, or un-Bible" (2001). Donna
White judges that "rather than a novel, *Always Coming Home* is a multimedia event. The book isn't even organized in any kind of standard fash-
ion: all the elements are mixed together in a carefully planned hodge-podge
. . ." [11] A hodge-podge might be another name for a "carrier bag," after all—
or a toolbox.

There is an advantage for Le Guin to call this work "novel": the novel is a
pretty slippery form, and by calling it "novel" she argues for its place in a
definable (albeit loosely defined and evolving) category of respectable literature. Le Guin's own notion of the novel is that it "is something non-intellec-
tual, though not simple; something visceral, not cerebral . . ." ("Preface," 3).
In other words, though White questions the layout, structure isn't the sole, or
even primary way, of identifying "novelness" for Le Guin.

Bakhtin is an ally of Le Guin's on matters of the novel. His theory of dialogism, which is centered on the study of the novel, defines the genre in terms
of what it does rather than simply how it looks. As one who breaks with
Russian Formalism regarding the primacy of structure, Bakhtin sees the
novel as "the sole genre that continues to develop, that is as yet uncom-
pleted." He goes on to say "we cannot foresee all of the plastic possibilities,"
as Le Guin's experiment shows.[12] He warns us that "everything works as
long as there is no mention of the novel" (1981, 8). But Le Guin's subtitle
does mention the novel, and by calling *Always Coming Home* a novel she
gives herself license to experiment—though many would argue that by 1985
she has earned that licensure through reputation. This book, she seems to
imply, is another of the plastic possibilities for the genre "novel."

The novel is the exception to the literary rule, the thorn in the side of
genre, and Le Guin, as we know, enjoys sticking it to genre. As if he were
thinking of *Always Coming Home* rather than the novel up to the early twentieth century, Bakhtin's novel is described as "whatever force is at work
within a given literary system to reveal the limits, the artificial constraints of
that system."[13] Le Guin's novel does this, though it may be more accurate to
say that she isn't so much acting in defiance as she is illustration. *Always*

Coming Home is a novel that shows the continuum of other genres (as listed above) that is itself the definition of "novel." The novel is, indeed, a quality of language rather than a fixed form reducible to rules for length or of story or character. As we see in *Always Coming Home*, "the novel as a whole is a phenomenon multiform in style and variform in speech and voice."[14] "In principle," Morson and Emerson argue, "any genre could be included in the construction of the novel . . . All these genres, as they enter the novel, bring into it their own language" (320-21). So the novel is, as a genre, a continuum of genres from the "nonliterary" to the literary, from the poetic to the prosaic, from the child's story to the adult's, even from the non-fictional to the fictional. There is no novel more perfectly suited to illustrate the habitability of the novel for other forms than *Always Coming Home*. The book both reifies the genres within it (history, autobiography, and poetry) and shows the limits of those western forms within the decidedly non-Western cultural context of the Kesh. Surely Bakhtin uses an appropriate analogy for Le Guin's work when he claims that "compared with [other genres], the novel appears to be a creature from an alien species"—at the very least a creature from a future world (Bakhtin 1981, 4).

Stone Telling

Within its own blurry boundaries, *Always Coming Home* presents us with a particular kind of novel. Stone Telling's autobiography is a *bildungsroman* set within the larger context of the Kesh culture and is presented in three pieces throughout the novel, roughly cutting the book into halves. Part One comes very early on, before we hear from Pandora. The second part appears midway through the book after Pandora has spoken to us thrice and we have been exposed to a great deal of Kesh literature and culture, and the concluding section brings up the rear near "The Back of The Book" after all but the last section of poetry.

The Stone Telling story is an example of a *bildungsroman* more in keeping with young adult literature not only because it is told by a character narrator, but it is told through the consciousness of the child-becoming-adult. At first Stone Telling seems to want to tell the story in retrospect, though she still shares childlike feelings, as when she depicts her wonder at Corruption's magic, which makes her "laugh with surprise" (*ACH*, 15). But she lets us know in Part One that a respected elder, Giver, suggested to her a strategy for telling her tale: he "suggested to me . . . that in writing the story I try to be as I was at the time of which I am writing" (30-1). Just as Frank McCourt's Pulitzer Prize-winning *Angela's Ashes* (1996) is powerful because it is told in the voice of the child who experiences the action, the Stone Telling sections, like good young adult literature, allows the reader to not only hear the voice but inhabit the consciousness of the young character.

Stone Telling abdicates commentary out of Le Guin's recognition of her own ignorance: "All I can write is what I saw, what I learned, what I did, and let wiser people find a name for it all" (*ACH*, 205).

What this technique accomplishes, other than creating the potential for a young adult reader to empathize with another young adult, is that it portrays different ways of being through a doubtable narrator. These ways of life are the conclusions of a young adult not entirely mature, not entirely equipped to reflect as an adult. And like young adult literature, an adult who defers her own wisdom and elects to restrict herself to the realistic mature limitations of her adolescent character narrator writes the story. While there are clear values choices in the novel that adults will discern, those values exist in juxtaposition with other possibilities, and the reader *can* take the Condors and the Kesh for what they are as portrayed by the relatively non-judgmental young narrator. Bakhtin warns us that "some critics, enslaved by the content of individual heroes' ideological views, have attempted to reduce these views to a systematically monologic whole, thus ignoring the fundamental plurality of unmerged consciousness which is part and parcel of the artist's design."[15] While it is easy for the reflective adult reader to say Condor equals bad, Kesh equals good, we have to remember as mature readers that we are given the world through a doubtable narrator, one who has told us that she doesn't feel competent to judge accurately what she sees. The naïve presentation of material softens the sense that what Stone Telling offers us about the Condor is slander, for instance. "There is no argument to present a particular practice as preferable; rather the data are presented as just the way the Kesh are," Warren Rochelle concurs.[16] No mature narrator's voice, if Pandora can be called that, engages in a value comparison between the Condor and the Kesh. Stone Telling is viewing the exotic in the Condor City, and views it as an immature outsider. "Exoticism presupposes a deliberate *opposition of what is alien to what is one's own*, the otherness of what is foreign is emphasized, savored, as it were, and elaborately depicted against an implied background of one's own ordinary familiar world," and Stone Telling is subject to that as well (Bakhtin 1981, 101). Le Guin has given us ample opportunity to see the immaturity of the teller by making her self-conscious about her ability to judge, a technique the author uses effectively in both *Very Far Away from Anywhere Else* and *The Beginning Place*, her young adult novels published before *Always Coming Home*.[17]

Not only are we shown the coming of age of a character from age eight onward to old age, we see through Stone Telling's eyes what Le Guin wants us to see about the Condor: they themselves live in a culture stuck in adolescence. During her own adolescence, Stone Telling lives with the Condors, an aggressive, masculine society. This provides the reader with a quality of male adolescence that Stone Telling herself, as a participant of a yin culture and as a young, inexperienced woman, would be hard pressed to provide us otherwise. Le Guin says of her novel that "*Always Coming Home* was a rash attempt to imagine such a world, where the Hero and Warrior are a stage adolescents go through on their way to becoming responsible human beings."[18] In *Always Coming Home* the Hero and Warrior are stuck in adolescence, but Stone Telling escapes the Condor City to go home to Sinshan to resume growth as a mature person.[19]

Stone Telling possesses four distinct identities throughout her story.[20] She begins her story as "North Owl." When she goes with her father to the city of the Condor she takes the name he gives her, "Ayatyu," a Condor name meaning "well-born woman" (*ACH*, 197). On her escape from that city and on the way back to Sinshan she adopts the name "Woman Coming Home" (381). By the time she writes this tale, she has become "Stone Telling," which is her final identity and the second name she gives herself. The Kesh typically possess three names throughout their lives as a way to mark the movement from childhood to young adulthood and finally to maturity later in life. Stone Telling's second and alien identity is what makes her able to see both worlds from two perspectives.

As the main character in the longest narrative section of Le Guin's book, Stone Telling is, as Bernard Selinger points out, "atypical in her story, which is typical in Le Guin's fiction" (133). She is the person who doesn't fit in because of her difference, the actuality or perception of which is the main fuel for the *bildungsroman*—the conflict of coming to terms with an identity. Le Guin tells us that "the novel is a fundamentally unheroic kind of story" (1989b, 168), and the *bildungsroman* typically is not about heroism as much as it is about survival, though we might argue that the successful quest for identity is the most heroic thing we ever do.

Stone Telling is the child of two cultures: her mother, Willow, is Kesh; her father, Terter Abhao, is Condor. Her father is of "no house" according to the people of Sinshan, and that makes Stone Telling's job of constructing a sense of self very difficult—and all the more necessary. "All that grieved me," she tells us, "was that I was half one thing and half another and nothing wholly." This, she qualifies, "was the sorrow of my childhood, but the strength and use of my life after I grew up" (*ACH*, 31). She begins by embracing her difference out of defiance: "If I had to be different from other people, then let my difference be notable, I thought" (27), an attitude which ultimately leads her to journey with her father to the City of the Condor when she turns seventeen. She never feels quite a person as Ayatyu, however. She tells us, "it is almost as hard to write about being Ayatyu as it was to be her" (*ACH*, 204). She observes that "not being entirely a person, [she] could not become a different person," so she will have to return home to finish becoming (*ACH*, 204). The reason that she has been asked to tell her story is so that people will understand the Condor, though for us—and for her—the point is to tell the story of her adolescence in a culture devoted to adolescence, but tell it *as* an adolescent, as she says she has chosen to do at the advice of Giver. Oliver Scheiding argues that *"Always Coming Home* is a book about living in the 'between,'" which is not just a matter of living between cultures but of living between stages of life.[21] In any case, her time with the Condor juxtaposed with her Kesh life shows the reader, as Sarah Jo Webb calls it, "an alternative way of being human" during a time in our development when we feel least human—adolescence.[22] When Stone Telling enters her middle life as a Kesh woman, taking the name "Woman Coming Home," she returns to her life in Sinshan as someone able to see with both eyes, as she calls it—an important part of what Le Guin argues throughout her fiction is fundamental to being truly mature—but she tells of the time before her double vision and with that single vision of the young adult. Like Tenar in Earthsea, Stone Telling be-comes herself by having become other for a time. Like *Always Coming Home*, Stone Telling is simultaneously multiple things, which might be seen as sorrow or strength.

The Child

By having a journey of home-away-home, Stone Telling engages in a pattern common to children's literature, which actually separates it from the *bil-dungsroman*. Instead of lighting out for the territories as Huck Finn does, Stone Telling comes home. This is one pattern Le Guin uses, as others have noted and discussed earlier in this book.[23] While in children's books the re-turn home is often perceived as a way to convince both child and reader that home is the place one really ought to be, Le Guin shows us that home is a place where we take what we've learned and improve life.[24] Home isn't to be overcome, it's to be developed and embraced. In fact, Le Guin had to go home to write this book—return to the Valley of her childhood summers: "to write the book I had, at last, and entirely, without reservation, to come home" (Le Guin 1988a, 9). She recalls that when she was a child she would play "in the adobe dirt with [her] little houses and cars and people . . . (1988a, 10); she returns to play in that home soil as a writer. It is Le Guin's belief that "the six directions can meet only in lived time, in the place people call home, the seventh direction, the center."[25] This novel is, like many books for the young, a celebration of that "seventh direction" called "home." Again, while the novel/autobiography featuring Stone Telling is not categor-ically either a children's book or a young adult novel, the qualities it shares with those genres are significant because of the rather fuzzy nature of the implied reader for this story and the whole book.

Apart from patterns of home and coming-of-age, the entire novel of *Always Coming Home* features the child—her presence, voice, and texts. It is through this child that we find a way into the Valley; in fact the child is "the only way" in (*ACH*, 5). To find the Valley "you take your child or grandchild in your arms, or borrow a young baby, not a year old yet, and go down into the wild oats" and wait patiently for a voice from "home" (*ACH*, 5). In "First Note" we are told that "what was and what may be lie, like children whose faces we cannot see, in the arms of silence. All we ever have is here, now" (n.p.). Selinger tells us that the children described in this "First Note""are in the arms but they aren't—they have no faces, no identity" (130). Later in the book, in the expository section called "Living on the Coast, Energy, and Dancing," the ephemeral quality of the child is made clearer: "A baby existed more in physical energy and relationship . . . than a person" (*ACH*, 526). Children represent a way of seeing rather than only being particular children in the community, though they are clearly that too. "Children often drew maps . . . " (480), we are told; and they also serve as maps.

Carol Franko has observed that there is a "recurring metaphor of children" in this novel, and it is an important statement on childhood for Le Guin.[26] Margaret Hostetler, too, has noted that "children in *Always Coming Home* function as polysignifiers, participating in several systems of representation," as well as "mediators between past, present, future."[27] Children, like birds in the Valley, are messengers, conduits for communication with us and for the dead outside the Valley. We learn that "in Sinshan babies' names often come from birds, since they are messengers" (*ACH*, 7). Later in an expository section of *Always Coming Home* called "The Serpentine Codex," we discover that that birds "may speak for the dead and bear messages to them, and their feathers are the words that the dead speak" (45). When as a child Stone Telling finds a feather, Cave Woman tells her that her "hands are a child's hands, they are running water through the wheel. They don't hold, they let go, they make clean" (*ACH*, 26), and are therefore a suitable medium because of their purity. In "How to Die in the Valley" the editor informs us that "children at the funeral might be given seeds or grains to scatter on the grave, so that birds would gather there to carry the mourners' songs to the Four Houses" (*ACH*, 92). These children perform an important duty in the culture, and without them there would be less dialogue among the peoples of the Kesh. For Kesh, "children were at the center of their world" (*ACH*, 524), the hinge, and the center is the seventh direction: home. Since the center or "heya" is the most important idea to the Kesh, the child in *Always Coming Home* is especially important.

We recognize that the cultural metaphor of child-as-medium is an influence on the Kesh literature as well: the child in the novel fragment *Dangerous People* has a "moonfever" that is portrayed as a vision of his mother, who may well be dead (*ACH*, 359). At the end of the novel fragment, the child ends up looking for the mother with the help of Moondog, the mother's lifelong pet.[28] In the anonymous poem "Artists" we see a connection between the creative function of the artist and the child: "That is where they live, / Where they get their breath: / there, in the gap between, / the empty place" (*ACH*, 78). The children perform through their essential nature as mediums, as artists do. In Sinshan, then, children are artists to be listened to and respected. They are a way to see the past, as Hostetler has it. In the longer poem, "From the People of the Houses of Earth in the Valley to the Other People Who Were on Earth Before Them," the piece that immediately precedes "The Back of The Book," we are given more than a look into the past through the metaphor of children. We see a direct address to the past by the children of the future, the world of the Kesh: "We were among you: / the children, / your children, / dying your dying to come closer, / to come into our world, to be born" (*ACH*, 429). Pandora offers us a view of the future through the metaphor of the child as well: "Many as we are, there's still too much to carry. It is a dead weight. Even if we keep breeding ten babies every second to bear the load of Civilisation forward into the future, they can't take it. They're weak, they keep dying of hunger and tropical diseases and despair, puny little bastards" (*ACH*, 154).

But those "puny little bastards" are a fundamental strength of this novel. The child, thematically and structurally, is fundamental to the work to a degree exceeding almost any novel for adults since Victorian England.

Children's Stories

Apart from the presence of children as characters and metaphors for communication, *Always Coming Home* contains texts written *by* child characters —clearly a hallmark of children's literature. The greatest presence of such texts is in the poetry sections, as far as we can tell. There's no reason to believe that the editor would know the authorial source of all of the texts she has found in Sinshan, after all, so many more may be by children than she knows. Le Guin makes it clear that she is trying to appeal to a larger audience than the usual reader of poetry: "In *Always Coming Home* I was trying to do a very, very unformidable kind of poetry that wouldn't frighten a prose reader. Our poetry has been so difficult and so intense in this century; an awful lot of people don't read it because they're scared off by it."[29] Two strategies for alleviating formidability is to present children's texts or have children write the texts—or both. After all, they are hardly the same thing.

The editor tells us that "rhyme is characteristic of children's songs" as a way to define that subgenre (*ACH*, 82), but a good deal of all of the poetry in the book contains internal rhyme. And all of the poetry, including those written by and/or for children, contains repetition. It is the editor, after all, that tells us that certain songs or poems are children's songs; the categories are, then, our own (*ACH*, 73). Indeed, any decision about their status comes from the editor rather than the culture from which it originates. For instance, "Boso" is "a children's counting-out song of Sinshan," we are told, though it is hardly more playful than other Kesh poems not for or by children. "All in the Western Land" is described as a children's dance and contains the common Kesh theme of the gyre, internal rhyme, and repetition, as do many other poems not designated "for children." The poem also contains the line "O who will be my lover / all in the western land," which we wouldn't ordinarily expect in a children's text (82). The first section of poetry mixes children's songs with pastoral, bawdy songs, insults, laments, and love songs. In fact, any of the poems in the third section of poetry could be for children if internal rhyme and repetition are markers, though they are not designated as "children's." The poems also don't contain what we might consider questionable language, but it is clear throughout this book that the Kesh do not share our sense of the profane.

What is for and by children is made ambiguous—as ambiguous as the larger book's relationship to the child reader. But it is important, I think, that Le Guin sets up this ambiguity while making it clear that some of the texts *are* likely by children. If Le Guin's editor hadn't raised the subject of category or origin, we would as likely supply the default "adult" or "Kesh." As it has been argued we in this culture fall back on "male," "Christian," or "white" when the possibility of an alternative isn't directly suggested. Le Guin, through her editor, makes the child visible, and therefore an alternative; the ambiguity and mixture of all types of texts forces us to keep from relegating that which is for, by, or about the child to the hinterlands of the book.

There are, in addition to the stories for children, those stories actually told by children and young adults. "The Train," a story told by Enough of Sinshan, a seven-year-old girl, is presented alongside other life stories told by people much older, and it is offered with the confidence that others in the community will consider it worthy and significant (*ACH*, 281). "She Listens" is narrated by the eponymous character, an adolescent woman who has just recently taken her middle name in life. And as Stone Telling told her tale through the consciousness of her younger self, "Junco" is written by an older man about his time as a young man, a "record of a vision quest by a spiritual athlete" (*ACH*, 281). Because the whole book is an anthropological collection of tales by the whole community, the children's and young adult tales are included without apology or qualification beyond the ages of the tellers—information that may not be as important to the Kesh as it is for our culture. In truth, the vast majority of the stories in the book don't seem to be age-specific for the Kesh, perhaps a comment on the importance of all stories and poems regardless of the ages of the tellers or the age of the implied reader. Perhaps *Always Coming Home* is at its most utopic in the way that children are respected and listened to.

It seems certain that even the most language-conscious contemporary adults could read most of these poems and many of the stories to their young children given the concrete nature and rhythmic quality of the works. We might say that Le Guin offers her readers—the young, the adolescent, and the adult—literature under the guise of an "adult novel." Elizabeth Cummins is right on the mark when she observes that "this 'cross-dressing,' one genre in the guise of another, in *Always Coming Home* obviously draws attention to the literary creative act and all that it entails—the writer, the audience, the social contests of both, the subject and form of the story or poem, and sometimes the performance of the telling."[30] This novel is a supreme example of crossover through its telling, its form, and its construction of an implied audience through those first two things.

Pandora

Always Coming Home is, as Donna White asserts, a "multimedia event" (95) that includes the authorial voices of the composer, Todd Barton, the illustrator or "artist," Margaret Chodos, and, most inscrutably, the Geomancer, George Hersh.[31] Newer editions come complete with a compact disc full of songs and poems. The maps are "drawn by the author," according to the title page.[32] Between the beginning and ending there is a perceptible authorial presence, where we hear all of the narrative voices in the text: Pandora the editor, Pandora the childlike worrier, Pandora the indignant Aunt, Thorn and the archivist (who are sources from within the Valley about the Valley), Stone Telling, and other Kesh speakers through the "primary" material. And in the middle of this narrative continuum is the hinge, the multi-hinged book itself. Across the hinge is the narratee who is also a generalized implied reader position: readers of the novel in 1985. Other implied readers, as I discuss above, include adults, young adults, and children—known and unknown to the author. This collaboration among real and created "speakers" avoids a single-voiced narrative presence even though the author is more perceptible in this book than in any of her other works. This is "from us all" to "all of you," it seems to say.

The rich and layered narrative relationships keep us from fixing on any one narrating voice in the presentation of this anthropological text. The narrating voice is multiple, inclusive, and as varied as the implied readers by age and the real readers of any text by happenstance. Jim Jose argues that in *Always Coming Home* "a dominant narrative voice is lacking"—a single voice, yes, but narrative voice itself is, in its polyphony, the project of the book.[33] Elizabeth Cummins is right to conclude that "Le Guin finds that one narrating voice is not enough" (1990b, 188). With Pandora we have in one character multiple narrative voices.

Naomi Jacobs speculates that "perhaps the fatal dullness, and the ethnocentrism, in so many utopias comes from a thinker's refusal to learn to 'sing' with the people she creates . . ."[34] Le Guin does "sing" with her creation, literally, and in her creative juxtaposition of ways of seeing, avoids both dullness and ethnocentrism. The authorial presence is remarkably perceptible, though not uniform. Bakhtin tells us that "the idea of the author can be scattered sporadically throughout the whole work . . . without, however, merging with the characters' individual personality," and this is true of this novel (1984, 84). While Le Guin merges with Pandora, our editor is also not Le Guin, and clearly the book carries many of the subtexts dear to Le Guin in the voices of other narrators who still remain their own people. The "First Note" is offered to us by the author, who conflates herself with Pandora, the editor. The identity of the speaker is revealed when she tells us she's "coming at [her] work as a novelist" rather than as the anthropologist Pandora (*ACH*, n. pg.). The work is book-ended by the author's voice, a voice that clearly combines Pandora and the Author in "Pandora No Longer Worrying" in which thanks are given to Le Guin's friends. We could argue that the very last text, one that comes after the glossary, "Stammersong," is Le Guin fully "drunk" on Keshness ("I have drunk the water of that river. / I am drunk my life long, my tongue is thick, / and when I dance I stumble and fall over"), as well as on the authorial act. It is easy to see the author as the song ends: "There is a valley, high hills around it. / There is a river, willows on its shores. / There are people, their feet are beautiful, / dancing by the river in the valley."

But critics don't agree on the identity of Pandora. For instance, Naomi Jacobs presents Pandora as someone "who might or might not be the editor" (42). Kristine Anderson, in contrast, takes for granted "the presence of Pandora as editor and translator."[35] Carol Franko, however, acknowledges the conflicted sense of Pandora's identity. If we consider the confused and developing sense of identity that characterizes the relationship among the three we needn't worry about separating. What is behind the narrative confusion and self-consciousness, the bold rule-breaking, is the same thing that is behind the self-consciousness of Stone Telling in her story. In both cases we are dealing with an identity narrative told at different levels of narration by speakers who both are and are not characters. We might even say that Pandora is, like Stone Telling, going through her own coming-of-age, though more in the manner of Ged in *Tehanu*—as an adult. Carol Franko claims that the key to the structure of *Always Coming Home* is "Le Guin's self-conscious, multifaceted narrator, Pandora" (57), and I agree. There is no real introduction to Pandora, as there is to Stone Telling by Pandora, so there is no context given for the "story" of Pandora. If we piece together her experiences throughout the book we'll see that hers and Stone Telling's are the only chronologically continuous parts of the book. The difference is that Stone Telling's tale is easily recognizable as a traditional narrative. Pandora's story fights through her own conflicted and shifting sense of identity without the luxury of a super-narrator to present it as such. Pandora's *bildungsroman* is a carrier bag experience rather than a linear tale like Stone

Telling's, an experience not yet "cleaned up" for convenient and easy consumption by a reader.[36]

One of the reasons there is confusion about Pandora's identity as simultaneously editor, author, and character is the way she speaks—like a child taking on roles, playing. Her voice shifts with the role, as do all of our voices; the problem is that we can't visualize the speaker to verify it. Heinz Tschachler sees Pandora as one "who occasionally casts off her role as anthropologist and addresses us as the author."[37] He sees her as someone putting on masks. I think, rather, that Pandora isn't assuming roles separate from her own: she *is* at different times the author, the editor, the anthropologist, the aunt, and the singer of poems. She is, like my five year old, simultaneously a big girl and a little girl when it fits or suits, which can be in the space of a single sentence. And like Stone Telling, Pandora is known by different names. This isn't a matter of a real face covered by false ones but of multiple real faces. Pandora herself is a set of narrative continua that runs from the most objective to the most subjective, from the most adult to the most childlike, from the most identifiable to the most indiscernible.

Pandora begins her story of identity as Stone Telling does—by being troubled. She is "worrying about what she is doing," as the title of her first section tells us. She begins by speaking of herself in the third person as though looking at herself. She fights the lure of the Kesh with objectivity, the third-person address of the social scientist. She doesn't want to "look into the big end of the telescope" and see it all as far away, but she will for now. She concludes the section by softening, by telling herself to "let the mind draw its energy. Let the heart complete the pattern" of what she sees, though she'll fight that further in the book (*ACH*, 56). She begins in the position of the distant intellectual in control as she has presented the native material in the book up to this point, but then she becomes visible in her discomfort. She wants to hold it all "in her hand" rather than just watch and take notes. Later in the book she, as editor, alludes to herself, as Pandora, as a part of herself already "gone native." Giving us an example of the modes of speech in the section "The Modes of Earth and Sky," the "editor" uses her Pandora identity as the subject: "So in actual conversation one would say, 'Pandora, are you living in Sinshan now?'—Pandora, Sinshanzan gehovzes hai ohu," (*ACH,* 535) and the answer to that is an emphatic yes. She *is* living in Sinshan now, in spirit—not an accidental linguistic example, I think. To typify her pre "no longer worrying" state, however, she provides the reverse as an example of the negative form: "Pandora is not living in Sinshan now," which is literally true since she is a contemporary of ours (535). She won't be "no longer worrying" for a few sections yet.

I get ahead of myself, however, which is the mad joy of reading this nonlinear book. Following her opening section is the half-page selection "Pandora Sitting by the Creek," in which she provides us with a metaphor for her becoming. Almost 100 pages into the text, after exposing readers and herself to Kesh stories and poems, as well as to their burial practices, she becomes lyrical. Sitting by the creek, observing the water, she is of a mind to see things in transition: "the rib-bone of a steer lies half in the water," "the tail feathers of a dead bird lie moving slightly in the water," "half the branches that cross the creek are dead and half alive and some it's hard to say" (*ACH*, 99). The illustration at the bottom of the page shows water striders, creatures that travel through water and air simultaneously—crossover bugs. Things are half here, half there; the world is half one thing, half another—like Stone Telling's lament. Pandora, in her lyrical musing, finds it hard to say where she is—half dead observer looking from "not here," half person beginning to live in Sinshan.

In "Pandora Worrying About What She Is Doing: She Addresses The Reader With Agitation," she has lost her trance and, after relating Kesh romantic tales, poems, and histories, she is in angry denial. She speaks now through character narration, or first-person address, losing the safety and feigned objectivity of external narration and third-person address. She asks whether it was she who burned the libraries of Babel, she who killed the babies by loading them with the weight of civilization. She is conflicted as "a daughter of the people who enslaved and extirpated the peoples of three continents" (*ACH*, 154). She becomes flippant, angry, and a gloomy adolescent addressing the reader as a "fellow maggot" (*ACH*, 154). Her self-consciousness is increasing and, as the adolescent who begins to see the dark side of the world in which she lives, she has a royal fit.

Following "Time and the City," Stone Telling's Part Two, and dramatic works of the Kesh, Pandora returns still "worried" but again lyrical and musing. In "Pandora, Worrying About What She Is Doing, Finds a Way into the Valley Through the Scrub Oak," she contemplates relinquishing her role as one who demarcates culture. The bushes, scrub oak, and chaparral "evades" and are "innumerable." She tells us "I read scrub oak. But I don't, and it isn't here to be read, or burnt" (*ACH*, 256). She acknowledges the messiness of life, of Kesh life, and resigns herself to it. She is still solitary (except for her momentary scream at her contemporary, the reader) and she goes back to simply observing the world.

The next section moves us from the third-person distance of the beginning and then the first-person musings and rants of what follows to the dialogic interaction between Pandora and one of the Kesh, the archivist of the library of the Madrone Lodge at Wakwaha-na. There, after exposition on "dancing the moon," more Kesh poems, some Kesh autobiographies, and some "brief Valley texts," Pandora can let go of some of her anxiety and anger and begin to ask questions. It is here that familial address creeps into Pandora's discourse: she is "aunt" and the archivist is "niece." Though the relationship seems to put Pandora in a superior position, it is she who seeks help from the niece. Shocked at the words of the archivist regarding his world being an "Up Yours" to Pandora's consumer culture, Pandora chides him by saying "You can't talk that way!" "True," the archivist responds, and then teaches Pandora to sing "like any savage" (*ACH,* 336). They sing together to end the section. Here Pandora does several things: she faces a representative of the culture into which she seeks entrance, she engages in dialogue, she moves from combat to song, and through it all she grows closer to sharing her own Kesh-like poems at the end of the book. She ultimately gives herself fully to her new identity.

Relatively soon after this section, following the novel fragment from *Dangerous People,* Pandora returns to this time speak "gently to the gentle reader" rather than to her "fellow maggot." Now instead of being ruled by guilt and a sense of betrayal, she is ruled by the generosity of one at peace with herself. She tells us, now irrevocably in first person—as a character and narrator, that she'll take us to the Valley. She wants to be in, with, and part of the Valley but wants us to go along. For her to go, she believes, we must go, too. She is grown up, but serves as children do in this narrative: she is our way in. She tells us: "we have a long way yet to go, and I can't go without you" (*ACH,* 360). By now Pandora is on her way to living in the Valley, though her identity as editor continues into "The Back of The Book" as she does her job. By the time we get to "Lodges, Societies, and Arts," not marked as a Pandora section, she is comfortable conversing with Thorn of Sinshan about Kesh life and drops all combativeness. She has learned to learn from the archivist, and this section has Pandora asking questions, letting Thorn educate her. She doesn't react. It is in this last part that she shares "three poems by Pandora," poems which speak from her new position as one of the Kesh. The poems mark a movement from third person early in the book to first-person address outside dialogue, to accusatory second-person address, to dialogue (itself from combat to acceptance), and finally to poetry that is written in first person plural form. She has attained "we." She has grown up as Stone Telling has. It is only then that editor/anthropologist/author Pandora shares her "no longer worrying" section in which we see the voice, the face of the author thanking her real friends in the real world for helping her grow up Kesh.[38]

As Stone Telling's section portrays a character narrator sharing her coming-of-age as one from two worlds, the Kesh and the Condor, Pandora/Le Guin shares her coming-of-age as a character-narrator from two worlds: Portland and the California Valley of her youth. Stone Telling merges here in the narration with the author/narrator Pandora as one who has left the Valley, lived in the city, and has returned to the Valley. Donna White argues that "the Stone Telling chapters are the closest thing to a narrative in *Always Coming Home,* so reviewers and scholars both tend to focus on those sections, even though they constitute at most one-fifth of the book" (98). Perhaps this is only because we haven't considered the relationship between the stories of Stone Telling, Pandora, and Le Guin. Despite the potential confusion of metalepsis, or transgression of hierarchy in narration, if we consider the different layers of narration as actually merging, telling the same story of coming-of-age, the relationships become clearer and confusion is alleviated. They are interweaving strands of the same project as well as different levels of narration.

The Reader

As we've seen above, and as Robyn McCallum reminds us, "there is always a potential dialogue embedded within the speech of characters and narrators in relation to an authorial context or position."[39] How is the reader positioned in this dialogue, though? What are we being asked to do? Who are we supposed to be? We are comforted in the beginning of the book when we are told that for the reader who is willing to deal with unfamiliar terms, "they will all become clear at last" (*ACH*, 3); that is, if we decide to read in a linear way, which the book seems to defy us to do.

If we do read in a linear way, we take on the position of the ignorant reader who must be willing to learn slowly, as a child in Sinshan would, as Pandora learns to do. The straight-through reader has to struggle with the alien nature of the Kesh culture before she gets any anthropological exposition. Take the Stone Telling pattern as an example of this. The reader approaches each section with a different degree of ignorance about Kesh culture. In Part One, Mouse Dance tells Stone Telling that a feather she found "was spoken to [her]"(26). We don't learn that birds are messengers of the dead or that their feathers are words until later in *Always Coming Home*. We have to let that vague reference wash over us until we learn what it means, much as Stone Telling must let meanings flow around her as she learns how the world works. This scripted ambiguity is a technique Le Guin uses to make us feel alien in the culture, as any child does—at least for a while. This facilitates the sense of confusion on the part of the narrator Stone Telling, which also creates a sense of empathy for the young adult reader. So, we are given only the concrete reality Stone Telling experiences in Part One, not the anthropological exposition that will precede Part Two. Le Guin argues that "there's no use in talking in abstractions if what you're trying to get at is exactly the opposite, a way of thinking that is utterly concrete, local, fixed in place like a spring of water or a mountain" (1988a, 6). It is the job of the novel to raise us in the culture about which it speaks, which often means deferred explanation, if it provides it at all.

If we decide to read the book as a textbook on Kesh culture, however, we might jump around it, reading what interests us first and then return to other parts, equipping ourselves with the appropriate knowledge to understand the primary texts in the first part of the book. But even if we do that, unless we read all of the exposition before any narrative or poetry or discussion by the Kesh, we may not know all we need to know, though all reading strategies result in *some* understanding. The book allows us to be as ignorant as we want to be, then, allowing us to play the role of child and adult in various degrees rather than separating those positions by kind. All *does* come together if we finish the book in whatever order we read. McCallum goes on to say that "texts which use dialogic narrative structures and techniques, such as multi-voiced and multi-stranded narration, and/or a range of genres and extraliterary discourses, generally construct more active reading positions. With the case of inexperienced readers, this is of particular importance, since these techniques can implicitly equip readers with a wide range of reading strategies and skills for ascribing meanings to texts" (259). The book allows actual younger readers to be active in constructing the sense of this text rather than simply permitting us to assume the role of child implied reader.

Elizabeth Cummins characterizes the relationship between storyteller and listener/reader as one "analogous to that which makes community possible" (1990b, 185). What makes community possible? One way we achieve community is through collaboration. We can't be isolated as readers of this book. To be a part of the community we have to be given some choice, some role to play, a sense of belonging. In the Kesh community, the role of listener to oral tales does not mean that the characters always know what is to come. The translator's note to "Some Stories Told Aloud One Evening in the Dry Season at the Summer Place Above Sinshan" explains that "the listeners did not know what was coming next, but collaborated in the invention and performance by their responses and laughter" (*ACH*, 60). The Kesh themselves give us a model for interaction. The listener/reader collaborates and becomes part of the community of the book by interacting, by responding honestly to what is presented in order to decide what will come next.

Heinz Tschachler argues that "by offering her readers a collaborative role in realizing the text, Le Guin reinforces the impression that *Always Coming Home* is an experimental, nonlinear fiction" (100). As Tschachler argues above that Pandora assumes a role separate from her primary identity, here he argues that the nonlinearity of the book is an impression created by the author. I don't think it's about impression—about masking what's really there. Rather, the construction of the text is ours to respond to and create in our individual reading, not an "impression" at all but the most concrete of realities. Cummins makes that connection when she points out that in *Always Coming Home* "the narrative techniques . . . call upon the reader to interact with the novel more as one interacts with the experiential world—or with consensus reality.[40] The book is constructed by individual interaction with the nonlinear arrangement, one that allows us varying degrees of ignorance as we move through our "responses and laughter." Bakhtin argues that "the idea begins to live, that is, to take shape, to develop ... only when it enters into genuine dialogic relationships with the other ideas, with the ideas of the *others*" (1984, 88); the idea of the book takes shape only as we engage in dialogue with it as the readers that we choose to be at each reading. Warren Rochelle notes that "The reader's interpretation, his sense of what is true—all is contingent and subject to revision," and we will move about the book, constantly revising our conclusions (152). We play as children in this text, no matter the degree of ignorance we choose, as we move among the primary material from Kesh culture. The implied reader of the book skates along the continuum of age from child to adult by varying degrees.

Pandora helps us understand the arrangement of the book that results in these reader positions. As she describes the scrub oak in the Valley she also describes the book she narrates: "It's a mess. It's littered. It has no overall shape ... There's no center and no symmetry" (*ACH*, 254). But she also makes it clear that "it is not accidentally but essentially messy" (254). There is some sense of relationship among the pieces, if not of order exactly. In a novel that, as Oliver Scheiding puts it, employs "a narrative discourse of non-ending reversals," there are ways back and forth through narrative direction, if one chooses to take them over the course of different readings (647). The book, like any dictionary of culture or language, is filled with cross-references. In "Serpentine Codex," we are referred back to a poem 77 pages earlier (*ACH*, 492). There is also an allusion in the preface to the section "Spoken and Written Literature" that refers us back to "How to Die in the Valley" (*ACH*, 539) just as the first section of poems refers us ahead to "Spoken and Written Literature" (73). There is a method to the madness, as we've seen. Again, as if in reference to the book as a whole, the editor observes that "a story has a beginning, a middle, and an end, Aristotle said, and nobody has proved him wrong yet; and that which has no beginning and no end but all middle is neither story nor history. What is it, then?" (*ACH*, 172) It is an opportunity for the reader to participate in the construction. The (dis)order of the book ultimately makes us feel like Stone Telling herself, who confesses that she "liked learning in the heyimas, taking part in a structure larger than my own knowledge, in which I could find relief from feelings of fear and anger which unaided I could not understand or get past" (*ACH*, 9).[41] The effect of the order of *Always Coming Home* is the effect of culture on the young person—there is a sense of one's place in a larger system that can be liberating as well as nerve-wracking. The reader becomes what the text makes her, but then the text becomes—as does a culture—what the participant makes of *it*.

Multiple Dialogues

There is, because of the order of the text, or its disorder, a dialogical relationship between reader and text that is on par with the relationship between author and text. The reader is co-creator, and readers of a wide range of ages are marooned on the same island making do with the materials at hand.

In *Always Coming Home*, as in anything considered "simultaneous," "the concepts of 'earlier' and 'later' lose their substance," (Morson and Emerson, 400). While the book has an order, it doesn't direct us, and even a section called "The Back of the Book" makes up for placement with its attraction to a reader for information. A reader of the "front" of the book needs the back more than the reverse. In this way Le Guin makes her book as much a non-linear, simultaneous experience as possible for a linear medium. Michael Holquist, in his discussion of Bakhtin's notion of simultaneity, points out that "simultaneity is found in dialogue between an author, his characters, and his audience, as well as in the dialogue of readers with the characters and their author."[42] And *Always Coming Home* is not a novel of shifting genres presented in order as much as it is a collection of genres existing in perpetual dialogue with each other, unlike a traditional anthology that places genres exclusively in their own hermetically sealed sections of the book. The dialogic quality of the book can be attributed to the way that information occupies "*simultaneous but different* space," as things do on a continuum (1990, 30).

The first hint we get of the dialogic quality of the book, its interest in the simultaneity of points on a line, is in "Quail Song," the first Kesh text in the book. The poem comes "from the Summer Dance" of the Kesh and makes it clear that what we are to experience in this book is dance, a form of expression that is the ultimate example of two bodies occupying simultaneous but different space in dialogue with each other: "in the meadows by the river / two quail run / Run two quail / rise two quail / two quail run / two quail rise / from the meadows by the river" (*ACH*, n. pg.). Even the aural quality of it forces the reader to experience something of a tongue twister, blending the words themselves even as they occupy their own space.[43] While we can see two quail as two individual birds, it is futile, as Yeats would have it, to separate the dancers from the dance.

The two principal figures in the book point to the nature of simultaneity in the book. Stone Telling and Pandora, in their respective coming-of-age stories, try to come to terms with a duality that needn't be binary but is dialogic. For Stone Telling we see multiple opportunities for dialogue. The most difficult to reconcile is the dialogue between Kesh and Condor, which is complicated by the fact that the great difference between them is the matter of dialogue itself. What she discovers, despite her interest through her own dual nature to reconcile the two cultures, is that the Condor are hierarchical, pyramidal, and patriarchal: "to be the Condor is to be outside" (*ACH*, 373). Stone Telling finds that she is "living among people who were going the wrong way," away from dialogue, which is a choice the Condor makes (*ACH*, 375). Because one side won't engage in dialogue it seems that nothing is accomplished, but through internal dialogue as Kesh and Condor she manages to learn to see with both eyes, as do Myra from "Buffalo Gals" and Tehanu in *Tehanu*. As she leaves the City of the Condor she notes that she now "had two eyes to see [her father] with" (*ACH*, 368). When she is told by her Condor father to forget one life for the other, she replies: "My mind is not that small . . . It holds the Valley and the City and still I don't know where the end of it is" (*ACH*, 369).

She comes to peace with her duality by the end of the book, as do the townsfolk back in Sinshan. She notes even early in the book that "what is seen with one eye has no depth" and that "the sorrow of [her] parents' life is that they could see with one eye only" (*ACH*, 31). When she, herself both Kesh and Condor, is in the Condor City she is an adolescent displaced from home and in a culture Le Guin herself describes as adolescent in nature; it is the ultimate dialogic situation. In retrospect she notes that "almost everything is double like that for adolescents; their lies are true and their truths are lies, and their hearts are broken by the world. They gyre and fall; they see through everything and are blind" (*ACH*, 195). Adolescence is, like "Quail Song," a metaphor for the experience of both the characters and the readers of the book, and adolescents live in the hinge where balance needs to be learned (*ACH*, 526).

In "Some Brief Valley Texts" we are provided the aphorism "to be single-minded is to be umindful. Mindfulness is keeping many different things in mind and observing their relations and proportions" (331). Pandora takes that to heart by the end of the book when she offers us the poem "Not Being Singleminded." In it she notes of her adopted people that they are "Some people, not very many, / trying to keep a lot of things in mind" (*ACH*, 523). She, like Stone Telling by the end of her story, has made her peace with the simultaneity of culture and of their respective conditions as multi-positioned people. Do we as readers? Yes, if we read like the young and are like Stone Telling who, as a child, "was able to forget fifty things while doing fifty others" (*ACH*, 187). Readers of the book are actually most successful if they read like children and young adults: children are not fazed by dealing with untraditional, nonlinear texts because they haven't yet been trained to expect them, and this book doesn't penalize one for having a short attention span; the adolescent is practiced in dealing with his or her consciousness of a world filled with conflicting messages. The most difficult position from which to read this book is from the Condor's position in which we demand hierarchical and linear sense to be offered us through our experiences living or reading. We need to read this book inside the hinge, the place where artists, children, and young adults live.[44]

Is *Always Coming Home* a children's book? No. But much of what Le Guin does in this book presents the question of what a novel for adults would need to do in order to create a true crossover text in the form most would, on first glance, deem only a novel for adults. In this story we have, as the most dominant narrative, a young adult's story. A narrator undergoes her own coming-of-age as an inhabitant of the Valley in a story that is illustrated with sketches to make unfamiliar objects and animals clear to the reader as is done in children's picture books. There are children's stories and poems alongside "adult" stories and poems themselves accessible for a young audience, and I have read some of the stories and poems to my own appreciative five year old. Finally, there are stories by children that share a similar relationship with tales told by adults; there is the accompanying CD-ROM that provides the texts in oral form for the easy consumption for even the preliterate child; and there is a narrative structure that puts the reader in the position of childhood not unlike many fantasy texts that put the child in the position of the "native" rather than anthropologist (and Pandora converts from anthropologist to native, gives herself up to the children's way if you track her "development" in a linear way). It isn't uncommon for adults to decide that certain children's picture books are for adults for their postmodern qualities of intertextuality, or because of decentered or fragmented narratives, or for the presence of "surprising" subtexts, but how unusual it is for anyone to decide that a book that isn't a picture book—a book that seems "obviously for adults"—might actually be "really for children?" It is true that Le Guin doesn't consider this a children's book, but it is hard to imagine what other narrative techniques one might use intentionally to make this book cross from adult to young adult to child readers as this one does. *Always Coming Home*, written at a time when Le Guin was focused on the young reader, sets the standard for a book that travels the continuum from child to adult reader.

6

Ethics and the Continuum of Hope

Genre and Audience

There are precisely as many genres as we need, genres whose conceptual shape is precisely determined by that need.

Adena Rosmarin
The Power of Genre

Genre is a representative of creative memory in the process of literary development. Precisely for this reason genre is capable of guaranteeing the unity and uninterrupted continuity of this development.

Mikhail M. Bakhtin
Problems of Dostoevsky's Poetics

I will claim no more for fantasy than to say that I personally find it the appropriate language in which to tell stories to children—and others.

Ursula K. Le Guin
"The Child and the Shadow"

In previous chapters, I invited readers to consider the ways Ursula K. Le Guin's work operates on different continua mostly indifferent to genre. Finally, I'd like to consider the question of genre more directly, especially the less investigated question of age-based genre. It seems to me that age-based genre is where we really see the most distinctions in Le Guin's fiction. Le Guin uses genre as her ethical compass to guide the audience. Her sense of genre enables her to do the right thing for certain readers. There is a continuum of hope in her work. The stories that are the most consistently hopeful are her children's stories, and those children's stories are always fantastic; she considers fantasy the genre that *guarantees* a hopeful outcome, no matter what her original plans are for a work and despite where she might go as she writes. As we move down the line toward the less hopeful, we find predominantly hopeful science fiction and rather bleak realism.

Children's Authors and the Claim of Audience

Writers who claim that they write only for themselves deny the influence of either genre or readership guides the writing. These writers argue by implication that they neither communicate with readers nor observe generic traditions; they simply write to/for themselves. They are self-proclaimed literary isolationists. In their commentaries on writing for children, Jill Paton Walsh, Katherine Paterson, P. L. Travers, Mollie Hunter, and Michael Steig directly point to themselves as at least partial, but they don't all go so far as to claim that they don't write for children.[1] Arthur Ransome made "the reiterated denial that he wrote for children," but he ultimately "made a distinction between writing *for* children and writing *to* children," claiming the latter occupation for himself.[2] Peter Hollindale believes that Ransome is less interested in child readers than he is childhood, which Hollindale considers a feature of the genre of children's literature.[3] In any case, writers for children who would deny both interest in, and consciousness of form and audience, argue that theirs is children's literature entirely by accident. However, a book becomes a children's book—intended by the writer or not—when critics identify generic features (text), and/or children find that the book speaks to them (context).

I'm more interested in the children's writer who claims both to write children's books and to write books for children—those writers who conflate text and context. When the children's author describes "writing to children," we are invited to see a rhetorical relationship between a writer and a reader; when the children's writer discusses "writing children's literature," we are invited to consider the text as a member of a particular genre or text type. We shouldn't be surprised when these authors sound like rhetors at one moment, and the next moment—perhaps in the next sentence—they go on to talk about, and even define their work, in textual terms only. The authorial tendency to combine textual and contextual definitions of children's literature frustrates critics eager to distinguish clearly between "book people" and "child people."

The authors who have primarily (though not solely) a rhetorical view of what they do see the text as a conduit for the delivery of their own message to real children.[4] Beyond mere lecture, Betsy Byars, Mollie Hunter, Katherine Paterson, and C. S. Lewis all claim to engage in a dialogue with actual children.[5] Byars's sense of audience comes, she claims, directly from her own children, who also give her the ideas for her books (7). She is amused by the "theory today that we must never write for children" (7).

Hunter, too, credits dialogue with her children for her success (8–9). Paterson makes her process and aim clear: "I write for my own four children and for others who are faced with the question of whether they dare to become adult" (109). C. S. Lewis is perhaps the most well-known critic of the cult of the generalized child: There needs to be, he says, a dialogue between an author and *a* child, a real person with whom one either actually consults or about which the author can predict responses based on the history of acquaintance. Lewis points out that the "participants modify each other" and form "a community."[6]

Authors for children don't always make clear distinctions between audience and genre. Authors as influential as those above seem to shift their gaze from genre to reader. For example, Lewis claims he writes in the particular genre of "children's literature" in the cases when children's literature "is the best art form for what [he has] to say" (1075). Lewis shows that he is as much engaged in a dialogue with genre as with some individual person, careful never to which or whom he speaks? There's no small bit of irony in the fact that Lewis's "art form" is as general as the generalized concept of the child audience that he cautions writers to avoid. Katherine Paterson also makes a shift from audience to genre in one breath, blurring the distinction between them. As if in response to Zohar Shavit's claim that "writing for children usually means that the writer is limited in his options of text manipulation,"[7] Katherine Paterson writes, "'Don't you feel constricted writing for children?' they'll ask. William, don't you find fourteen tightly rhymed lines an absolute prison? Ah, Pablo, if you could just yank that picture off that lousy scrap of canvas! You get the point" (33). What Paterson and Lewis illustrate is that it is both easy and sensible to combine the notions of genre and audience when one is writing in a genre named for an audience—text and context necessarily become conflated. Genre and audience are combined rather than confused with each other. These authors haven't made an error, they have made an erasure. They erase the distinction between audience and genre in children's literature.[8]

Perhaps it isn't odd to talk about genre as an audience. Genre is an audience in its own way, an audience to which people write. It is a living tradition with clear rules and expectations for discursive behavior. It is as much a context for conversation as that provided by an audience of children. The dual audience in this case is composed of children and tradition, rather than of children and adults.

The critic's impulse, however, is to make a distinction between categories —between texts and contexts. Peter Hunt suggests that "the critic of children's literature has only two choices": She can either decontextualize the text by ignoring the audience, or she can grant the primacy of the audience as the foundation of the genre and communicate to that audience, however perceived.[9] Hunt's position is that there is an absolute and necessary choice. Lewis's and Paterson's conflation shows that such easy distinctions may actually be impossible.[10]

Respected critics can be as ambivalent about the differences between texts and contexts as successful authors can. Peter Hollindale considers "the author's textual negotiations with the child" to be what makes children's literature "unique, and different in kind from other forms of literature" (12), yet he questions that negotiation when he says that "the adult children's author is always obsolete" (22) and that "children" is "an increasingly unstable concept" (25). Jacqueline Rose maintains that "there is no child behind the category 'children's fiction,' other than the one which the category itself sets in place," yet she is concerned about the potential for unethical authorial control over real child readers which might result in a sort of "molestation."[11]

The tension is evident in Barbara Wall's important narratological work *The Narrator's Voice*, as well. She notes that there is a "substantial barrier of age" between adult writers and child readers which "may be surmounted or traversed" but never removed as authors attempt to "serve . . . their chosen audience" (20). Wall's ultimate concern is with the implied audience rather than the real one, which is fitting in her narratological approach. Can an implied audience, the author's own construct, be "served?" Wall insists that "the real author knows only the implied reader, a presence his or her text inescapably calls into being" rather than the real audience that can be served (7). "Implied audience" is a textual feature, not a contextual reality like a real reader. The implied audience that can be served other than the author herself is the genre to which she speaks, a construct of tradition that exists in a context and has "needs" and expectations. She asks us to remember "the physical parties in the transaction, whose existence cannot be legislated away by theories of narration, for without them there would be no transaction, nor any reason for the transaction" (4). This is important, but it isn't really the province of her narratological approach, one that is concerned with not "what is said, but the way it is said, and to whom it is said" (2). The "chosen audience"(20)—the implied audience of genre—is the audience to whom the author speaks if she cannot, or will not, speak to the "real" audience of children. Other than herself, genre *is* an audience that the author knows.

Children's writers who claim to write to an audience of actual children (generalized or specific) may more comfortably link textual issues with audience by invoking the issue of ethical fiction. John Gardner links them in one sentence: "If I'm going to write for these [ghetto] kids, I'd rather deal with them in a fantasy world where everything's not bleak or where there's a hint of sunlight in the background."[12] Claudia Mills, prolific both as a writer and critic of children's literature, argues that those who study children's literature "are more willing than many other critics to concede that one aim of a children's book is to shape the evolving character of its readers."[13] In fact, even Jacqueline Rose, someone who denies the existence of the audience category "children," claims that "writers for children must know and understand children" (70). Katherine Paterson, like Gardner, makes it clear that she cares about that real child: "I cannot, will not, withhold from my young readers the harsh realities of human hunger and suffering and loss, but neither will I neglect to plant that stubborn seed of hope" (38). The distressing is not omitted; it is merely treated in a way that Paterson believes will work for a child audience, an audience that includes her own children. "Hopeful realism" then, becomes a combination of structure and audience concern under the banner of ethical fiction and informs Paterson's vision of the genre of children's literature. Paterson refuses to water down issues, but she also insists that there be a sense of hope by the end of the story. This is why we see her, as well as Lewis, speak about form and audience simultaneously. She doesn't divorce them.[14]

Writers who claim that they are only concerned with the art form often write fiction similar in structure and ethical quality to writers who conflate audience and genre. This is because the genre itself is the implied audience, and the genre has expectations for ethical art that have evolved for centuries. Writers less rhetorically/ethically conscious are affected because of their concerns for satisfying the genre's ethical tradition. As if in response to a rhetorically conscious author like Paterson, Jill Paton Walsh asks, "How can I feel any responsibility to my audience when I don't know who my audience are?"[15] Because Walsh doesn't "know" the actual readers, and because the readers, whoever they are, don't have a responsibility to the writer, Walsh is "responsible to nobody" except to the book itself as an artistic product (Walsh 1973, 32, 35). Sandra Beckett notes that the French crossover author, Michel Tournier, insists that he doesn't write children's books at all. "Can an author write for children without writing children's books, as Tournier claims to do?"[16] It is entirely possible that what one writer considers a matter of audience, another writer without rhetorical concerns might find to be a textual feature of children's books. If Walsh doesn't consider children as she writes her children's books, she then writes with an eye aimed at generic tradition. For her to write what she considers "children's literature," although ignoring a sense of audience, necessarily means that her guideline—her context—is genre, however she perceives it. Even if such authors claim to write for themselves, or for art, the question of how the work finally achieves the form of children's literature is one that can't be ignored.

Both Walsh and Paterson are known for their hopeful, yet unflinching social realism. Paterson's self-consciousness about an audience is the reason she writes hopeful literature; Walsh writes hopeful realism because she's conscious about the demands of children's literature. Wayne Booth argues that "the distinction between genuine literature (or 'poetry') and 'rhetoric' or 'didactic' literature is entirely misleading if it suggests that some stories . . . are purged of all teaching" (151–52). The idea that all good art is ethical—accidentally through form or intentionally through a rhetorical awareness—enables writers for children to serve both children and children's literature. We see the same conflation of audience and art, text and context, ethics and genre in Le Guin's self-critical discourse.

Le Guin's Ethical Equation of Children's Literature and Fantasy

The idea of the crossover writer, or the writer who writes for both children and adults, has been on children's literature critics' minds lately. Critics are seeing the worth of examining the nature of children's literature at the site of the successful crossover writer because such writers actually perform the genre distinctions in question. Mitzi Myers's question about the crossover writer seems a natural one to ask of Le Guin: "What continuities or divergences mark the writings of those who create separate works for child and adult?"[17]

Le Guin, like Paterson and Hunter, is concerned with the real live child audience who reads her books. In fact, Susan Wood claims that for Le Guin to recognize a book to be about ethics "is Le Guin's highest praise."[18] Le Guin describes her duty to her much younger audience by defining what she won't do in the particular genre of children's literature: "There's a certain type of hopelessness that I just can't dump on kids. On grown-ups sometimes; but as a person with kids, who likes kids, who remembers what being a kid is like, I find there are things I can't inflict on them. There's a moral boundary, in this sense, that I'm aware of in writing a book for young adults."[19] Like Hunter and Paterson, Le Guin refuses to absolve herself of any responsibility. She shows here a rhetorical awareness regarding her writing to children. Le Guin claims that "a denial of authorial responsibility, a willed unconsciousness, is elitist, and it does impoverish much of our fiction in every genre, including realism."[20] This, written to introduce a collection of short stories for the adult market, seems to reinforce her comment above that ethical art isn't at all a matter restricted to the child audience. Le Guin tells us that children "need to be—and usually want very much to be—taught right from wrong."[21] Once a child knows the difference, according to Le Guin, a child "[knows] what bad is. Grown-ups get confused."[22] We all need moral art, Le Guin seems to be saying, though perhaps in different degrees based on age. She marks the distinction between being preachy and being ethical. In the introduction to *The Word for World Is Forest,* Le Guin notes that those writers who yield to the temptation of didacticism "forget about liberty . . . and instead of legislating in divine arrogance, like God or Shelley, they begin to preach."[23] So, although Le Guin has a special concern for children, the difference of concern between adults and children would seem to be one of degree rather than kind: "Writers for children write with as much concern about audience as writers for adults—indeed, usually with a more conscious and perhaps more ethically alert concern. They have to; writing can damage people. Writers for kids don't want to damage kids."[24] If we are all in need of ethical art, then, how does ethics affect Le Guin's distinction between adult and children's literature?

Le Guin claims that she doesn't "know of anything you 'do' for kids that is different than [what] you do for adults" (McCaffrey and Gregory, 82). Despite her observation that she has a stronger sense of her fiercely loyal readership now than she did years ago, Le Guin still maintains that to think of the reader "is fatal."[25] "Ultimately, you write alone," she tells the readers of her new book on the craft of writing.[26] Consider, however, this important qualification to her insistence that one shouldn't write with an audience in mind: "While *planning* a work, the writer may and often must think about readers; particularly, if it's something like a story for children, where you need to know whether your reader is likely to be a five-year-old or a ten-year-old. Considerations of who will or might read the piece are appropriate and sometimes actively useful in planning it, thinking about it, thinking it out, inviting images. But once you start writing, it is fatal to think about anything but the writing."[27] Le Guin is adamant that stories "are, in their strange way, acts of communication—addressed to others," and we have to care about the addressee.[28] The initial consideration of audience is important. She is forceful about foregoing audience worries *after a work is started,* however. She is concerned about damaging children, and begins a work considering the possibility that children will be her audience. What keeps that work "on track" as ethical art for children once the process begins and audience concerns go out the window? How does she keep the baby and the bath water?

Ultimately, as I'll show below, Le Guin is communicating with two audiences, or, rather, she writes for one audience by writing to another. She addresses a particular generic tradition rather than a generic group of children. By doing this, Le Guin can have her ethics and child audience, too, without having to think about the age of her audience after she plans and as she writes. Consider how Le Guin personifies genre as an audience with needs, expectations, and demands, and explains the risk one runs by running counter to the demands, the "needs," of this audience:

> The beauty of your own tradition is that it carries you. It flies, and you ride it. Indeed, it's hard not to let it carry you, for it's older and bigger and wiser than you are. It frames your thinking and puts winged words in your mouth. If you refuse to ride, you have to stumble along on your own two feet; if you try to speak your own wisdom, you lose that wonderful fluency. You feel like a foreigner in your own country, amazed and troubled by what you see, not sure of the way, not able to speak with authority.[29]

Regardless of whether she has tried to defy genre or write to it, Le Guin has always used literary genre to guide her efforts; in fact, by constantly bringing our attention to her defiance of it, she reveals how she uses genre to define herself and to give herself authority, even if it is all (or mostly) by opposition. Because she has claimed that there are few definitions of children's books, what is the established tradition to which Le Guin can speak that simultaneously satisfies her requirement for ethical fiction for children and guides her once the writing has begun?[30]

Le Guin has discussed the special moral dimensions of another genre: "Fantasy is the natural, the appropriate language for the recounting of the spiritual journey and the struggle of good and evil in the soul" (Le Guin 1989c, 64). In fact, she points out that "realistic fiction for children is one of the very hardest media in which to [teach children right from wrong]" (Le Guin 1989c, 65), highlighting the difficulties she faces in finding a sure-fire ethical address to children. Where else but in fantasy can the child best be served?

There are no science fiction tales for children among Le Guin's texts and few outright fantasies for adults. Realism cuts across the two groups, however, with the qualification that the one children's story of hers that is realism is a frame for a fantasy within the tale.[31] Hollindale makes a similar observation about the genre of children's literature, in general, and, in a gesture that calls Le Guin to mind, uses the tradition of fantasy for his comparison: "There is an implicit definition of children's literature which has little *necessarily* to do with children; it is not the title of a readership, but of a genre, collateral perhaps, with fable and fantasy."[32] Le Guin implies the equation of fantasy and children's literature: "And I also rejoice in the privilege of sharing this honor, if I may, with my fellow writers, not only in the field of children's books, but in that even less respectable field, science fiction. For I am not only a fantasist, but a science fiction writer, and odd though it may seem, I am proud of both.[33] She also makes the link between fantasy and children's fiction when she asserts that "fantasists are childish, childlike. They play games,"[34] though fantasy is a game "played for very high stakes" because of its focus on moral matters.[35] Le Guin's use of the words "adult" and "children's" seem to serve as synonyms for "our world" (present or future) and "alternative world" (fantasy), respectively. The genre of children's literature is the same as the generic tradition that, according to Le Guin, is implicitly moral when it is well-written, Good when it is good. It is good to avoid didacticism, which one can do if one gives up the control of what gets written to the work itself, which Le Guin claims is essential (1998, 149). If control is given over to the "winged words" put into the writer's mouth by generic tradition, Le Guin can write good fantasy, write moral tales for children, and not end up preaching to children. She can trust the genre in which she has put trust. The degree that she can be less hopeful in stories for adults is accounted for by her choice of genres that don't put a premium on hope—science fiction and realism.

From the time of the essays reproduced in *The Language of the Night* on fantasy and science fiction (1972 to 1988) until her interview with me in November of 2001, Le Guin has stayed consistent about her views on fantasy, children's literature, and the special role of morality in those genres. The consistency becomes, in effect if not in intent, a conflation of fantasy and children's literature, which is a conflation of text and context not unlike that practiced by Lewis, who wrote fantasy for children and science fiction for adults.

Le Guin claims that she "finally got [her] pure fantasy vein separated off from [her] science fiction vein, by writing *A Wizard of Earthsea* and then *The Left Hand of Darkness*."[36] Since 1973, when she wrote the words above, Le Guin has continued to pursue various generic paths. Having worked out the "different veins," she continued the fantasy vein by starting to write specifically for young children through picture books. From her first picture book, *Leese Webster* in 1979, up through her 2002 publication of *Tom Mouse*, she has written 12 picture books. All these texts, all for young children, have clear and necessary elements of fantasy if they aren't fantasy outright. Interestingly, *Very Far Away from Anywhere Else* (1976), *The Beginning Place* (1980), and *Tehanu* (1990)—her books usually recognized as those for young adults—clearly represent a range from realism to high fantasy with mixing going on in between. Young adult literature—a literature of transition from age to age—may well mark where Le Guin allows her age-based genres to blur regarding morality and literary genre. In any case, in the 37 years from *City to Illusions* (1967) to *Gifts* (2004), Le Guin has kept her adult readers firmly in the genres of realism and science fiction. Even the stories of Orsinia, set in a fictional country, are meant to play in the affairs of Eastern Europe, not Earthsea.[37]

Gerard Genette observes that all genres contain several other genres;[38] in Le Guin's case, rather, certain genres exist *as* other genres, or as parallel, as seen in the fantasy/children's literature relationship. However, although Le Guin's fantasy is also known as her literature for children, it is also appropriate for everyone—an inclusive definition of children's literature that is as old as its status as a field of study. "Fantasy is the great age-equalizer," she tells us (1989f, 49). Is this simply another fly in the ointment of demarcation? Not because adults are more than free to read her picture books; in fact, adults are usually the ones reading them to children anyway. She pulls in the adults, as well, after all. Although fantasy doesn't exclude adult readers (as all good children's literature doesn't), it is fantasy that enables Le Guin to talk about children, children's literature, and morality. Ironically, fantasy and science fiction might be two genres that help Le Guin discover a genre otherwise invisible: "Adult literature." Famous for both her treatment of the "other" in literature and for defying genre, Le Guin may have found herself first confronted with the "other" when she was introduced to age-based genre with the publication of *A Wizard of Earthsea*. Before Ged, what had been simply different genres—realism, poetry, short fiction, science fiction, the essay—suddenly became subcategories of "adult literature(s)"—genres that she wrote when writing to adults. Despite Le Guin's discourse on morality and the inclusion of older readers, we continue to recognize Le Guin's children's books by the code word "fantasy"; we recognize her books for adults by the code words "realism," "poetry," "science fiction," and "nonfiction."[39] Maureen Thum's description of Wilhelm Hauff seems an apt description of Le Guin: Le Guin, like Hauff, explores the "area of wonder, of free-floating potentialities and magical intercessions associated with the child's 'unreal' world of fantasy, and with . . . the 'real' world of the adult."[40]

Brian Attebery reminds us that Le Guin's "first three books of fantasy appeared interspersed with her science fiction novels," and so "it is not surprising . . . that her fantasies share the same concerns as her science fiction";[41] David Galef argues that thematic parallelism is seen in a number of crossover writers, as well.[42] Le Guin's shared set of themes (freedom, home, journey, identity, otherness as seen in the beast and alien, and the courage to construct a self in the world) surface in all of her writing; they are merely articulated in different kinds of texts. Perry Nodelman reminds us that "many readers, both children and adults, seek out further texts by authors they have enjoyed, because they expect a common thread, a consistency in subject and style, in all the texts an author produces."[43] This is certainly true of Le Guin's readers. Readers of *The Dispossessed* follow Le Guin *to Always Coming Home*, perhaps to come home in different ways in different genres; the young readers *of A Ride on the Red Mare's Back* will find in Ged's story and then in Shevek's the same concerns about always coming home, though they travel from folklore to high fantasy to science fiction to get there.[44] However, given the clear generic alliances Le Guin makes between fantasy and realism (traditional or science fiction) and age, her "approaches to the themes vary considerably" (Attebery, 166).

Though genre isn't a barrier to Le Guin's themes, genre is an influence felt from her earliest foray into children's literature with the publication of *A Wizard of Earthsea*.[45] Her entry into the realm of heroic fantasy with the Earthsea series was allowable, she observes, because they were published as children's books. "So long as [she] behaved [herself], obeyed the rules, [she] was free to enter the heroic realm" (1993, 7). Le Guin found that she needed to challenge genre's influence in order to speak as herself. Until she realized she was the mouthpiece of tradition, she confused security with freedom; once she realized this, she says, the long succession of "genre-busting" texts began—texts for adults, that is. As a writer writes *within* a given genre, "She begins to write *against* the genre, thus changing and renewing it. The rigid system of genres and modes [begins] to disintegrate."[46] By bucking tradition, Le Guin gives up the authority vested in her as a duly appointed officer of traditional genres and creates a new authority for herself. *Always Coming Home* defies demarcation; *Malafrena* asks us to consider a fictitious country in a Europe we know. Her children's literature, however, remains genre-faithful. She simultaneously plays with genre in her adult texts and respects the integrity of the children's literature/fantasy relationship. All of her fantasy stories for children are hopeful tales. The science fiction novels are stories of hope, though many of her science fiction short stories such as "The New Atlantis," "Vaster Than Empires and More Slow," and "Mazes" deal in despair.[47] Her realism in both novel and short story form, however, seems to be predominantly bereft of hope.

So, despite all of her "genre-busting," Le Guin keeps genre clear in her sights (or watches it over her shoulder.) Todorov notes that "it is . . . considered a sign of authentic modernity in a writer if he ceases to respect the separation of genres."[48] Rosmarin, too, argues that "to be a modern writer and to write generically is a contradiction in terms."[49] "We forget," Scholes reminds us, "that when we attribute total freedom of choice to an artist, we are constructing a fiction of freedom, projecting our own needs and desires upon a figure who is far less free than we may assume."[50] As much as Le Guin defies genre expectations and tradition, as much as she "seems to contain within herself a multitude of writers,"[51] she also respects the rules as one price to pay to satisfy a need—the need to provide moral literature for young readers, the need to have a clear sense of audience that combines people and tradition, and the need to put the notion of audience behind her once her plan is completed and her writing begun. Perhaps, then, we underestimate the influence of genre on Ursula K. Le Guin. Moreover, perhaps we overestimate the ability of writers and critics of children's literature to separate matters of audience from matters of genre and matters of literary communication from matters of "art." Although it is certain that there are very successful writers who lay claim to moral relationships with child readers, those acts of literary communication are also simultaneously hopeful communiqués to a demanding and clear tradition.

Should genre be separated so neatly from audience in our consideration of children's literature? Le Guin's own writing of all kinds illustrates the problems, perhaps the dangers, of doing so. In the most significant ways, Le Guin's notion of the child is her notion of the genre of fantasy; the "conceptual shape" is the same. Her themes remain the same for all audiences, but the genres do not. Although Le Guin may be a crossover writer "trying out identities,"[52] she isn't creating a "colloquy between past and present selves" (Knoepflmacher and Myers, vii) but rather is engaging in a dialogue between multiple present selves, genres, and audiences. Although it would be foolish to discount the importance that individual children have played, and do play, in the writing contexts of many authors, the context and expectations of genre are more accessible for writers and seem to match the needs of those children's writers to find a distinctive form of address. Markers like "hope" and "morality" can serve to guide the author who would write in a genre named for an audience that will remain largely unknown. Separations by fantasy and realism (including science fiction) can help the ethical crossover writer to keep some lines straight while allowing herself to write in the direction the genre allows. The conflation of audience and genre, as seen in the commentaries of Le Guin, Paterson, Lewis, and others, is a phenomenon that itself marks literature for children as a unique genre shaped in part by its own demands.

7

An Interview with Ursula K. Le Guin

Portland, Oregon, November 9, 2001, 10 A.M. to 12 P.M.

At the beginning of my visit with Ms. Le Guin, I gave her the two-page breakdown of her works by age group found after this interview. I began our conversation by commenting on the even distribution of her works by age group. I did not know at the time of this conversation about the scheduled publication for the spring of 2002 of either *Tom Mouse* or *The Birthday of the World and Other Stories*. I have since added those last two titles, as well as her newest collection of short stories, *Changing Planes* (2003), and her soon-to-be released young adult fantasy novel, *Gifts* (2004), to the that follows for the reader's benefit.

Mike Cadden: I think that people who read your work more selectively— people who just read the science fiction or the children's books—would probably be surprised to see how evenly split it is between adult, young adult, and children's books. They'd be surprised, I'd guess, because there hasn't been a lot of criticism that connects them.

Ursula K. Le Guin: Yes, particularly with the actual children's books, which have barely been mentioned.

MC: In his study on people who write for both children and adults, David Galef notes that there are few authors who have written for both children and adults all through their careers and have been successful in both of those areas. He uses A. A. Milne as an example of somebody who does that. What I was curious about is what has enabled you to move back and forth so frequently? You've moved between them pretty regularly. Why do you think that you have moved so freely between them over the years?

UKL: You know, partly I'd have to say it's because I had an agent who was willing to sell both kinds. The effect of the market is very powerful. I think a lot of writers aren't able to. They might want to write both kinds or several kinds. This is also true of other genres. I had one of the very few agents in the United States, or in the world, who was willing to handle any genre. And not only willing to, but she could do it. She was good at it. She knew her stuff, which freed me to do what I wanted to do, which was apparently never to be pinned down into being a type of writer—except basically fiction and poetry.

MC: Is it disorienting as a writer to move back and forth from children's to young adult to adult work?

UKL: No more than it would be to write string quartets and symphonies, I think. They're slightly different arts. They're definitely different forms. You're putting slightly different stuff into it, but it's all writing stories.

MC: If you use your example of the string quartet and the symphony, I would imagine that the process, or even the goals, might be a little different as you move from one to the other.

UKL: Well, sure. Someone like George MacDonald: Who was he writing for? He was writing for children and adults, there's no doubt about it. I read *At the Back of the North Wind* when I was eight, and I read it when I was 58, and I thought it was a pretty weird book both times. But it is accessible and rewarding to both kids and adults. I am always uncomfortable when we start drawing absolute lines between things. There are differences, yes, sure. You know, there's a difference between realism and science fiction, and realism and magical realism, and so on. Your readers' expectations are different and you're trying to meet those. And, of course, the difference between a book for kids and a book for anyone over 11 and 12 is partly ethical. There are certain things you don't do to kids. You can really beat up on an older reader and scare them to death without really hurting them. It's like if I get an idea for a story, it carries with it its own sense of what kind of story it is. If it's about four kittens with wings, there's probably no way that this is for grownups. Just in itself, this is something for kids. But if it's about religious terrorists, then it's definitely not for kids.

MC: You were mentioning before the ethical distinction about there being a moral boundary between adult and children's fiction.

UKL: A very vague one, and a sort of troubling one. You hate to think of doing moral censorship on your own writing: "I can't do that because it's for kids." But the fact is all children's writers do.

MC: Jill Paton Walsh is one who says that she writes and is responsible to the art rather than to an audience. You're somebody, like Katherine Paterson or Mollie Hunter, who has talked about there being an ethical or moral distinction.

UKL: I think that if you pin Jill down . . . I mean, look at her books. She wrote a book about the bombing of London for young adults, which is probably accessible to a nine-year-old reader: *Fireweed*. That's a tough subject for a kid, but she made it endurable for a child. She didn't do anything that would damage the child.

MC: I wonder if that was because she was following what children's or young adult books tend to do, which means she's writing toward generic expectations rather than worrying about actual readers.

UKL: Well, like many children's book writers, she is a parent. We behave differently with children.

MC: Then there's a behavioral difference between approaching age-based genres and, say, making a move from *Searoad* to *A Fisherman of the Inland Sea*, where you're moving from realism to science fiction.

UKL: I think the behavioral difference is between adults and kids. And I mean kids—people under 12, because "young adult" is such a vexed question. Basically, to me, a "young adult" novel is a novel with a young protagonist.

MC: Which explains why *Tehanu* is where we might begin rethinking the Earthsea series as young adult fiction.

UKL: Yes, it doesn't have a young protagonist. The protagonist is a woman in her fifties.

MC: Well, we could argue that Ged is going through adolescence in that book.

UKL: Well, yeah, but that's metaphorical. He's not a child. He's a very grown up man. But back to genre difference. Science fiction is a good one to talk about because science fiction readers are experienced in reading science fiction, and one of the things that affects you when you're writing it is that you know you don't have to explain a lot. You've got very savvy readers. There's a kind of literary writing which takes a certain kind of reader. Umberto Eco's highly intellectualized fiction needs a certain kind of reader, and is written for that kind of reader.

MC: You would draw the distinction of "implied reader" between the age-based genres in terms of ethical responsibility rather than across other genres like science fiction and fantasy where you might simply say, "Well, I've got a group of people here who won't tolerate an 'expository lump' because when they see that, they just bristle."

UKL: That's where it seems to come out, yes, and those science fiction and fantasy readers don't need it. And I never, ever have written with a person in mind as a reader, except private things that I did for my own children, which I never published.

MC: C.S. Lewis claimed that there are two good ways of writing for children. One was to write for a particular child. The other is to write children's literature because it's the best vehicle for what you want to say. So you're in that second group?

UKL: Yes, that's what I'm trying to say. Definitely. And that varies according to the writer. Wasn't Kenneth Grahame writing for a particular child?

MC: Yes, he was writing for his son just as Milne was writing for *his* son. And Lewis uses those as examples. He says you're in deadly trouble when you try to start writing for a generalized child. That's the bad way.

UKL: Yes, and that's the problem editors have. They start tampering with your vocabulary. They say, "Children don't know those words." And I grew up with Kipling. That *incredible* vocabulary that he uses even in the "Just So" stories. I won't have anything to do with that kind of generalized child.

MC: I noticed that in *Steering the Craft*, in that first chapter where you're talking about the love of and the use of sound, you use crossover writers exclusively as examples. You use Kipling, yourself, Twain, and Gertrude Stein. I thought that was interesting that all of your examples come from people who write for different ages, not simply in different genres.

UKL: Genre-busters, yes.

MC: I wondered if there's any kind of connection between being somebody who writes for children and adults and developing the sense of sound.

UKL: I think what's more interesting with all of those writers is that they are very hard to fit into any genre at all. What did Mark Twain write? He wrote a lot of different things. The word "crossover" bothers me because "crossover" I've known for years as a genre term, not a children and adult term. It means you cross from science fiction to realism or fantasy to science fiction. It's a horizontal term. It has nothing to do with age. Now, it can certainly be used that way, but to limit it to meaning somebody who writes both for children and adults, I think, is going to cause confusion.

MC: Not if we make it clear that we're borrowing a term from elsewhere. For instance, it's used in music, as well. Although there is that question of the value of the hierarchy of genre. It can sometimes be up and down rather than across.

UKL: Oh yes. The age thing. I do suspect that most of us who write both for children and adults also bust other genre rules. Probably we move more freely from the fantastic to the non-fantastic, like Kipling, who moves back and forth so that you can hardly catch him.

MC: So the crossover writer will ignore genre rather than move across it? And what stays consistent is not register, not genre, not anything that has to do with categories as much as what they continue to say? That seems to remain similar. You're talking about similar things—how you use what you're good at in your life—but you're simply talking about them in different places.

UKL: And different genres offer different metaphors. Science fiction gives you the spaceships, the other planets, the alien beings, and fantasy gives you a whole other set of metaphors. Realism gives you yet another set. Why limit yourself unless you wanted to do so temperamentally?

MC: Does children's literature offer particular metaphors?

UKL: No, because you can write it in any genre.

MC: So it's the traditional genre metaphors that make a difference rather than the age of the implied reader?

UKL: I think so.

MC: To follow up on that, *A Visit from Dr. Katz* is an exception in your children's books as something set exclusively in a realistic setting, although if you were to look at the pictures and read the book separately, you would have different realities—the pictures show that "Dr. Katz" is two cats rather than a doctor.

UKL: It's a linguistic ploy. A language ploy. It comes from the old joke, "Do you know the woman who sleeps with cats? Mrs. Katz." I thought, hey, you could do a story with it. In other words, it's a joke. But that's in character with my work.

MC: And it's in character with a lot of children's books, the idea that what one reads in the picture and what one reads in the words has an ironic relationship.

UKL: There's this hint, then, that it's not quite realistic in that sense.

MC: I really enjoyed the children's songs in *Always Coming Home*, and I noticed that the editor tells us that "Rhyme is characteristic of children's songs" in the Kesh tradition. Other than the poems found in *Always Coming Home*, you don't have any poetry collections for children. I wondered whether you'd ever tried writing poetry for children.

UKL: Leese Webster, my first picture book, was done with a friend up the street. We didn't realize that it was very unusual to be able to sell an already illustrated children's book. We were so ignorant. I told him, I've got this idea for a spider, Jim. I wrote this thing, a poem. And it was Dr. Seuss—all language and rhythm. Of course, I had been reading a lot of Dr. Seuss to my kids. He gets in you. The book was just terrible, just ghastly. It was a horrible, horrible thing, and Jim tried to draw some pictures for it. They were awful pictures with big fat spiders. They were cartoonish. Months and months later, all of a sudden, I began to write the same idea about a spider in a palace, but there wasn't a king anymore. It was an empty palace. I was very pleased with how it came out in very plain, simple prose. I don't think I have the gift for kids' poetry.

MC: Leese Webster is very spare.

UKL: It's austere, and that fit Jim's talent. I'm very pleased with the little book.

MC: So you had tried children's poetry and backed off?

UKL: Backed off and realized I was just doing derivative stuff, and I didn't seem to have that gift.

MC: So there might be something more structurally different about poetry for children?

UKL: I'm not sure I believe very strongly in poetry for children, because what I read when I was a kid were anthologies of real poems. Poetry was something that you approached as a child, an adult thing that you just got what you could from it. The language was rich and appealing, like Shakespeare's "Ding Dong Bell."

MC: In the last few decades, there has been a lot done in the area of poetry for children.

UKL: You know, I don't find it terribly interesting. I've looked at it for my grandkids, and I usually end up getting one of the old collections with the real stuff.

MC: You've written picture books for children, and novels and novellas for young adults and adults. Another forum that I haven't seen you approach is the novel for the young elementary school reader.

UKL: The realistic school story? Pioneer stories, stuff like that? I tried to write one. Part of my family used to live in southeast Oregon. I tried to write a story from a story my great aunt told me, and it just wouldn't get off the ground. That's not a gift I seem to have.

MC: A great, austere, very short book is *Sarah, Plain and Tall*.[1]

UKL: Yeah, I was thinking of that. That's a wonderful book to give a girl. I love that kind of thing, but it's not one of my gifts. The Catwings books are chapter books. That's a nice age group, though—the kids that I get letters from about the catwings. I was very touched to find that they use those a lot in inner city schools.

MC: Sandra Lindow, a reading specialist who works with abused children, wrote an article talking about how useful those books are. There tends to be—if you look at Catwings or *Tehanu* or "Buffalo Gals"—the damaged child, or the physically-challenged child in your work. I wonder why you're drawn to that? Is there something you're trying to communicate about kids or is it that there's something kids are useful for in fiction?

UKL: You and somebody else recently have made me realize that I have, repeatedly, put at or near the center of a story, a child who has been abused in one of many ways.[2] With *Tehanu*, and certainly with "Buffalo Gals," I tried to keep it very light-handed, but the fact is that Myra [from "Buffalo Gals] had not been well-treated and was being handed back and forth between parents like a football. I hadn't thought about this. This is really weird. Is it because perhaps I had about as far from an abused childhood as it's possible to have? Does it gives me some take on this that I feel something has to come out? It's very strange because I had a good childhood.

MC: When Professor Mellon at Stanford interviewed you, you had talked about your happy childhood and the effects of that on your writing, but you also, in that same interview, talked about how you write about men as a way to achieve distance. The damaged child seems to make for double distance: You aren't a child anymore trying to write for children, and you had a happy childhood. Do you feel that distance when you're writing children's books just as you do when you write about men and aliens?

UKL: I don't know. The male characters in my books tend to be isolated and are often under considerable stress and difficulty. They're kind of being abused by life. I do write about underdogs all the time, and the abused child is an extreme example of an underdog. I'm the daughter of privilege in most ways—in the most privileged country in the most privileged time that has ever been: upper middle class with affectionate, kindly parents. But I wonder if because I didn't have to struggle and fight and claw at anybody, it just allows me to empathize.

MC: You've said before that you remember what it's like being a teenager and a child.

UKL: All teenagers are abused. They're abused by life; they're abused themselves. And boy, I had a long hard teenage experience, like most of us—like most writers did, I think. I think distancing is not the key there, because thinking particularly of Therru, the fact was that this was my guide into the book. I couldn't get into the book until that child appeared and, as it were, took me by the hand, which was kind of an appalling experience. Why is this the key? Of course, it took three books to find out. But it's the opposite of distancing; it's being let in.

MC: In that book we're seeing through Tenar. In *Steering the Craft*, you write at length about the importance of point of view.

UKL: Well, so many students seem to be so totally unaware of it!

MC: You point out that "all myths and legends and folktales, [and] all young children's stories" employ what you call the Involved Author or Omniscient Author, which you say is tough to pull off.

UKL: I find students who are just unable to write the omniscient point of view. They've never read anything except third-person limited omniscient. They think it's the only way to tell a story—from within one of the characters. It makes it so easy. The omniscient point of view is way harder, actually. And they find it out when I make them try it.

MC: Isn't it interesting that such a difficult form is used in writing for children?

UKL: And in myth and legend. I think what my brother Karl wrote about that in *Retelling/Rereading* explains why I do it that way.[3]

MC: I'm rereading *Malafrena* right now. You use [Omniscient Author] in that story, I notice. We go everywhere in that book.

UKL: The strongest influence on me in some respects, especially for the Orsinian books, is Russian literature. Tolstoy is a master at just dropping into somebody's mind and moving out again so that you never even notice him go.

MC: It has that effect, even in Dostoevsky, that you never quite know what it is that you're supposed to believe. I'm reading *Malafrena* right now and wondering, "Who's right?" Luisa seems to have every right to feel this way, but I'm not quite sure that I believe that she should. It's a wonderful effect. And it's interesting that this omniscient point of view can therefore be disorienting if you choose not to come down on a particular point of view.

UKL: It can be as disorienting as the fly-on-the-wall thing where you ostentatiously don't judge, whereas in the omniscient mode, the agendas are merely implied or even contradictory. You can really confuse things nicely.

MC: If people use an entirely omniscient perspective in children's books, do you think they simply choose to have readers come to a particular conclusion about events?

UKL: One of the points that Karl [Kroeber] makes in his book is that that is the storyteller's voice. And he discusses *Vanity Fair*. When people generalize about Victorian literature they're actually talking about *Vanity Fair*. The others don't do it nearly as much as Thackeray. He's always coming in and saying, "Well, you may think such and such about this character, but I will tell you . . . " This is absolutely the oral storyteller. He's so perceptible, he's in your face to the extent that you almost want to push him aside. It's a very interesting trick.

MC: In *Malafrena*, the narrator is imperceptible.

UKL: Yes, but in kids' books, it is perceptible. And it's in Kipling. I think he wrote better for kids than almost anybody does, in the *Jungle Book*, particularly in the non-Mowgli ones. There's a lot of the author or the storyteller telling you, and he's not in your face, or he's not telling you what to think, but he's telling you about things.

MC: Which is different from Lewis, who wants to tell you not to think badly of Edmund because he's had bad experiences with progressive education and general permissiveness.

UKL: He's a bit coarse. And I felt that. It was one of the things that put me off those books. Now in the *Just So Stories*, which are for younger children, that is the voice of the oral storyteller: "Now, Best Beloved . . . " and those are stories to be read aloud. The magic of it is that he managed to combine the two.

MC: And Milne has that wonderful ambivalence about to whom he's really speaking.

UKL: Oh, now there's poetry for children. It's adorable and unforgettable. I can still recite a lot of it.

MC: And it always has that sideways wink at the reader.

UKL: Oh, yeah. The grown-up is enjoying it just as much as the child.

MC: Have you experimented much with children's books in terms of what you could pull off in terms of narrative, or had you thought about children's books that way?

UKL: I didn't think about them at all. Not until I was asked to write a young adult book. No, I wrote little private stuff for my kids, but I never thought of it as leading anywhere.

MC: Did any of those appear? Those that you wrote for your own children?

UKL: No. They were private things for the kids. See, I make that difference. If it's written for a specific kid, it belongs to that kid. It's theirs. It's not public.

MC: So you were writing for your children at the time you were also writing the original Hainish novels? Yet you were saving a space to write for you children.

UKL: Yes. Little stuff.

MC: I had wondered since it was 1979 before *Leese Webster* came out whether you were writing for your children and simply keeping it in the family.

UKL: Not much, but yes. Little picture books.

MC: What about for the grandchildren? Are they the audience at all for the catwings?

UKL: I'm too shy to try things out on kids. I feel like I'm coercing the kids. And also, I can't ask, "Do you like what mummy wrote, dear?" You know? You can't do that. I know that a lot of writers do, but I just can't do it. I have given manuscripts to my friends to read to their kids. There's a non-coercive situation.

MC: Did the kids know that you had written the stories?

UKL: It was just "a friend of momma's." And then I would get the feedback, which was always useful. Sometimes very funny. Kids can be brutal critics.

MC: Another form that you've used is that linked story.

UKL: I've finally got a name for it. I was listening to the Bach cello suites and thought, "Of course, they're story suites." The stories are separate. The movements in a suite do stand alone. The suite is very much an entity. That is the closest parallel I've ever gotten to.

MC: And that's why the crossover metaphor keeps coming back. I wondered if you found something in that suite form that just simply allowed you to do something that you couldn't do otherwise?

UKL: Yeah. It's almost like a different approach to the novel. I was getting more and more interested in choral writing—having many voices. And there's a certain disintegration there. *Four Ways to Forgiveness* certainly could have been a novel. I could have pulled it all together and kept a central character or two or three, you know. Apparently, I just didn't want to. I wanted to take that openness and have a lot of space between.

MC: The effect, though, when you're done reading it is like watching a movie in subtitles. When you remember it, you remember it in English. And when you're done reading *Searoad*, well, it's the "carrier bag." It's that associative jumble—not linear. It all makes sense as a whole when I'm done.

UKL: I'm very leery of questions of influence because I think they're too complicated to talk about, but I think there's undeniably an influence from Virginia Woolf here. From *The Years* and *The Waves*. I had a lot of trouble giving my Virginia Herne the Pulitzer. Typical woman thing [laughs].

MC: Though it doesn't appear in the story. It's just in the back of the book. What should we call that "back?" You have it in *Always Coming Home* . . .

UKL: Back matter.

MC: Back matter. Should we look at *Always Coming Home* as linked stories?

UKL: No, it's a grab bag. Medicine bag.

MC: In the back of those books, including *Tales from Earthsea*, you have to have something at the end of it all. Does the back matter create the connections that you're worried aren't there?

UKL: Some readers want the "fictional facts." A lot of readers don't look at that stuff. That's fine. The precedent there, again, is very clear: It's Tolkien. All that back matter in *The Lord of the Rings* which many readers don't pay any attention to. But some of us adore it because it keeps telling us. Some of us really want to know how far it is from here to there. So it's the pseudo-factuality thing. It's very important to me. I think Tolkien deserves more notice, both as an acknowledged and unconscious influence on me as an example of what you can do. There's an epic—*The Lord of the Rings*—with this enormous back matter. I wonder if Tolkien hadn't done that if I would have had the courage to do it? He didn't influence me in the way the things you read as a child influence you. But he influenced me as an example of how to do a lot of things right. And he's fearless about whether he's writing for kids or adults. He's completely indifferent. He's a precedent.

MC: I can see it in *Always Coming Home* where it's got that anthropological feel.

UKL: That whole book becomes, in a sense, back matter.

MC: When I was rereading *Searoad* I ended up—because you have things so achronic in the Herne section—listing all the names on a legal pad with the year the section takes place and the age of the character at that time.

UKL: I could have Xeroxed it for you because I had such a chart!

MC: I wanted to know how old characters were when they were thinking similar things.

UKL: Yes. Have you seen Tom Shippey's book on Tolkien? He's got a chart showing where characters are when other characters are being talked about. My god, it's complicated.[4]

MC: Well, that would be tough in *Malafrena*, wouldn't it? I was wondering, while Itale is in prison, who is doing what? What's the father doing? What's Luisa doing?

UKL: Oh, yeah. You know, I'm sure I had that charted out at the time of writing. You have to. I'm told that Emily Bronte worked out very carefully how Heathcliff made his money, which wasn't pretty. It was by slave trade. None of it is in the book. But when he comes back a wealthy man, she knew what he'd been doing. And that sort of charting makes complete sense to me.

MC: In that time between *Malafrena* and *A Fisherman of the Inland Sea*, you were doing a lot of work for young children, and *Always Coming Home* and "Buffalo Gals" also appear in that time, but after some children's books had been published. We talked about those two books having damaged children in them, but they also feature children. Are those books indebted to the influence of the children's books, or is it the other way around?

UKL: There was also a good deal of poetry written in there. No, I just moved from one thing to the other, and whatever the subterranean links are, I'm unaware. You perceive much more childishness in *Always Coming Home* than I do.[5] There are a lot of children in it, partly because it's a *bildungsroman*, and we start with a child, because it is a whole society where children and adults live together, and therefore children are not "outside"— the way they are with us. But there is very little by or for children in *Always Coming Home*.

MC: No, I would never make the case that it's a children's book.

UKL: But I think you perceive more of the poetry and other stuff as being for children. I'm fairly specific. If it's by a child, I say so. I try to make the point that it doesn't matter that much, which is kind of a hard point to make explicit, because once you make it, it matters. Of course, you can just slide it into the fiction.

MC: You'd written recently about leaving the children out of *The Left Hand of Darkness*, your story "Coming of Age in Karhide."

UKL: Yes, it was silly. I should have shown Estraven with the children so that one could believe "he" was a mother. So I made up for that in "Coming of Age in Karhide."

MC: I was struck this last time reading *Always Coming Home*, how the boy and Moondog in Wordriver's *Dangerous People* are like the girl and mare in *A Ride on the Red Mare's Back* as children accompanied by animals on a mission to rescue a family member. In anybody's work you're going to see parallels.

UKL: I think that that's a *little* bit far-fetched, to tell you the truth.

MC: Maybe so, but I did honestly think of the one when I read the other. I wouldn't make the case that there's an influence between them, but it made me wonder whether there were cases when you consciously said, "You know, I can tell this again by using a different metaphor." Have you ever taken a situation or plot from one of your works for older readers and refashioned it for younger readers, or the reverse?

UKL: No, that would happen subliminally. I would find myself partway through or almost finished saying, "Oh, for heaven's sake. That's one of my one or two stories that I keep telling." But when I'm doing it, I think it's the most highly original thing that's never been done before by anybody. Particularly me.

MC: Michael Tournier, a French children's writer, does this all the time. He consciously does this.

UKL: I am singularly and deliberately unconscious about my intentions when I write. Many writers are much more conscious of what they are doing. I seem to cultivate unconsciousness. I don't mind talking about it afterwards, but often it's not very helpful because I did cultivate unconsciousness of what I'm doing. I simply work best that way. It's like not plotting too carefully, not being too sure of where I'm going. I just write best under those circumstances. And if I know exactly what I'm doing, I would get bored doing it. I pick up ideas from my own stuff and develop them, like *churtening* . . . which I thought was going to go on. You know, make a whole series of its own. And then it stopped. Apparently, it doesn't work. Well, since they did it a couple of times, I can't really say it doesn't work, but I got no more stories about it. I sure would like to know what's going on in Orsinia. But I have no messengers. Nobody is arriving from Orsinia to tell me. No news. Of course, that was my earliest. Discovering Orsinia was how I really began writing serious fiction.

MC: Well, *Malafrena* feels very different from the other works. It's so very dramatic!

UKL: Well, fundamentally it's a book by a 21-year-old . . . infinitely revised. But the literary romanticism is there. I still love the 1820s. I just read a wonderful book by Robert Harvey called *Liberators*, about the five major liberators of South America. It's all 1812 to 1830. It was a fascinating time.[6]

MC: So you don't know whether we're going back to Orsinia, eh?

UKL: I'll go back if I get an invitation.

MC: Is there any invitation from the Kesh? I wouldn't be surprised to see a Kesh novel.

UKL: Well, I did work on one. There are two chapters.

MC: We get the second chapter of that novel in *Always Coming Home.*[7]

UKL: Yes, but I got stuck. It would only be a three-chapter novel. I worked on it and then something warned me off. So I don't know whether that will get done or not. It's sitting there. Getting deep enough into Kesh culture to write as a Kesh writer took a long time. It was a lot of fun. Also, I was there when I wrote the book. I was in the Valley. But we'll see.

MC: Being home is important, then? There's a big subtext in your work, after all, one of the things that I see which doesn't fall into the usual pattern. In adult and young adult books, you often see this sort of "lighting off for the territories" that we see in *The Adventures of Huckleberry Finn*. And in children's books, to use Twain as an example, we get *The Adventures of Tom Sawyer*—we return or we never left. But your books that are for young adults, adults, and children, don't follow that pattern. Some of the adults stay, some go; some of the children stay, some go.

UKL: I liked the way you wrote about that.[8] I thought, "Yeah, he's right." I didn't realize how anomalous it is.

MC: If subtext is the way that a lot of successful crossover writers are successful—because they don't worry about genre, they simply try on the different forms saying something very similar—it's really hard to know whether there's any way to think of "home" differently by age in your work. What I end up wondering is what makes it necessary for anybody of any age to leave or to stay or to return? Is age at all a useful way to think about the differences between the homes?

UKL: I think that age is not much of a key there.

MC: People who travel by themselves are in trouble.

UKL: Yeah, people who travel by themselves *are* in trouble.

MC: Would you say that there's something that provokes your characters to either leave or return? Things that they have to do or have to discover in order to come back?

UKL: I wonder if the whole concept of home-leaving and homecoming is important to me because I had, again, so unusually settled a home life as a child? Absolutely the same house—two houses, which is kind of important.

MC: How far apart?

UKL: Sixty miles. That was a big trip when I was a little kid. If my parents had to leave, my great-aunt was there. There was just this total continuity, which is very rare. And the rest of my life, until I was 50, my mother had the house in Berkeley. Same house. And my children own the house in the Napa Valley. It's our house; we can still go there. 72 years. How many Americans have a place that they can know all their lives that is still in their family? There are not many people like that, particularly in the West. Just the massive solidity of that experience is unusual.

MC: So does that make it hard for people to get away from home in your fiction?

UKL: No, it's just that it's important. I think that the whole concept of "home" is a vexed one for many Americans. And there are these weird descriptions, like "Home is where they have to let you in." What? That's a hell of a way to describe it. And, of course, there's the guy I got my title from: Novalis. "Where are you going? Always home." But that's spiritual. You're always heading there. Always home. You're not there; you're always *going* there.

MC: It's not like some children's writers who might say, "We have to have them come home because we have to have that certain Dorothy-returns-to-Kansas feeling." Even though there may be an ethical boundary for how you treat subjects, how home plays out seems to be wherever it takes you. Even if they do come back in your fiction, it isn't to the same place. It isn't Kansas anymore.

UKL: Yeah, my line about "It's okay to come home as long as you realize you've never been there before"—that line goes pretty deep through a lot of my stuff. I can give you a very strong childhood influence, by the way. It's *The Wind in the Willows*, the chapter when Moley goes home. I adored that. My favorite is actually when the little otter gets lost. It's very sentimental. I can't read it now, but as a child, I didn't realize it was sentimental, and I just loved it. The English are good at this. In Tolkien, the Shire is home in this sense. I think everybody likes the Shire because they know they're home. And that's a little bit like Mole and Rat. And, of course, there's a sense of security that's obviously involved.

MC: The reason I raise the question of home is because some people try to define the genre of children's literature by this issue. A children's book is one in which you have that Odyssean pattern. And not only do they come home, they realize that that's where they ought to be—not so much because they need to do a next thing, but because it reinforces what they should have known all along. Dorothy realizes she should be there.

UKL: Home is best. East or West, home is best [Laughs]. That's terrible reductionism.

MC: And you do have various ways of handling home.

UKL: Well, look at Odysseus. He gets home, but my god, his wife is old, everybody has died—the dog has died. It's not the kingdom he left.

MC: I'd like to talk a bit about your "carrier bag" theory. You make the case that it's a way of thinking about narrative that gets us away from that linear, spear-like quality, and we certainly see that in something like *Searoad*. I'm wondering whether children's books fit into that carrier bag?

UKL: Well, children's books are like short stories. They're short. You can't get too confused. It is a narrative, after all. If you're writing for kids—and they rightly want a story—you're going to have to move more or less directly. It's a quality of the short piece. It really had better move.

MC: I guess the "suites" are the opportunity to provide the linear in the carrier bag.

UKL: Yes, it makes it nonlinear. I don't have to follow a character.

MC: Well, the Catwings books do that.

UKL: Yes, well, when I suddenly jumped off to Alexander, and then followed Jane, I was kind of surprised by that myself. I expected to write something about the first four cats.

MC: All bets are off, as far as I'm concerned, about where that story stops because we keep going back and forth, and different things happen along the way, and they're not necessarily connected. I'm sure that at some point the Catwings books will all be published in one volume.

UKL: Yes, we could put them in a nice little box! Kids love those. But that's Scholastic, and Scholastic is all Harry Potter now. I don't know if there is going to be any more catwings. My bet would be a little against. Jane broke loose and came back. Jane is the favorite of the kids that write me. It's very interesting. When they write their own stories, they tend to feature Jane. Though the boys write about the boy cats and they have gun battles [laughs] . . . they fly airplanes. They're wonderful.

MC: So the kids rewrite your stories?

UKL: Yeah, they tell me what to write, and sometimes they show me. Oh, in *Catwings*, where the narrator says something like "that's what cat families do," when the mother sends her kittens away, I didn't originally have that in there. That was my wonderful editor, Dick Jackson, a very experienced children's book editor. And he said that kids will be horrified, that I was frightening children. And I thought, "I don't want to do that. But it is what cats do." And he said just to say that. So I did. I get letters from inner city kids who say, "I hate Mrs. Jane. She sent her kids away." They're very human cats. The kids identify with the kittens. There was a real flaw there that Dick caught and patched up as well as he could, but it remains an ethical catch in the book. Sending them away is for their own good, but it's necessary that they get back together again. They might have just gone on off and never come back. Jane, apparently, really has gone back. Jane ends up back in the city with her mother.

MC: I wondered about *Jane on Her Own*—whether you were more self-conscious about the question of "How do I say this for children so that they aren't frightened?"

UKL: I think to some extent I was. It was a problematic idea. I don't want to be "anti-rat," but, of course, rats are terrible ogres to a kitten. Rats kill kittens, and so I had to kind of demonize the rats. And then in *Jane on Her Own*, the whole television thing came up. I had to think about that a good deal, and I tried not to demonize the guy [who keeps Jane, who has flown into his window, and puts her on television]. He just sees a good thing when it flies in his window.

MC: I'm amused by the lack of shock he shows.

UKL: And I really like the way Schindler drew him. Schindler is wonderful. We have no communication. He doesn't want to hear from me. I had been in close touch with Julie [Downing] for *A Ride on the Red Mare's Back*. She came up here and we spent an afternoon talking about it. And she did *Tom Mouse*. She likes to relate to the author. So it varies.

MC: It seems like it would be a tough thing—to have the picture and text wedded so well.

UKL: Schindler was just a choice of genius, I think. And it feels so strange to me to have these little books be so successful and never be able to write a 'thank you' for the pictures. He draws his own cats, and that's his farm in the books. He dedicated the books to his cats.

MC: Speaking of attaching wings to things, I notice in *Fish Soup* that there are flying mice.

UKL: That was Patrick Wynne, who I met at Orycon. He's an excellent draftsman. I bought one of his pictures, and we got to talking. He said that he was very envious of Schindler because he would have loved to draw the winged cats, and he drew a little winged mouse. So I said, "Okay, I'll write you a book." And so we presented that as a finished book. It was a fun collaboration.

MC: Fish Soup is just so much more metaphoric than your other children's books.

UKL: Yeah, I think grown-ups like it better.

MC: It may be that it's the children's book of yours most clearly a crossover to an audience other than the one for which it was produced.

UKL: Last summer, I came on some books I read as a child by James Stephens, the Irish writer. He was very well known in the '20s and '30s, and some of them are real Irish myths, and some of them are fake Irish myths. And I realize that much of my tone comes from those things I read as a kid. They're grown-up books; they're not for children. And it just got down in me. And I thought, "Yea! I'm pulling a James Stephens!"

MC: The *Fish Soup* book made me think of the crossover issue as I reread *Tehanu*. I thought that *Tehanu* is sort of a transition from the series that you began for young adults and it simply changed in the sense that it didn't have the young adult protagonist.

UKL: Well, there's 17 years between *The Farthest Shore* and *Tehanu*, and after those 17 years, I was finally able to write the book I had started within the year after *The Farthest Shore* and couldn't write. I didn't know why Tenar was doing what she was doing. All I knew was that she was marrying this farmer. I wrote a chapter or two and then got nowhere. "I don't know how to write this book. I don't know what Tenar is doing or who she is." And it took 17 years to find out. One of the reasons I couldn't write the book was because Tenar would have been growing up and getting married. She wouldn't be a young adult; she would be, literally, in her 20s or 30s. The first three books were dimly conceived of as young adult books—the first one *clearly* conceived as a young adult book, and the second two progressively less. At last, I realized, "I don't have to cater to these kids." If they're going to read fantasy they're going to read it at nine or 10. They're going to read *The Hobbit*, and then they're going to read *The Lord of the Rings*. Nobody is going to keep them from it. I don't have to write to them. This is a free category, fantasy is. It is the real age crosser. *The Hobbit* is an interesting example because it was definitely written for children. And there are many things in it that are traditional for-children locutions. And then they asked him to write a sequel. The beginning of *The Lord of the Rings* is a little more child-like, and then he really found his direction and got going.

MC: So if you catch them when they're young, they'll just follow you?

UKL: That's right. With fantasy they do. And it's amazing where they'll follow you. By the time *Tehanu* got going, I wasn't thinking in those terms at all. I just was thinking that I've got this fantasy to write. The readers are with me or they're not. This is the book I have got to write, even if it's about old people, or people getting old.

MC: By the time we get to *The Other Wind*, it is such a choral piece, as you put it, that it really is about a lot of different people of different ages. Maybe it's just getting hard to write about Earthsea selecting a particular age.

UKL: I democratized the trilogy. The second trilogy is democratic; the first trilogy is hierarchic.

Apparently, we don't have an Archmage. The King is The King, but that's not quite as important as it seemed.

MC: I was struck that at the end of *Tehanu* with the feeling that we're going to come back here. And Kalessin at the end of *Tehanu* is dropping hints as he does at the end of *The Other Wind*, and I had this readerly feeling that the Master Patterner and Irian want to get back together, as impractical as it is—but if you can have a giraffe and a boa constrictor hanging out together in the ocean in *Solomon Leviathan*, you can have a dragon and a man together.

UKL: [Laughs.] Well, I was 20 then. I don't know if I'm that agile anymore. I really don't know.

MC: But it felt like, "I'm going to leave this so I can come back to it."

UKL: I do like to leave the door open. It doesn't mean that *I* will go through it.

References

Ursula K. Le Guin's Fiction for Adults, Young Adults, and Children

For Adults	For Young Adults	For Children
Planet of Exile (1966)		
Rocannon's World (1966)		
City of Illusions (1967)		
	A Wizard of Earthsea (1968)	
The Left Hand of Darkness (1969)		
	The Tombs of Atuan (1970)	
The Lathe of Heaven (1971)		
	The Farthest Shore (1972)	
The Dispossessed (1974)		
The Wind's Twelve Quarters (1975)		
The Word for World Is Forest (1976)		
Orsinian Tales (1976)	*Very Far Away from Anywhere Else* (1976)	
The Eye of the Heron (1978)		
Malafrena (1979)		*Leese Webster* (1979)
	The Beginning Place (1980)	
The Compass Rose (1982)		*Cobbler's Rune* (1982)
		Solomon Leviathan (1983)
Always Coming Home (1985)		
Buffalo Gals and Other Animal Presences (1987)		*Catwings* (1988)
		A Visit from Dr. Katz (1988)

For Adults	For Young Adults	For Children
		For Children
		Catwings Return (1989)
		Fire and Stone (1989)
Tehanu (1990)		
Searoad (1991)		*Fish Soup (1992)*
		Red Mare (1992)
		Wonderful Alexander (1994)
A Fisherman of the Inland Sea (1994)		
Four Ways to Forgiveness (1995)		
Unlocking the Air and Other Stories (1996)		
		Jane on Her Own (1999)
The Telling (2000)		
Tales from Earthsea (2001)		
The Other Wind (2001)		*Tom Mouse (2002)*
The Birthday of the World and Other Stories (2002)		
Changing Planes (2003)		
	Gifts (2004)[a]	

[a]This title is not yet in print; it is due out in September of 2004. Harcourt lists this title under its teen/young adult division, listing it for ages 12 and up.

Fiction by Decade:
1966 to 1969: 5 books (4 for adults, 1 for young adults, 0 for children)
1970 to 1979: 11 books (7, 3, 1)
1980 to 1989: 10 books (3, 1, 6)
1990 to 1999: 9 books (5, 0, 4)
2000 to 2004: 7 books (5, 1, 1)
Total of all years: 42 books of fiction (24 for adults, 6 for young adults, 12 for children)

Notes

Preface
1. Ursula K. Le Guin, "A Citizen of Mondath," *The Language of the Night: Essays on Fantasy and Science Fiction,* ed. Susan Wood and Ursula K. Le Guin, Rev. ed (New York, NY: HarperCollins, 1989), 22.
2. Sandra L. Beckett, "Introduction," *Transcending Boundaries: Writing for a Dual Audience of Children and Adults,* ed. Sandra Beckett (New York: Garland Publishing, Inc., 1999), xiii-xiv.
3. Helma van Lierop-Debrauwer, "Crossing the Border: Authors Do It, but Do Critics? The Reception of Dual-Readership Authors in the Netherlands," *Transcending Boundaries: Writing for a Dual Audience of Children and Adults,* ed. Sandra Becket (New York: Garland Publishing, Inc., 1999), 6.
4. Suzanne Elizabeth Reid, *Presenting Ursula K. Le Guin* (New York: Twayne Publishers 1997), 3.
5. Ursula K. Le Guin, *Steering the Craft* (Portland, OR: The Eighth Mountain Press, 1998), 121.
6. Ursula K. Le Guin, "Introduction," *Buffalo Gals and Other Animal Presences* (New York: Penguin, 1990), 10.
7. Donna White, *Dancing With Dragons: Ursula K. Le Guin and the Critics* (Columbia, SC: Camden House, 1999), 2, 106.
8. Richard Erlich, *Coyote's Song: The Teaching Stories of Ursula K. Le Guin.* A Science Fiction Research Association Digital Book, 2001. http://www.sfra.org/Coyote/CoyoteHome.htm.

Chapter 1
1. Harold Bloom, "Introduction," *The Left Hand of Darkness: Modern Critical Interpretations* (New York: Chelsea House Publishers,1987), 2.
2. Ann Swinfen, *In Defence of Fantasy: A Study of the Genre in English and American Literature Since 1945* (London: Routledge & Kegan Paul, 1984), 232; hereafter cited in text.
3. John H. Crow and Richard D. Erlich, "Words of Binding: Patterns of Integration in the Earthsea Trilogy," *Ursula K. Le Guin* (New York: Taplinger Publishing Company, 1979), 220.
4. Ursula K. Le Guin, *The Word for World Is Forest* (New York: Berkley Publishing Co., 1976), 107; hereafter cited in text as *Word*.
5. Le Guin even personifies the book itself: a book comes to her not "as an idea, or a plot," but "as a person. A person seen, seen at a certain distance" ("Science Fiction and Mrs. Brown," *The Language of the Night: Essays on Fantasy and Science Fiction,* ed. Susan Wood and Ursula K. Le Guin, rev. ed. [New York: HarperCollins, 1989], 107).
6. Wayne Cogell makes the claim that Le Guin refutes Sartre's notion regarding identity in just this way in the story "A Trip to the Head." *The Wind's Twelve Quarters* (New York: Bantam Books, 1976). See Wayne Cogell, "The Absurdity of Sartre's Ontology: A Response by Ursula K. Le Guin," *Philosophers Look at Science Fiction.* Ed. Nicholas D. Smith (Chicago: Nelson Hall, 1982), 143–51.
7. Ursula K. Le Guin, "American SF and the Other," *The Language of the Night: Essays on Fantasy and Science Fiction* (New York: HarperCollins, 1989), 95.

8. Ursula K. Le Guin, "Introduction," *Buffalo Gals and Other Animal Presences* (New York: Penguin, 1990), 12; hereafter cited in text as *1990c*.

9. Roger Sale, *Fairy Tales and After: From Snow White to E. B. White* (Cambridge, MA: Harvard University Press, 1978), 77.

10. Margaret Blount, *Animal Land: The Creatures of Children's Fiction* (London: Hutchinson & Co., 1974), 17; hereafter cited in text.

11. For a discussion on the continuum of animal/human consciousness through animal focalizers see William Nelles, "Beyond the Bird's Eye: Animal Focalization," *Narrative* 9.2 (May 2001): 188–94.

12. William Magee, "The Animal Story: A Challenge in Technique," *Only Connect: Readings on Children's Literature* (Toronto: Oxford University Press, 1980), 224.

13. Consider other sources that treat the related issues of anthropomorphism, children, and children's texts: Jay Blanchard, "Anthropomorphism in Beginning Readers," *Reading Teacher* 35.5 (February 1982): 586–91; Roy A. Gallant, "Pitfalls of Personification," *Science and Children* 19.2 (October 1981): 16–17; Juliett Kellogg Markowsky, "Why Anthropomorphism in Children's Literature," *Elementary English* 52.4 (April 1975): 460–2; Anne Royall Newman, "Images of the Bear in Children's Literature," *Children's Literature in Education* 18.3 (Fall 1987): 131–38; Belle D. Sharefkin and Hy Ruchlis, "Anthropomorphism in the Lower Grades," *Science and Children* 11.6 (March 1974): 37–40; John Morgenstern, "Children and Other Talking Animals," *The Lion and The Unicorn* 24 (2000): 110–27.

14. Ursula K. Le Guin, *The Altered I: An Encounter With Science Fiction*, (Victoria, Australia: Nostrilia Press, 1976), 9.

15. Clyde Kilby, *An Anthology of C. S. Lewis: A Mind Awake* (New York: Harcourt Brace Jovanovich, 1968), 20.

16. Le Guin is also an "arboreal" writer, to be sure, and deals with plant life in stories like "Vaster than Empires and More Slow" (*The Wind's Twelve Quarters* [New York: Bantam Books, 1976], 166–99) and "Direction of the Road" (*The Wind's Twelve Quarters* [New York: Bantam Books, 1976], 244–50). While these raise issues of anthropomorphism as well, this study attempts to make sense of only those instances of animal and alien anthropomorphism. For some insight into the issue of vegetable sentience in Le Guin's work see Ian Watson, "The Forest as Metaphor for Mind: The Word for World Is Forest and 'Vaster Than Empires and More Slow,'" *Ursula K. Le Guin: Modern Critical Views*. Ed. Harold Bloom (New York: Chelsea House Publishers, 1986), 47–56. See also Lynda Schneekloth, "Plants: The Ultimate Alien," *Extrapolation* 42.3 (2001): 246–54.

17. Ursula K. Le Guin, "The Wife's Story," *Buffalo Gals and Other Animal Presences* (New York: Penguin, 1990), 69, hereafeter cited in text. Interestingly, here Le Guin plays with an old idea that the child and animal, as those closer to nature, are more likely than the adult to sense when someone is essentially bad or "wrong."

18. Ursula K. Le Guin, "Horse Camp," *Buffalo Gals and Other Animal Presences* (New York: Penguin, 1990), 147; hereafter cited in text.

19. Ursula K. Le Guin, "The White Donkey," *Buffalo Gals and Other Animal Presences* (New York: Penguin, 1990), 142; hereafter cited in text.

20. Ursula K. Le Guin, "May's Lion," *Buffalo Gals and Other Animal Presences* (New York: Penguin, 1990), 181; hereafter cited in text.

21. Ursula K. Le Guin, "Buffalo Gals, Won't You Come Out Tonight?" *Buffalo Gals and Other Animal Presences* (New York: Penguin, 1990), 17–51; *Tehanu: The Last Book of Earthsea* (New York: Atheneum, 1990); hereafter cited in text as *Tehanu*.

22. Margaret Chang, "Heroism Revisioned: Girls, Wildness, and Mothers in Ursula K. Le Guin's Recent Writing," Ursula K. Le Guin panel (paper presented at the MLA Convention, Grand Hyatt Regency Hotel, Chicago, IL, 27 December 1995), 3; hereafter cited in text.

23. Tenar's foster child is known both as "Therru" and "Tehanu"; because she is more significant as Tehanu I will use that name throughout.

24. The narrator also observes that Aunty Moss "had a smell as strong and broad and deep and complicated as the smell of a fox's den" (*Tehanu*, 35) and imposes on Heather, Aunty Moss's girl, a view of Tehanu as "another goat; a lame kid" (*Tehanu*, 33). This habit of reading people in terms of animals, in other words, is not restricted to *Tehanu*.

25. Ursula K. Le Guin, *The Tombs of Atuan* (New York: Bantam, 1975 [orig. publ. 1970]), 96.
26. Ursula K. Le Guin, *The Other Wind* (New York: Harcourt, 2001).
27. Ursula K. Le Guin, *Earthsea Revisioned* (Cambridge, U. K.: Green Bay Press, 1993), 18; hereafter cited in text as 1993.
28. The only other impressions of Tehanu we receive are from men: Ogion simply indicates that "they will fear her" (*Tehanu,* 23); Aspen refers to Tehanu as "monster" or as Tenar's witch's "familiar" or "whelp" (*Tehanu,* 240); Ged vaguely worries about Tehanu's fate, never giving us an indication, specifically, of how he sees her. Those who are still mages of power, Ogion and Aspen, see Tehanu in terms of threats to a current system of male magic, though Ogion accepts the inevitability while Aspen mocks it along with Ogion's and Ged's "old" magery. In Aspen's eyes Tehanu must be the familiar of a witch (or some aberration); the man without magery, Ged, sees her as one who will have trouble in a patriarchal society. These men construct her according to the limits of their vistas.
29. Michael Holquist, *Dialogism: Bakhtin and his World* (London and New York: Routledge, 1990), 20.
30. Ursula K. Le Guin, "Buffalo Gals, Won't You Come Out Tonight?" *Buffalo Gals and Other Animal Presences* (New York: Penguin, 1990), 54; hereafter cited in text.
31. *Buffalo Gals Won't You Come Out Tonight,* illus. by Susan Seddon Boulet (San Francisco: Pomegranate Artbooks, 1994) 25, 34, 50. Susan Seddon Boulet's illustrations for Le Guin's "Buffalo Gals," imply a different view of Myra's perspective than the textual descriptions, it seems to me. Boulet's dedication of her work to the author reveals the degree to which an alternative view has been offered: "Ursula, who gave me the freedom to create from an already complete and wonderful story." Boulet's "creations," her depictions of Owl (25), Deer (34), and Horse (50) illustrate an uneasy synthesis of human and animal—almost reminiscent of H. G. Wells's *The Island of Dr. Moreau*; Le Guin's story makes it clear that while the "old people" have animal-like traits, they are not, visibly, part animal. Despite this tension, Le Guin comments that "the feeling of Susan's work was right; though her approach is opposite, I think we are going to the same place; so I am very happy with those pictures" (Letter to the author. 26 November 1995).
32. This list could be the mediation between self and other on a number of ideological planes, including the idea of humanity, gender, eastern and western thought, and more. These texts seem to lend themselves to a discussion of both of the continuums of civilized and wild and human and alien. Here "human" is defined through Ged's placement on one end of the scale in very patriarchal terms, however. The women's alliance with the wild in these tales invites more theorizing—not to mention the more specific parallel of cats and women if we continue to consider the juxtaposition of "Buffalo Gals" and *Tehanu* with the Catwings books.
33. Le Guin indirectly calls against pinpointing a position on a spectrum in her children's book *Solomon Leviathan's Nine Hundred and Thirty-First Trip Around the World.* Damon, the giraffe, asks of his friend Ophidia, a boa constrictor, a "personal question":
    "Where does your tail begin? Where does the rest of you leave off? Does your tail begin where the back of your head stops? That seems peculiar, but where does one draw the line?"
    "My friend," said the boa constrictor, "I am an indivisible entity to which such hypotheses are irrelevant."
    "I see," said the giraffe. (*Solomon Leviathan's Nine Hundred and Thirty-First Trip Around the World,* illus. Alicia Austin [New York: Philomel Books, 1983], 8).
34. Ursula K. Le Guin, *Buffalo Gals and Other Animal Presences* (New York: Penguin, 1990), 139; hereafter cited in text as *Buffalo Gals.*
35. Ursula K. Le Guin, *A Wizard of Earthsea* (New York: Bantam, 1975 [orig. publ. 1968]), 87; hereafter cited in text as *Wizard.*
36. Ursula K. Le Guin, *The Farthest Shore* (New York: Bantam, 1975 [orig. publ. 1972]), 159; hereafter cited in text as *Farthest Shore.*
37. Ursula K. Le Guin, "Tabby Lorenzo," *Buffalo Gals and Other Animal Presences* (New York: Penguin, 1990), 152.
38. Ursula K. Le Guin, "She Unnames Them," *Buffalo Gals and Other Animal Presences* (New York: Penguin, 1990), 194–96.

38. Ursula K. Le Guin, *Catwings* (New York: Scholastic, 1990); *Catwings Return* (New York: Scholastic, 1991); *Wonderful Alexander and the Catwings* (New York: Orchard Books, 1994); *Jane On Her Own* (New York: Orchard Books, 1999).

40. There are mice with wings in *Fish Soup* (New York: Atheneum, 1992), but they are only fancy irrelevant to the story, and they do not exhibit human consciousness. The Milts in *The Adventure of Cobbler's Rune* are monstrous amalgamations of different creatures meant to be ridiculous and poorly designed.

41. Sandra Lindow argues convincingly that Le Guin is accurately depicting Jane's traumato-phobia—the fear of the fear felt during the trauma. Jane, Lindow argues, "is surely experiencing the effects of post-traumatic stress disorder" (Sandra Lindow, "Trauma and Recovery in Ursula K. Le Guin's *Wonderful Alexander*: Animal as Guide through the Inner Space of the Unconscious," *Foundation: The International Review of Science Fiction* 70 [Summer 1997]; 34). Alexander is not only a friend but a good therapist because "he recognizes that Jane's language holds the key to her recovery" (35). This is another expression of Le Guin's interest in the community of individuals. As we saw in chapter three, home isn't to be found by isolated individuals. Lindow points out that this children's book makes it clear that "trauma cannot be healed in isolation" (37). Tehanu and Jane are also comparable to children who suffer trauma and are silenced by it.

42. Ursula K. Le Guin, *Wonderful Alexander and the Catwings* (New York: Orchard Books, 1994), 13.

43. Ursula K. Le Guin, *Leese Webster* (New York: Atheneum, 1979); *A Visit from Dr. Katz* (New York, NY: Atheneum, 1988); *Tom Mouse* (Brookfield, CT: Roaring Brook Press, 2002).

44. Sinclair makes a useful observation that "Le Guin has, essentially, two modes for presenting her protagonists as outsiders: either they are true aliens [. . .] or they are natives of a society, yet their perception of social life nevertheless sets them apart" ("Solitary Being: The Hero as Anthropologist," *Ursula K. Le Guin: Voyager to Inner Lands and to Outer Space,* ed. Joe De Bolt [London: Kennikat Press, 1979], 52). Either condition marks the protagonist-as-outsider as "other" in Le Guin's sense of the word: "someone who is different from you." Yet, as useful a distinction as this is, the observation doesn't make a distinction between the nature of the "apartness" of the alien from another "other."

45. Crow and Erhlich claim, on the contrary, that Le Guin's "vision is essentially one of integration" (200).

46. Charlotte Spivack makes it clear that she sees logic in *Word*, asserting that "the dialectical structure [of the book] is based on diametrically opposed characters" (*Ursula K. Le Guin* [Boston: Twayne Publishers, 1984], 67) and that this "dialectical structure is the central feature of *The Word for World Is Forest*" (68). Crow and Erlich see evidence of dialectics in Le Guin's fiction, but argue that the synthesis happens outside the text: "It is up to the reader to provide whatever synthesis is possible in Le Guin's dialectics" (221). Seen as a dialectic, then, the major characters in *Word*—Davidson, Selver and Lyubov—can only be concluded to be "essentially one-dimensional" (Spivack, 71) and, therefore, aesthetic disappointments. But depth may not be the best metaphor for considering the efficacy of characters in a narrative. Rather than privileging the fleshing-out of particular stances held by characters or insisting that they should take unified and clear stands, the notion of breadth might be a better consideration than depth for a round character that is a site for dialogue.

47. Keith Hull, "What is Human? Ursula Le Guin and Science Fiction's Great Theme," *Modern Fiction Studies* 32.1 (1986), 65.

48. Of course, Mark Twain would have it that Davidson's cruelty *makes* him human. Only humanity is cruel. Twain argues this most directly in *The Mysterious Stranger*. It isn't my intention to analyze this particular philosophical point here, however.

Chapter 2

1. Because later essays devoted to Earthsea and The Valley of the Kesh, respectively, feature their narrative strategies, I won't discuss them here. I'll leave it to the reader to decide whether those books present exceptions to what I present here. Likely they will, for there

isn't any one pattern that can be so neatly offered to explain the way Le Guin's stories work.

2. Mieke Bal uses "external narrator" and "character narrator" rather than "third-person" or "first-person" narrator. I prefer her terminology because it makes better sense in conjunction with the idea of focalization; see Mieke Bal, *Narratology*, 2nd ed. (Toronto: University of Toronto Press, 1997). It's important in Le Guin's fiction to understand when one sees through a character from "outside" or from "inside." Genette calls any narration from outside the story "extradiegetic" and narration from within "intradiegetic." A character telling her own story is "autodiegetic" narration; see *Narrative Discourse: An Essay in Method*, trans. Jane E. Lewin (Ithaca: Cornell University Press, 1980).

3. Ursula K. Le Guin, *Malafrena*, (New York: Berkley-Putnam, 1979).

4. Ursula K. Le Guin, *Steering the Craft* (Portland, OR: The Eighth Mountain Press, 1998), 86; hereafter cited in text as 1998.

5. Ursula K. Le Guin, *Planet of Exile* (New York: Ace Books, 1966); *The Lathe of Heaven* (New York: Charles Scribner's Sons, 1971) [hereafter cited in text as *Lathe*]; *The Word for World Is Forest* (New York: Berkley Publishing Co., 1976) [hereafter cited in text as *Word*]; *The Eye of the Heron* (New York: Harper & Row, 1983, [originally published by Delacort Press, 1978]). See Richard Erlich's observations in *Coyote's Song* about the parallel patterns of narration in some of these novels: http://www.sfra.org/Coyote/CoyoteHome.

6. Again, narratology is rife with different terms for similar phenomena. Maria Nikolajeva discusses the use of free indirect discourse in children's books in her recent article "Imprints of the Mind: The Depiction of Consciousness in Children's Fiction," found in *Children's Literature Association Quarterly* 26.4 (Winter 2001–2002)—but uses Dorrit Cohn's term "narrated monologue." She concedes, however, that "free indirect discourse," Genette's term, is "more common." It should be said that Dorrit Cohn's *Transparent Minds: Narrative Modes for Presenting Consciousness in Fiction* (Princeton, NJ: Princeton University Press, 1984) offers an important early discussion on the subject.

7. Consider free indirect discourse as a way to be "double voiced" in contrast to what we see as characters with multiple vision in other Le Guin works. Tehanu, from the book of the same name, and Myra, from "Buffalo Gals Won't You Come Out Tonight," *Buffalo Gals and Other Animal Presences* (New York: Penguin, 1990) each see simultaneously from two points of view—Tehanu as both person and dragon; Myra as both person and wild animal. Free indirect discourse is a more subtle way for a character to gain authority based on vision. It's duality is hidden, and hence a bit more difficult for a reader to challenge.

8. Ursula K. Le Guin, *The Beginning Place* (New York: Harper & Row, 1980).

9. Carol Franko says of the final section "where neither angle is dominant" that the text is "a quiet yet powerful culmination of the storyteller's enactment of intersubjectivity through narrated angles of vision." See Carol Franko, "Acts of Attention at the Borderlands: Le Guin's *The Beginning Place* Revisited," *Extrapolation* 37.4 (1996), 304.

10. Ursula K. Le Guin, *Rocannon's World* (New York: Ace Books, 1966); *City of Illusions* (New York: Ace Books, 1967); *The Dispossessed* (New York: Avon, 1974); *The Telling* (New York: Harcourt, Inc., 2000) [hereafter cited as *Telling*].

11. For a discussion on journey in *Rocannon's World, The Left Hand of Darkness*, and *The Dispossessed* from a Jungian perspective, see Peter Briggs, "The Archetype of the Journey in Ursula K. Le Guin's Fiction," *Ursula K. Le Guin*, ed. Joseph Olander and Martin Harry Greenberg (New York: Taplinger Publishing Company, 1979), 36–63.

12. I am indebted to Thomas Dunn's argument that "Le Guin's employment of the folded narrative . . . provides a kind of Argument by Design to the concepts running throughout the novel." Though his attention is mainly on the Odonian concepts, he does acknowledge the parallel between the structure of the novel and temporality. See Thomas Dunn, "Theme and Narrative Structure in Ursula K. Le Guin's *The Dispossessed* and Frederik Pohl's *Gateway*," *Reflections on the Fantastic: Selected Essays from the Fourth International Conference on the Fantastic in the Art*, ed. Michael R. Collins (New York: Greenwood Press, 1986), 91.

13. This seems to be a parallel to Mao's Cultural Revolution during which the texts and tradition of the Tao were in great danger.
14. Richard Erlich, "From Shakespeare to Le Guin: Authors as Auteurs," *Extrapolation* 40.4 (1999): 341–50.
15. Ursula K. Le Guin, *The Left Hand of Darkness* (New York: Ace, 1969) [hereafter cited as *Left Hand*]; *Very Far Away from Anywhere Else* (New York: Bantam Books, 1976) [hereafter cited as *Very Far*]. The Stone-Telling sections of *Always Coming Home* are presented as character narration. I'll discuss the implications of this in chapter five.
16. John Stephens, "Maintaining Distinctions: Realism, Voice, and Subject Position in Australian Young Adult Fiction," *Transcending Boundaries: Writing for a Dual Audience of Children and Adults*, ed. Sandra Becket (New York: Garland Publishing, Inc., 1999), 189.
17. Roberta Seelinger Trites argues that "when an adult assumes narrative authority within the text for the purposes of communicating an ideology of maturity, the adolescent implied reader is at least temporarily displaced" (*Disturbing the Universe: Power and Repression in Adolescent Literature* [Iowa City: University of Iowa Press, 2000], 74). It is the case in this novel that Owen's character narration potentially isolates him as much as other forms of narration, notably approaches Le Guin uses in other novels that more easily facilitate connection among characters.
18. Just as in *The Dispossessed* where the structure of the narrative echoes the subject—simultaneity of time and place—in *Very Far Away From Anywhere Else* Owen's academic interest is consciousness and is presented in the highly self-conscious form of character narration.
19. Le Guin likes to connect heavenly as well as human bodies. Consider the relationships between Werel and Yeowe, Urras and Annares, Hain and Ve, Terra and the worlds of Aka and Athshe. It is as if these worlds, like Le Guin's characters, derive purpose from each other.
20. See the interview that concludes this volume for Le Guin's discussion of this matter. Nick Gevers interviewed Le Guin "by letter in November/December of 2001" just after my visit with her in early November and found Le Guin interested in talking about "story-suites" with him as well (November/December 2001. wysiwyg://63/http://www. sfsite.com/03a/ul123.htm). She seems to have stumbled upon the idea right around that time. She addresses this in her foreword to *The Birthday of the World and Other Stories* (New York: HarperCollins, 2002), xi–xii: "There's a sneering British term 'fix-up' for books by authors who, told that collections 'don't sell,' patch unconnected stories together with verbal duct tape. But the real thing is not a random collection, any more than a Bach cello suite is. It does things a novel doesn't do. It is a real form, and deserves a real name. Maybe we could call it a story suite? I think I will."
21. Ursula K. Le Guin, *Orsinian Tales* (New York: HarperCollins, 1976); *Searoad* (New York: HarperCollins, 1991); *Four Ways to Forgiveness* (New York: HarperPrism, 1995).
22. Ursula K. Le Guin, *Unlocking the Air and Other Stories* (New York: HarperCollins, 1996).
23. Ursula K. Le Guin, "Old Music and the Slave Women," *Far Horizons*, ed. Robert Silverberg (New York: Avon Books, 1999), 7–52. Subsequently collected in *The Birthday of the World and Other Stories* (New York: HarperCollins, 2002).
24. Ursula K. Le Guin, *The Wind's Twelve Quarters* (New York: Bantam Books, 1976); *The Compass Rose* (New York: Bantam Books, 1982); *A Fisherman of the Inland Sea: Science Fiction Stories* (New York: HarperPrism, 1994); *Changing Planes* (New York: Harcourt, Inc., 2003). One reviewer of *Unlocking the Air* notes that "instead of gathering her short works according to subject matter, as she has previously done, Le Guin has tossed them together here, as if to say all of these worlds represent the same writer; do you too see a single vision?" See Charles Nicols, "The Very Different Worlds of Ursula K. Le Guin," review of *Unlocking the Air*, by Ursula K. Le Guin, *Chicago Tribune* 25 Feb. 1996, Books Section 5.
25. Ursula K. Le Guin, *Buffalo Gals and Other Animal Presences* (New York: Penguin, 1990).
26. While each story in each suite deserves a detailed explication, it is my intention, rather, to show how each suite as a whole manages to use the strategies of narration and focalization to connect characters—or keep them apart. In the first two suites, especially, with so many tales offered, I attempt to keep commentary on individual stories to a minimum so that the point about narrative strategies can be advanced without belaboring the discussion.

27. I will refer to the twelve short stories as "Orsinia Tales" or "Tales of Orsinia" since "Unlocking the Air" is not in fact a part of the collection called *Orsinian Tales*.

28. James Bittner makes the argument that because the tales about Orsinia were written over the course of many years, and because publication dates of these tales—so difficult to get published—don't tell us much about when they were actually written. "We cannot, therefore, try to understand [them] as a discrete stage or step in Le Guin's development"; see "Persuading Us to Rejoice and Teaching Us How to Praise: Le Guin's Orsinian Tales," *Science Fiction Studies* 5 (1978): 216.

29. See the interview that concludes this volume on Le Guin's not having been asked into Orsinia for a while, despite her curiosity about what is going on there.

30. Ursula K. Le Guin, "The Barrow," *Orsinian Tales* (New York: HarperCollins, 1976), 14; hereafter cited in text.

31. Ursula K. Le Guin, "The Road East," *Orsinian Tales* (New York: HarperCollins, 1976), 77; hereafter cited in text.

32. Ursula K. Le Guin, "The House," *Orsinian Tales* (New York: HarperCollins, 1976), 186.

33. Ursula K. Le Guin, "Ile Forest," *Orsinian Tales* (New York: HarperCollins, 1976), 71.

34. Ursula K. Le Guin, "Brother and Sisters," *Orsinian Tales* (New York: HarperCollins, 1976), 127.

35. Ursula K. Le Guin, "Unlocking the Air," *Unlocking the Air and Other Stories* (New York: HarperCollins, 1996), 139.

36. Ursula K. Le Guin, "The Ship Ahoy," *Searoad: Chronicles of Klatsand* (New York: HarperCollins, 1991), 13.

37. Ursula K. Le Guin, "Geezers," *Searoad: Chronicles of Klatsand* (New York: HarperCollins, 1991), 41.

38. Ursula K. Le Guin, "Bill Weisler," *Searoad: Chronicles of Klatsand* (New York: HarperCollins, 1991), 59.

39. Shirley bristles at Jen's use of the word "lover," or at the use of any "euphemism" to describe a relationship for which "there aren't any words that mean anything." Shirley observes, "we can't say who we are . . . Nothing means anything but proper names. You can say Barbara was survived by Shirley. That's all you can say"("Quoits," *Searoad: Chronicles of Klatsand* [New York: HarperCollins, 1991], 106); hereafter cited in text as "Quoits."

40. Ursula K. Le Guin, "Crossroads," *Searoad: Chronicles of Klatsand* (New York: HarperCollins, 1991), 118.

41. Ursula K. Le Guin, "Sleepwalkers," *Searoad: Chronicles of Klatsand* (New York: HarperCollins, 1991), 90; hereafter cited in text.

42. It isn't clear whether they are journal or diary entries, interior monologue, or even a one-sided unburdening to a counselor—but they seem not to be letters. Each entry begins with a name and a date: "Lily, 1931" ("Hernes," *Searoad* [New York: HarperCollins, 1991], 148). What follows is in character narration, or first-person address. Each of the four speakers has monologues of a couple of pages, on average, arranged randomly in the story, though Le Guin tends to show us these characters' thoughts at roughly similar points in their lives.

43. Ursula K. Le Guin, "In and Out," *Searoad: Chronicles of Klatsand* (New York: HarperCollins, 1991), 57.

44. Ursula K. Le Guin, "Hand, Cup, Shell," *Searoad: Chronicles of Klatsand* (New York: HarperCollins, 1991), 15.

45. Le Guin cautions us that the Werel in the Forgiveness story-suite "is not the Werel of the early novel *Planet of Exile*. It's a different one" ("Foreword," *The Birthday of the World*, xii). She claims to have forgotten about that one. See the interview that concludes this volume.

46. Ursula K. Le Guin, "Betrayals," *Four Ways to Forgiveness* (New York: HarperPrism, 1995), 7; hereafter cited in text.

47. Ursula K. Le Guin, "Forgiveness Day," *Four Ways to Forgiveness* (New York: HarperPrism, 1995), 46, 76; hereafter cited in text.

48. Ursula K. Le Guin, "A Man of the People," *Four Ways to Forgiveness* (New York: HarperPrism, 1995), 106; hereafter cited in text.

49. Ursula K. Le Guin, "A Woman's Liberation," *Four Ways to Forgiveness* (New York: HarperPrism, 1995), 198; hereafter cited in text.
50. Ursula K. Le Guin, "Old Music and the Slave Women," *Four Ways to Forgiveness* (New York: HarperPrism, 1995), 7; hereafter cited in text as "Women."
51. Maria Nikolajeva, *Children's Literature Comes of Age: Toward a New Aesthetic* (New York and London: Garland Publishing, Inc., 1996), 100.
52. See not only *Steering the Craft* (87) but the interview that concludes this volume on Le Guin's thoughts regarding the difficulty of these extreme forms of narration for both professional and novice writers.
53. Ursula K. Le Guin, *Catwings* (New York: Scholastic, 1990); *Catwings Return* (New York: Scholastic, 1991); *Wonderful Alexander and the Catwings* (New York: Orchard Books, 1994) [hereafter cited as *Wonderful*]; *Jane On Her Own* (New York: Orchard Books, 1999) [hereafter cited as *Jane*].
54. See Nikolajeva's discussion of the limits and arcane qualities of quoted monologue (Winter 2001–2002, 175).
55. Ursula K. Le Guin, *The Adventures of Cobbler's Rune* (New Castle, VA: Cheap Street, 1982); *A Ride on the Red Mare's Back* (New York: Orchard Books, 1992).
56. Ursula K. Le Guin, *Fish Soup* (New York: Atheneum, 1992); *A Visit from Dr. Katz* (New York, NY: Atheneum, 1988); *Solomon Leviathan's Nine Hundred and Thirty-First Trip Around the World* (New York: Philomel Books, 1983); *Fire and Stone* (New York: Atheneum, 1989).
57. Ursula K. Le Guin, *Leese Webster* (New York: Atheneum, 1979) [hereafter cited as *Leese*]; *Tom Mouse* (Brookfield, CT: Roaring Brook Press, 2002); hereafter cited as *Tom*.
58. Cobbler in *Cobbler's Rune* functions as focalizer not because he cannot communicate with humans—there are none in the book. He is Le Guin's only sole-traveler, and this from the very first children's book she wrote (though it was published after *Leese Webster*). We hear Cobbler's thoughts as he travels along, though there are fewer of these than one might imagine. He has a good deal of dialogue with helpers, villains, and allies along the way.

Chapter 3

1. Elizabeth Cummins, "The Land-Lady's Homebirth: Revisiting Ursula K. Le Guin's Worlds," *Science Fiction Studies* 17.2 (1990): 154.
2. Mikhail M. Bakhtin, *The Dialogic Imagination: Four Essays*, trans. Michael Holquist and Caryl Emerson, ed. Michael Holquist (Austin: University of Texas Press, 1981), 84; hereafter cited in text.
3. Ursula K. Le Guin, *Always Coming Home* (New York: Harper & Row, 1985), 160; hereafter cited in text.
4. Victor Reinking and David Willingham, "Interview: A Conversation with Ursula K. Le Guin," *Paradoxa: Studies in World Literary Genres* 1.1 (1995): 54.
5. Heinz Tschachler, "What if Arlington, Texas *is* Utopia? Ursula K. Le Guin, Postmodernism, and (In)determinacy," *Postmodern Studies* 11 (1995): 271.
6. Virginia L. Wolf, "From the Myth to the Wake of Home: Literary Homes," *Children's Literature* 18 (1990): 56.
7. Ursula K. Le Guin, "A Non-Euclidean View of California as a Cold Place to Be," *Dancing at the Edge of the World: Thoughts on Words, Women, Places* (New York: Harper & Row, 1989), 98.
8. Michael Holquist, *Dialogism: Bakhtin and his World* (London and New York: Routledge, 1990), 18; hereafter cited in text.
9. Ursula K. Le Guin, "The Shobies' Story," *A Fisherman of the Inland Sea: Science Fiction Stories* (New York: HarperPrism, 1994), 99.
10. Leonard Lutwack, *The Role of Place in Literature* (Syracuse: Syracuse University Press, 1984), 11; hereafter cited in text.
11. Scott Russell Sanders, *Staying Put: Making a Home in a Restless World* (Boston: Beacon Press, 1993), 114.
12. Ursula K. Le Guin, *The Dispossessed* (New York: Avon, 1974), 44; hereafter cited in text.

13. Ursula K. Le Guin, *The Beginning Place* (New York: Harper & Row, 1980), 167; hereafter cited in text as *Beginning*.

14. Maria Nikolajeva, *Children's Literature Comes of Age: Toward a New Aesthetic* (New York and London: Garland Publishing, Inc., 1996), 123.

15. Le Guin does feature space travel as the setting for much of her short fiction, however, most notably the churten stories from *A Fisherman of the Inland Sea*; real-road travel as well as memory and dream travel seem to be more acceptable for Le Guin's longer fiction.

16. Consider the short story "Coming of Age in Karhide." Sov: "Yet as I write I see how also nothing changes, that it is truly the Year One always, for each child that comes of age, each lover who falls in love" (Ursula K. Le Guin, "Coming of Age in Karhide," *New Legends*, eds. Greg Bear and Martin H. Greenberg [New York: Tor, 1995] 91 [subsequently collected in *The Birthday of the World and Other Stories* (New York: HarperCollins, 2002): 1–22]).

17. James Bittner makes the observation that "what Le Guin's characters learn on their quests is that freedom and wholeness are not to be found in individualism, but in partnership ..." ("Persuading Us to Rejoice and Teaching Us How to Praise: Le Guin's Orsinian Tales," *Science Fiction Studies* 5 [1978]: 218). He links this with the claim that Le Guin's tales employ journeys of Romantic circularity (216). My argument about the movement is different (because I make a case for the unimportance of return in some of these stories) but we agree—as Le Guin and Erlich state—that it is hard to succeed alone in the universe.

18. Ursula K. Le Guin, *Planet of Exile* (New York: Ace Books, 1966); *The Eye of the Heron* (New York: Harper & Row, 1983) [originally published by Delacort Press, 1978].

19. In her short story "The Eye Altering" (*The Compass Rose* [New York: Bantam Books, 1982], 154–68), Le Guin shows us how the first native generation of colonists on Zion see their world truly, unlike the generation before who knew Earth. Genya produces art—landscapes of Zion, seen "with the eyes and the heart"—that his contemporaries find beautiful, but which his elders find lacking because they measure it by the light of a different sun (167).

20. Ursula K. Le Guin, *Rocannon's World* (New York: Ace Books, 1966).

21. Ursula K. Le Guin, *The Left Hand of Darkness* (New York: Ace, 1969); *The Word for World Is Forest* (New York: Berkley Publishing Co., 1976); *The Telling* (New York: Harcourt, Inc., 2000); hereafter cited in text.

22. Frank Dietz says of Genly Ai that he "has to cross borders before he can fulfill his role as an envoy of the Ekumen of Known Worlds" ("'Home is a Place Where You Have Never Been': The Exile Motif in the Hainish Novels of Ursula K. Le Guin," *The Literature of Emigration and Exile*, eds. James Whitlark and Wendell Aycock [Lubbock: Texas Tech University Press, 1992], 110). Here Dietz discusses national borders, but equally important are the borders between city and wilderness.

23. See James Bittner's excellent essay, "Chronosophy, Aesthetics, and Ethics in Le Guin's The Dispossessed: An Ambiguous Utopia," (*No Place Else: Explorations in Utopian and Dystopian Fiction*, ed. Eric S. Rabkin et al. [Carbondale: Southern Illinois University Press, 1983], 244–70) for a discussion of the "palindromic" (258), "concentric" (261), or "contrapuntal" (263) qualities of the narrative layout and, hence, journey experience for the reader.

24. George E. Slusser, *The Farthest Shores of Ursula K. Le Guin* (San Bernadino: Borgo Press, 1976), 50.

25. Bernard Selinger documents in his book *Le Guin and Identity in Contemporary Fiction* (Ann Arbor, MI: UMI Research Press, 1988) that the relationship between Urras and Anarres, and hence between Shevek's conflicting sense of home, has been touched on and not resolved by several critics. It is interesting how resistant this award-winning novel seems to be to any approach.

26. The Werel of *City of Illusions* (New York: Ace Books, 1967) is not the same Werel that serves as the setting for the much later *Four Ways to Forgiveness* (New York: HarperPrism, 1995). Le Guin had forgotten that she had named a planet "Werel" already.

27. Ursula K. Le Guin, *Malafrena* (New York: Berkley-Putnam, 1979), 79.

28. Maria Nikolajeva, *From Mythic to Linear: Time in Children's Literature* (Lanham, MD: The Children's Literature Association & Scarecrow Press, Inc., 2000), 134.

29. Ursula K. Le Guin, *The Word for World Is Forest* (New York: Berkley Publishing Co., 1976), 33; hereafter cited in text.

30. Ursula K. Le Guin, *The Lathe of Heaven* (New York: Charles Scribner's Sons, 1971); hereafter cited in text.

31. In contrast to my argument that Heather is a partner, Bernard Selinger, using a Lacanian approach to *The Lathe of Heaven*, argues that George functions "relatively autonomously" by the end of the novel and that Heather (along with others) is made use of by George as "subjective objects" (88).

32. Carol Franko, "Acts of Attention at the Borderlands: Le Guin's *The Beginning Place* Revisited," *Extrapolation* 37.4 (1996): 302. Also, Maria Nikolajeva notes that "when we examine the evolution of the fantasy genre we discover that there is a prominent general tendency in all types of fantasy novels toward fluid boundaries between reality and the magical world or secondary time, and towards psychological depth" (2000, 124). See Nikolajeva on other applications of dialogics to fantasy using children's books.

33. Ursula K. Le Guin, *Very Far Away from Anywhere Else* (New York: Bantam Books, 1976); hereafter cited in text.

34. Ursula K. Le Guin, "Brothers and Sisters," *Orsinian Tales* (New York: HarperCollins, 1976), 85–127; "A Week in the Country," *Orsinian Tales* (New York: HarperCollins, 1976), 129–54; "Unlocking the Air," *Unlocking the Air and Other Stories* (New York: HarperCollins, 1996), 125–39.

35. Ursula K. Le Guin, "Winter's King," *The Wind's Twelve Quarters* (New York: Bantam Books, 1976), 86. I'll talk more about simultaneity in *Always Coming Home* in a later chapter. Carol Franko notes that "the Kesh prefer spatial to temporal images" ("Self-Conscious Narration as the Complex Representation of Hope in Le Guin's *Always Coming Home*," *Mythlore* 57 [1989]: 59) which is what makes reading *Always Coming Home* not unlike reading *Orsinian Tales*, or even *Searoad*. Time is subsumed by place—quite the opposite to Le Guin's "Ether, OR" (*Unlocking the Air and Other Stories* [New York: HarperCollins, 1996], 95–123) in which a town moves about over linear time.

36. The way the dates are arranged in the collection of short stories causes James Bittner to argue that there is a distancing effect. The arrangement of stories also, he says, causes the reader to circle back in time continuously, that circularity and linearity are, in fact, synthesized (1978, 216–18).

37. Ursula K. Le Guin, "Conversations at Night," *Orsinian Tales* (New York: HarperCollins, 1976), 71.

38. Ursula K. Le Guin, "The Fountains," *Orsinian Tales* (New York: HarperCollins, 1976), 4; hereafter cited in text.

39. Ursula K. Le Guin, "Hernes," *Searoad* (New York: HarperCollins, 1991), 123–93; hereafter cited in text.

40. Ursula K. Le Guin, "Quoits," *Searoad* (New York: HarperCollins, 1991), 99.

41. Batikam, a performer of the asset class on Werel, thinks of the freed slave world of Yeowe as "his home," even though he has never been there (Ursula K. Le Guin, "Forgiveness Day," *Four Ways to Forgiveness* [New York: HarperPrism, 1995], 62). "Home is a place where you have never been," Shevek tells us in *The Dispossessed* (44)—as long as you are in the process of moving toward it and away from it simultaneously. Since purposeful motion is between places, not simply being in space, the place is as important as the space, and the companionable motion among them is most important of all.

42. Ursula K. Le Guin, "A Man of the People" *Four Ways to Forgiveness* (New York: HarperPrism, 1995), 93–144; "Old Music and the Slave Women," *Far Horizons*, ed. Robert Silverberg (New York: Avon Books, 1999), 7–52 [subsequently collected in *The Birthday of the World and Other Stories*, (New York: HarperCollins, 2002), 153–212].

43. Ursula K. Le Guin, "A Woman's Liberation," *Four Ways to Forgiveness* (New York: HarperPrism, 1995), 172; hereafter cited in text.

44. Ursula K. Le Guin, "Betrayals," *Four Ways to Forgiveness* (New York: HarperPrism, 1995), 1–34.

45. Abberkam sees only the danger of the inductive chronotope, not seeing what might lie on the other side: "'Take your children on the wonderful ship and fly to our wonderful worlds!' and the children are taken, and they'll never come home. Never know their home. Never know who they are" (Le Guin, "Betrayals," 21). The one-way ticket is not a journey of purposeful movement, according to Abberkam, because it denies one of the places necessary for constructing a sense of home and self. He doesn't see that home isn't a place but a condition. See "The Fisherman of the Inland Sea" as a possible exception to this.

46. The Fabbres' tales in the Orsinia suite might be thought of as the romance in Orsinia. It would be interesting to have a suite of stories only about them.

47. It is interesting to note, however, that the only picture book Le Guin has written for children that is principally realism, *A Visit from Dr. Katz* (illus. Ann Barrow [New York: Atheneum, 1988]) is the only example of the chronotope of singular time and place.

48. Ursula K. Le Guin, *Fish Soup* (New York: Atheneum, 1992).

49. Ursula K. Le Guin, *A Ride on the Red Mare's* Back (New York: Orchard Books, 1992), 14; hereafter cited in text as *Red Mare*.

50. Ursula K. Le Guin, *Tehanu: The Last Book of Earthsea* (New York: Atheneum, 1990).

51. Leo Zanderer notes that "the idea of the forest as a kind of ultimate home, or as a primal, collective home, may well belong to a particularly Anglo-European rather than American conception of life" ("Popular Culture, Childhood, and the New American Forest of Postmodernism," *The Lion and The Unicorn* 11.2 [1987]: 15), and that our American myths "characteristically involve men who overcome the forest and the wilderness and make it inhabitable, civilized" (fn, 32). Le Guin's forests function as neither savage wilderness nor home in each tale. The tales span and mix genres and, therefore, the uses of the setting and symbolic matter of forest are varied. See also Ian Watson's "The Forest as Metaphor for Mind: *The Word for World Is Forest* and 'Vaster Than Empires and More Slow,'" *Ursula K Le Guin*, ed. Harold Bloom (New York: Chelsea House, 1986), 47–56.

52. In Le Guin's tale "A Fisherman of the Inland Sea," from the book of the same name, Isabo tells the narrator–protagonist "that a mother is connected to her child by a very fine, thin cord, like the umbilical cord, that can stretch light-years without any difficulty" (188). This thread seems to have little difficulty with time, distance, or dimension as it crosses into the frame narrative, the dream world. Stone Telling in *Always Coming Home* describes a similar condition: "I began to feel the Valley behind me like a body, my own body . . . That was my body, and I here lying down was a breath-soul, going farther away from its body every day. A long very thin string connected that body and that soul, a string of pain" (201).

53. Ursula K. Le Guin, *Catwings* (New York: Scholastic, 1990); *Catwings Return* (New York: Scholastic, 1991); *Wonderful Alexander and the Catwings* (New York: Orchard Books, 1994); *Jane On Her Own* (New York: Orchard Books, 1999).

54. A similar condition exists in C. S. Lewis's *The Magician's Nephew* (New York: HarperTrophy, 1955) in which Digory and Polly are sent to "another world" with the use of Uncle Andrew's magic rings. Together, in the "The Wood Between the Worlds," the children are able to convince each other that they must fight the sleepiness the woods induce and move on to either another world or back to their own. We are lead to believe that, independent of each other, they would have slept and forgotten their identities, as Polly claims: "This place is to quiet. It's so—so dreamy. You're almost asleep. If we once give in to it we shall just lie down and drowse forever and ever" (35). At another point, Digory is about to explore other worlds without "marking" the path back to their own. Polly points this out, to his horror, saving him and herself from a lifetime of searching for the way back. This proves another forest trap of stasis in children's fiction in which stasis is tantamount to death—a loss of home.

55. Ursula K. Le Guin, "From Elfland to Poughkeepsie," *The Language of the Night: Essays on Fantasy and Science Fiction*, ed. Susan Wood and Ursula K. Le Guin, rev. ed. (New York: HarperCollins, 1989), 79.

56. Ursula K. Le Guin, *The Farthest Shore* (New York: Bantam, 1975 [orig. publ. 1972]).

57. Ursula K. Le Guin, *The Adventures of Cobbler's Rune* (New Castle, VA: Cheap Street, 1982), 9.

58. Given Le Guin's interest in names, it seems somehow impossible for it to be an accident that "Damon" is "nomad" in reverse.
59. Ursula K. Le Guin, *Solomon Leviathan's Nine Hundred and Thirty-First Trip Around the World*, illus. Alicia Austin (New York: Philomel Books, 1983), 26; hereafter cited in text.
60. Ursula K. Le Guin, *Tom Mouse* (Brookfield, CT: Roaring Brook Press, 2002).
61. Again a name seems important. Ms. Powers certainly empowers Tom to travel his many roads as his purposeful partner. I can't help wishing that her first name were Emily; the idea of "Em Powers" is perhaps going a bit far, I admit.
62. Ursula K. Le Guin, *Leese Webster* (New York: Atheneum, 1979); *Fire and Stone* (New York: Atheneum, 1989).
63. Margaret R. Higonnet, "Narrative Fractures and Fragments," *Children's Literature* 15 (1987): 37–54; hereafter cited in text.
64. Christopher Clausen, "Home and Away in Children's Fiction," *Children's Literature* 10 (1982): 143.
65. Jon C. Stott, "Running Away to Home—A Story Pattern in Children's Literature," *Language Arts* 55.4 (1978): 473–77.
66. Perry Nodelman, *The Pleasures of Children's Literature,* 2d ed. (New York: Longman, 1995) 157; See Perry Nodelman's excellent topically arranged bibliography of children's literature criticism. One section is devoted to articles that deal with the phenomenon of home in children's literature: www.uwinnipeg.ca/~nodelman/resources/allbib.htm
67. Ursula K. Le Guin, "Dancing to Ganam," *A Fisherman of the Inland Sea: Science Fiction Stories* (New York: HarperPrism, 1994), 107.

Chapter 4

1. Ursula K. Le Guin, *The Other Wind* (New York: Harcourt, Inc., 2001); hereafter cited in text as *Wind*.
2. Ursula K. Le Guin, *Tehanu: The Last Book of Earthsea* (New York: Atheneum, 1990); hereafter cited in text.
3. Ursula K. Le Guin, *A Wizard of Earthsea* (New York: Bantam, 1975 [orig. publ. 1968]); hereafter cited in text as *Wizard*.
4. Reprinted in *The Wind's Twelve Quarters* (New York: Bantam Books, 1976), 65–72.
5. Ursula K. Le Guin, "The Word of Unbinding," *The Wind's Twelve Quarters* (New York: Bantam Books, 1976), 71.
6. Reprinted in *The Wind's Twelve Quarters* (New York: Bantam Books, 1976), 73–84.
7. Ursula K. Le Guin, "Dreams Must Explain Themselves," *The Language of the Night: Essays on Fantasy and Science Fiction,* ed. Susan Wood and Ursula K. Le Guin, rev. ed. (New York: HarperCollins, 1989), 45; hereafter cited as "Dreams."
8. Donna White, *Dancing With Dragons: Ursula K. Le Guin and the Critics* (Columbia, SC: Camden House, 1999), 10.
9. Ursula K. Le Guin, *The Tombs of Atuan* (New York: Bantam, 1975 [orig. publ. 1970]); *The Farthest Shore* (New York: Bantam, 1975 [orig. publ. 1972]); hereafter cited in text as *Tombs* and *Farthest*, respectively.
10. All characters in the series have more than one name. So rather than constantly representing them by those multiple names I will be settling on what seems to be the character's dominant identity. For instance, though the Prince of Havnor is both Arren and Lebannen, I refer to him as Lebannen throughout. While he is "Arren" for the most part in *The Farthest Shore*, he becomes more strongly known as Lebannen from the end of that novel through the rest of the series. Ged begins life as Duny and then is known as Sparrowhawk; but it is as Ged that he is most significant. Tenar's foster child is both Therru and Tehanu; since she is more significant as Tehanu I use that name throughout.
11. One example of Le Guin's interest in mythic traffic between the respective worlds of the living and the dead can be found in her short story "A Child Bride" in *Unlocking the Air* (New York: HarperCollins, 1996), 141–43. This is a story told from the consciousness of Persephone, though it never specifically mentions her name, taken from her mother Demeter by Hades to be his bride in the Underworld.

12. Lois Kuznets points out that "the first book is not about the development of a new king, but about his helper and prophet, the magician or wizard—in this case, Ged" ("'High Fantasy' in America: A Study of Lloyd Alexander, Ursula Le Guin, and Susan Cooper," *The Lion and the Unicorn* 9 [1985]: 30). While it is true that ultimately Lebannen will be King and Ged a goatherd come full circle, Ged is, as Archmage-to-be, on track for the most powerful position in the pre-Lebannen world. In fact, Lebannen is more Ged's successor than his superior since the Archmage position is never filled as the King takes over and Ged "abdicates" as Archmage. Ged's is the story of the coming-of-age of the hero–king, as Earthsea knows it at this time.

13. Ursula K. Le Guin, "A Description of Earthsea," *Tales From Earthsea* (New York: Harcourt, Inc., 2001); hereafter cited in text as "Description."

14. Ursula K. Le Guin, "The Finder," *Tales from Earthsea* (New York: Harcourt, Inc., 2001); hereafter cited in text as "Finder."

15. Ursula K. Le Guin, "Darkrose and Diamond," *Tales from Earthsea* (New York: Harcourt, Inc., 2001); hereafter cited in text as "Darkrose."

16. Ursula K. Le Guin, "The Bones of the Earth," *Tales from Earthsea* (New York: Harcourt, Inc., 2001); hereafter cited in text as "Bones."

17. Ursula K. Le Guin, "On the High Marsh," *Tales From Earthsea* (New York: Harcourt, Inc., 2001), 163; hereafter cited in text as "Marsh."

18. Ursula K. Le Guin, "Dragonfly," *Tales from Earthsea* (New York: Harcourt, Inc., 2001): hereafter cited in text.

19. One reason we don't know about this until this point in the series is that only Pelnish lore and the Kargs recorded it, and they and the dragons serve only as antagonists in the epic first series.

20. Michael Levy, "Re: Tales from Earthsea." Online posting. 28 June 2001. Child_Lit. www.rci.rutgers.edu/«simil»mjoseph/childlit/about.html; hereafter cited in text.

21. George Slusser, *The Farthest Shores of Ursula K. Le Guin* (San Bernardino: Borgo Press, 1976), 34; hereafter cited in text.

22. David Rees, *The Marble in the Water: Essays on Contemporary Writers of Fiction for Children and Young Adults* (Boston: The Horn Book, Inc., 1980), 78.

23. Consider the link between this scene at the end of "Dragonfly" and the second ever Earthsea story, "The Rule of Names," which preceded the publication of the first book in the series. In that story Yevaud kills a greedy wizard, like Thorion a pretender to power, by squashing him. In that tale the wizard, like Thorion, is taken by surprise by the fact that his opponent is, in fact, a dragon.

24. Mikhail M. Bakhtin, *The Dialogic Imagination: Four Essays*, trans. Michael Holquist and Caryl Emerson, ed. Michael Holquist (Austin: University of Texas Press, 1981), 13; hereafter cited in text.

25. Margaret Esmonde, "Beyond the Circle of the World: Death and the Hereafter in Children's Literature," *Webs and Wardrobes: Humanist and Religious World Views in Children's Literature*, ed. Joseph Milner O'Beirne and Lucy Floyd Morcock O'Beirne (Lanham, MD: University Press of America, 1987), 41.

26. Gerald Prince, "Introduction to the Study of the Narratee," *Narratology: An Introduction,* ed. Susana Onega and Jose Angel Garcia Landa (New York: Longman, 1996), 198.

27. There is at least one instance of present tense in the telling, which might be important to those who can make something of the choice. At one point Ged dismisses a point made by Vetch: "'Old Tales,' says Ged" (*Wizard*, 50). The "says Ged" seems an anomaly in the novel.

28. Ursula K. Le Guin, "Foreword," *Tales from Earthsea* (New York: Harcourt, Inc., 2001), xi; hereafter cited in text as "Foreword."

29. Ursula K. Le Guin, *Always Coming Home* (New York: Harper & Row, 1985).

30. Len Hatfield, "From Master to Brother: Shifting the Balance of Authority in Ursula K. Le Guin's *Farthest Shore* and *Tehanu*," *Children's Literature* 21 (1993): 43–65.

31. Gerald Prince, *A Dictionary of Narratology* (Lincoln: University of Nebraska Press, 1987), 34.

32. The later development of Ged's character "revises" that earlier set of foolish notions about power and what Odonians—Le Guin's Cetian anarchist group from her Hainish novels—would call "egoizing."

33. There are many places in which the narrator relies on the word "seems" in order to reinforce the feeling of appearance. This selection is one such place when it *seems* that the Archmage is the ninth master. There are several other places where the word is used in this way (*Wizard*, 5, 34, 35, 43, 100).

34. See Mike Cadden, "The Irony of Narration in the Young Adult Novel," *Children's Literature Association Quarterly* 25.3 (2000): 146–54.

35. Ursula K. Le Guin, *Very Far Away from Anywhere Else* (New York: Bantam Books, 1976); *The Beginning Place* (New York: Harper & Row, 1980).

36. Ursula K. Le Guin, *Earthsea Revisioned*, (Cambridge, U. K.: Green Bay Press, 1993), 12; hereafter cited in text as *Revisioned*.

37. George Slusser, "The Earthsea Trilogy," *Ursula K. Le Guin*, ed. Harold Bloom (New York: Chelsea House, 1986), 71.

38. Barbara Bucknall, *Ursula K. Le Guin* (New York: Frederick Ungar, 1981), 37.

39. Philip Pullman, "Carnegie Medal Acceptance Speech." Online posting. 2000. www/randomhouse.com/features/pullman/philippullman/speech.html. Pullman's *His Dark Materials* trilogy, a revision of Milton's epic, parallels Le Guin's work. He might be said to borrow the idea of characterizing a person's death as a shadow figure in his last volume, and Le Guin's latest volume seems to have a few parallels to Pullman's last work. Her portrayal of souls happily escaping a trap of an afterlife by dissipating into the air as they leave their walled Dry Land is very similar to what happens at the end of Pullman's trilogy. Also, Medra, the child-gatherer for the new Roke, is a positive reversal of Mrs. Coulter, the child-snatcher in the Pullman series. Stories about Medra say that he is "a dreaded sorcerer who carried children to his island in the icy north and there sucked their blood" ("Finder," 79); Coulter, in essence, does just that in her own story's icy north.

40. Perry Nodelman, "Pleasure and Genre: Speculations on the Characteristics of Children's Fiction," *Children's Literature* 28 (2000): 8.

41. Perry Nodelman, "Reinventing the Past: Gender in Ursula K. Le Guin's *Tehanu* and the Earthsea 'Trilogy,'" *Children's Literature* 23 (1995): 198.

42. On the series as a whole see Elizabeth Cummins, *Understanding Ursula K. Le Guin* (Columbia: University of South Carolina Press, 1990); on *A Wizard of Earthsea*'s focus on coming-of-age, see Ursula K. Le Guin, "Dreams Must Explain Themselves," *The Language of the Night: Essays on Fantasy and Science Fiction*, ed. Susan Wood and Ursula K. Le Guin, rev. ed. (New York: HarperCollins, 1989), 41–51; on the mixture of Campbell's and Pratt's respective models of gender-specific coming of age in *The Tombs of Atuan* see Gail Sidonie Sobat, "The Night in Her Own Country: The Heroine's Quest for Self in Ursula K. Le Guin's *The Tombs of Atuan*," *Mythlore* 81 (1996): 24–32; on Lebannen's development in *The Farthest Shore* as it mirrors Arthur's ascendancy see Lois Kuznets, "'High Fantasy' in America: A Study of Lloyd Alexander, Ursula Le Guin, and Susan Cooper," *The Lion and the Unicorn* 9 (1985): 19–35.

43. In *The Tombs of Atuan*, Le Guin argues with "some critics" by pointing out "neither can Ged get free without [Tenar]. They are interdependent. I redefined my hero by making him dependent, not autonomous" (*Revisioned*, 9).

44. Peter Hollindale, "The Adolescent Novel of Ideas," *Children's Literature in Education* 26.1 (1995): 91.

45. Roberta Seelinger Trites, *Disturbing the Universe: Power and Repression in Adolescent Literature* (Iowa City: University of Iowa Press, 2000), 10; hereafter cited in text.

46. Trites also notes that "adolescent literature is at heart a romantic literature because so many of us—authors, critics, teachers, teenagers—need to believe in the possibility of adolescent growth" (15). It is the romantic nature of both young adult literature and the epic that is another reason for the easy traffic between these genres in the Earthsea series.

47. Jeanne Murray Walker, "Rites of Passage Today: The Cultural Significance of *A Wizard of Earthsea*," *Mosaic* 13.3–4 (1979): 179; hereafter cited in text.

48. See W. A. Senior, "Cultural Anthropology and Rituals of Exchange in Ursula K. Le Guin's 'Earthsea," *Mosaic* 29.4 (1996), 101–13.

49. Ursula K. Le Guin, "Foreword," *Tales From Earthsea* (New York: Harcourt, Inc., 2001), xiv.

50. Ursula K. Le Guin, "The Shobies' Story," *A Fisherman of the Inland Sea: Science Fiction Stories* (New York: HarperPrism, 1994), 88.

51. Ursula K. Le Guin, "Dancing to Ganam," *A Fisherman of the Inland Sea: Science Fiction Stories* (New York: HarperPrism, 1994), 132; hereafter cited in text as "Ganam."

52. Ursula K. Le Guin, "The Carrier Bag Theory of Fiction," *Dancing at the Edge of the World: Thoughts on Words, Women, Places* (New York: Harper & Row, 1989), 169.

53. Mikhail M. Bakhtin, *Problems of Dostoevsky's Poetics,* trans. ed. Caryl Emerson, (Minneapolis: University of Minnesota Press, 1984), 81; hereafter cited in text.

54. This exists in Le Guin's stories for young children. Consider the catwings being adopted by the children at Overhill Farm in *Catwings* or the children adopted by the adults in *Fish Soup.* These parents and their children become families through mutual consent, not through biology or the institution of marriage.

55. Alder dreams of the kitten whose touch had kept him from the Dry Land in his dreams; Seppel, of Alder's wife, Lily, who tells him "You must send [Alder] to me" (*Wind,* 206–7); Onyx, of being caught in a web on the ship; Lebannen, of people starving in cellars and a child in darkness; Seserakh, of walking on the Dragon's Way, a taboo; Irian, of falling toward rocks; Tehanu, of dark tunnels and roots; Tenar, of crawling on the throne of Nameless ones, also taboo; Azver, of no stars or sunrise; the boys on Roke, of an army of dead that they must fight; and the Masters, of the ship's coming to them on Roke.

56. Lebannen's vision of the child in the darkness calls to mind the story "The Ones Who Walk Away From Omelas" (*The Wind's Twelve Quarters* [New York: Bantam Books, 1976], 251–59) in the sense that the question for those in Omelas is the same as it is for Lebannen: at what price do you allow the child to suffer? The Summoner himself will walk away from the Omelas of his wizardly world when he helps pull the wall to the Dry Land down. He recognizes that pulling the wall is the right thing to do even though it wasn't the right thing to do yesterday. He has always, and continues to do what he understands is right. Le Guin says something of the responsibility to do what you know is right even when "right" changes: "In my lifetime as a writer, I have lived through a revolution, a great and ongoing revolution. When the world turns over, you can't go on thinking upside down. What was innocence is not irresponsibility. Visions must be revisioned" (*Revisioned,* 12). Ged himself cautions Lebannen in *The Farthest Shore:* "Having choice, we must not act without responsibility" (67).

57. Ironically, Medra is saved by this voice from the Dry Land later in the story—something not possible had this taken place after the events of *The Other Wind,* or so it would seem.

58. Ursula K. Le Guin, "Science Fiction and Mrs. Brown." *The Language of the Night: Essays on Fantasy and Science Fiction,* ed. Susan Wood and Ursula K. Le Guin, rev. ed. (New York: HarperCollins, 1989), 106.

59. Even the witch Rose who names Irian has a double vision of sorts: "one always straight, the other cast off" ("Dragonfly," 166).

60. Ursula K. Le Guin, "Buffalo Gals, Won't You Come Out Tonight," *Buffalo Gals and Other Animal Presences* (New York: Penguin, 1990), 17–51.

61. Ursula K. Le Guin, *Planet of Exile* (New York: Ace Books, 1966), 29.

62. Warren G. Rochelle, *Communities of the Heart: The Rhetoric of Myth in the Fiction of Ursula K. Le Guin* (Liverpool, UK: Liverpool University Press, 2001), 52.

63. Here we see the lands west of Kargad not as the center of world, as they say of Havnor and as represented on the map, but as the periphery—further helping the reader see the relativity of the epic portrayal of Havnor. And in *The Tombs of Atuan,* Tenar/Arha describes the Tombs, as she must, as "the center of things" (26). For a Kargish perspective on the tale of Erreth-Akbe, see page 48 of *The Tombs of Atuan;* for the Kargish view of wizards in the first trilogy, see pages 49–51 of *The Tombs of Atuan.*

64. Ursula K. Le Guin, "American SF and the Other," *The Language of the Night: Essays on Fantasy and Science Fictio,* ed. Susan Wood and Ursula K. Le Guin, rev. ed. (New York: HarperCollins, 1989), 95.

65. Ursula K. Le Guin, "Winter's King," *The Wind's Twelve Quarters* (New York: Bantam Books, 1976), 105–6.

66. I say "dragon and person," but while we are given to understand that the two were once one, only women are portrayed as both dragon and person in the current age: The Woman of Kemay, Tehanu, and Irian.

67. Ursula K. Le Guin, "Myth and Archetype in Science Fiction," *The Language of the Night: Essays on Fantasy and Science Fiction,* ed. Susan Wood and Ursula K. Le Guin, rev. ed. (New York: HarperCollins, 1989), 75.
68. Gary Saul Morson and Caryl Emerson, *Mikhail Bakhtin: Creation of a Prosaics* (Stanford, CA: Stanford University Press, 1990), 335.
69. This is another way that Earthsea and Pullman's *His Dark Materials* series intersect. The dragon Yevaud is like the Bear king who embraces human ways only to have his borrowed humanity used against him.
70. Ged tells Lebannen in *The Farthest Shore* that "life rises out of death, death rises out of life; in being opposite they yearn for each other and are forever reborn" (136). This proves ultimately to be true in the series, but it always seemed incongruous with the model of the Dry Land. The Dry Land is unnatural even in the first trilogy because it is outside of Le Guin's usual vision. We might consider this another trap or influence of tradition: she takes a vision of death from western mythology rather than one that fits the system of equilibrium she has created in Earthsea. As Ged helps reestablish equilibrium, the place he has to seal off itself mocks equilibrium.

Chapter 5

1. Bernard Selinger, *Le Guin and Identity in Contemporary Fiction* (Ann Arbor, MI: UMI Research Press, 1988), 128; hereafter cited in text.
2. Ursula K. Le Guin, "Preface to the 1989 Edition," *The Language of the Night: Essays on Fantasy and Science Fiction,* ed. Susan Wood and Ursula K. Le Guin, rev. ed. (New York: HarperCollins, 1989), 4.
3. Ursula K. Le Guin, *Always Coming Home* (New York: Harper & Row, 1985) [henceforth cited as *ACH*]; *Tehanu: The Last Book of Earthsea* (New York: Atheneum, 1990).
4. Ursula K. Le Guin, "Buffalo Gals, Won't You Come Out Tonight," *Buffalo Gals and Other Animal Presences* (New York: Penguin, 1990), 17–51. A direct connection between Earthsea and *Always Coming Home* is the presence of a character named Alder. Alder appears in the latest Earthsea book, *The Other Wind* (New York: Harcourt, Inc., 2001), as a healer. The Alder of *Always Coming Home* is a healer and, like the Ged of *Tehanu* onward, an older man who marries the main character of the novel, a woman who is on her second husband and has a small daughter. Since the names of characters are important to Le Guin, it is reasonable to consider that she sees a connection between the three characters.
5. Ursula K. Le Guin, *Malafrena* (New York: Berkley-Putnam, 1979); *Fisherman of the Inland Sea: Science Fiction Stories* (New York: HarperPrism, 1994).
6. Ursula K. Le Guin, *Wild Oats and Fireweed* (New York: Harper & Row, 1988).
7. Ursula K. Le Guin, "Legends for a New Land," *Mythlore* 56 (1988): 10; hereafter cited in text as 1988a.
8. *Always Coming Home* is Le Guin's first experiment with a fiction compiled by pieces. Following *Always Coming Home* came *Searoad* (New York: HarperCollins, 1991), *Four Ways to Forgiveness* (New York: HarperPrism, 1995), and *Tales From Earthsea* (New York: Harcourt, 2001), each a collection of story pieces—called "story-suites" by Le Guin recently (see chapter seven). They all, interestingly, contain appendices as well.
9. Ursula K. Le Guin, "The Carrier Bag Theory of Fiction," *Dancing at the Edge of the World: Thoughts on Words, Women, Places* (New York: Harper & Row, 1989), 169; hereafter cited in text as 1989b.
10. Richard Erlich, *Coyote's Song: The Teaching Stories of Ursula K. Le Guin* (A Science Fiction Research Association Digital Book, 2001. www.sfra.org/Coyote/CoyoteHome.htm); hereafter cited in text.
11. Donna White, *Dancing With Dragons: Ursula K. Le Guin and the Critics* (Columbia, SC: Camden House, 1999), 95.
12. Mikhail M. Bakhtin, *The Dialogic Imagination: Four Essays*, trans. Michael Holquist and Caryl Emerson, ed. Michael Holquist (Austin: University of Texas Press, 1981), 3; hereafter cited in text.

13. Michael Holquist, "Introduction." *The Dialogic Imagination: Four Essays*, trans. Michael Holquist and Caryl Emerson, ed. Michael Holquist (Austin: University of Texas Press, 1981), xxxi.
14. Gary Saul Morson and Caryl Emerson, *Mikhail Bakhtin: Creation of a Prosaics* (Stanford, CA: Stanford University Press, 1990), 261; hereafter cited in text.
15. Mikhail M. Bakhtin, *Problems of Dostoevsky's Poetics*, trans. Caryl Emerson (Minneapolis: University of Minnesota Press, 1984), 8–9; hereafter cited in text.
16. Warren G. Rochelle, *Communities of the Heart: The Rhetoric of Myth in the Fiction of Ursula K. Le Guin* (Liverpool, UK: Liverpool University Press, 2001), 82; hereafter cited in text.
17. Ursula K. Le Guin, *Very Far Away from Anywhere Else* (New York: Bantam Books, 1976); *The Beginning Place* (New York: Harper & Row, 1980).
18. Ursula K. Le Guin, "The Fisherwoman's Daughter," *Dancing at the Edge of the World: Thoughts on Words, Women, Places* (New York: Harper & Row, 1989), 229.
19. Le Guin has played before with the idea of comparing a stunted masculine adolescent world to a more mature world view. *The Word for World Is Forest* (New York: Berkley Publishing Co., 1976) is such an exercise, as is her story "Pathways to Desire" (*The Compass Rose* [New York: Bantam Books, 1982], 175–207).
20. Despite the fact that Stone Telling's name shifts three different times, I refer to her as "Stone Telling" above and throughout for the reader's convenience and because it is the name of the selection.
21. Oliver Scheiding, "An Archeology of the Future: Postmodern Strategies of Boundary Transitions in Ursula K. Le Guin's *Always Coming Home*," *Amerikastudien* 41.4 (1996): 640; hereafter cited in text.
22. Sarah Jo Webb, "Culture as Spiritual Metaphor in Le Guin's Always Coming Home," *Functions of the Fantastic: Selected Essays from the Thirteenth International Conference on the Fantastic in the Arts* (Westport, CT: Greenwood Press, 1995), 156.
23. In the third essay in this volume I would place this under the threshold chronotope of the dream journey—actually not the most prevalent of Le Guin's journey patterns.
24. There is a collection of articles devoted to studying the role of home in children's literature. See my own "Home is a Matter of Blood, Time, and Genre: Essentialism in Burnett and McKinley." *ARIEL: A Review of International English Literature* 28.1 (1997): 53–67; Joel D. Chaston, "If I Ever Go Looking for My Heart's Desire: 'Home' in Baum's 'Oz' Books," *The Lion & the Unicorn* 18.2 (December 1994): 209–19; Christopher Clausen, "Home and Away in Children's Fiction," *Children's Literature* 10 (1982): 141–152; Jon Stott, "Running Away to Home—A Story Pattern in Children's Literature," *Language Arts* 55.4 (April 1978): 473–477; Jon Stott and Christine Doyle Francis, "'Home' and 'Not Home' in Children's Stories: Getting There—and Being Worth It," *Children's Literature in Education* 24.3 (1993): 223–233; Lucy Waddey, "Home in Children's Fiction: Three Patterns," *Children's Literature Association Quarterly* 8.1 (Spring 1983): 13–15; Virginia Wolf, "From the Myth to the Wake of Home: Literary Houses," *Children's Literature* 18 (1990): 53–67.
25. Ursula K. Le Guin, "A Non-Euclidean View of California as a Cold Place to Be," *Dancing at the Edge of the World: Thoughts on Words, Women, Places* (New York: Harper & Row, 1989), 82.
26. Carol Franko, "Self-Conscious Narration as the Complex Representation of Hope in Le Guin's *Always Coming Home*," *Mythlore* 57 (1989): 58; hereafter cited in text.
27. Margaret Hostetler, "'Was It I That Killed the Babies?', Children as Disruptive Signifiers in Ursula K. Le Guin's *Always Coming Home*," *Extrapolation* 42.1 (2001): 32.
28. This is an interesting image that predates Le Guin's children's picture book *A Ride on the Red Mare's Back* (New York: Orchard Books, 1992) in which an older sister seeks and finds, with the help of her magical animal friend the Red Mare, her younger brother who has been captured by trolls.
29. Jean W. Ross, "Interview with Jean Ross," *Contemporary Authors* 32 (1999): 253.
30. Elizabeth Cummins, *Understanding Ursula K. Le Guin* (Columbia, SC: University of South Carolina Press, 1990), 1182; hereafter cited in text as 1990b.

31. Other than on the title page, reference to this Geomancer is in "Pandora No Longer Worrying," which reads: "And behold the Geomancer, whose name measures the Valley, who shaped the hills and helped me sink half California, who went on the Salt Journey, caught the Train, and walked every step with Grey Bull . . . " (*ACH*, 544). Webster's Ninth New Collegiate Dictionary defines "geomancy" as "divination by means of figures or lines or geographic features." Le Guin told me that Hersh helped her envision the landscape by building a relief map of Northern California out of plaster and then changing it the way she had changed the landscape, digging out the central valley so that it would re-flood. He gave her photographs of that, materials Le Guin used to draw her maps in the book.

32. "Towards an Archaeology of the Future" follows "First Note" and the opening poem "Quail Song," in which the voice of the author continues. In it the narrator tells us, "I was studying yet once more the contours of my map of the region . . . " (*ACH*, 3). It is "her" map because it belongs to her, but also because she drew it. This is one of the ways the author connects herself with the inhabitants of the Valley, with the children who often drew maps (*ACH*, 480), with "the people of the Valley [who] drew maps—mostly of the Valley. They evidently enjoyed laying out and looking at the spatial relationships of places and objects they knew well. The better they know them, the better they liked to draw and map them" (*ACH*, 480). Le Guin might well be speaking of the cartographer of Earthsea here.

33. Jim Jose, "Reflections on the Politics of Le Guin's Narrative Shifts," *Science-Fiction Studies* 18 (1991): 190.

34. Naomi Jacobs, "Beyond Stasis and Symmetry: Lessing, Le Guin, and the Remodeling of Utopia," *Extrapolation* 29.1 (1988): 43; hereafter cited in text.

35. Kristine J. Anderson, "Places Where a Woman Could Talk: Ursula K. Le Guin and the Feminist Linguistic Utopia," *Women and Language* 15.1 (Spring 1992): 9.

36. W. H. Auden's poem "After Reading a Child's Guide to Modern Physics" (*W. H. Auden: Selected Poems*, ed. Edward Mendelson [New York: Vintage Books, 1979], 246-48) comes to mind here. The fourth stanza captures our first childhood encounter with the conflict between the comforting Newtonian myth of the linearity of the universe and the real sense of an expanding, non-linear existence: "Our eyes prefer to suppose / That a habitable place/ Has a geocentric view, / That architects enclose / A quiet Euclidean space: / Exploded myth—but who / Would feel at home astraddle / An ever expanding saddle?"

37. Heinz Tschachler, "Ursula K. Le Guin: Ethnic Fantasy as Political Parable," *Literature, Culture and Ethnicity: Studies on Medieval, Renaissance and Modern Literatures*, ed. Jurak Mirko (Ljubljana, Slovenija: Uene Delavnice, 1992), 100; hereafter cited in text.

38. In her short story "Mazes," Le Guin tells the tale of an alien caught in a scientist's rat maze. The tale is told by the alien just before he dies of starvation, and he starves entirely because the scientist doesn't understand either his biological needs or his dance language. The scientist doesn't try to understand the alien on its terms, only his own—as an old wizard of Earthsea might. The alien concludes by saying "And now I have to die. No doubt it will come in to watch me die; but it will not understand the dance I dance in dying" ("Mazes," *The Compass Rose* [New York: Bantam Books, 1982], 176). In *Always Coming Home*, Le Guin gets the scientist to step into the maze and dance.

39. Robyn McCallum, *Ideologies of Identity in Adolescent Fiction: The Dialogic Construction of Subjectivity* (New York: Garland, 1999), 27; hereafter cited in text.

40. Elizabeth Cummins, "The Land-Lady's Homebirth: Revisiting Ursula K. Le Guin's Worlds," *Science Fiction Studies* 17.2 (1990): 161.

41. Sov in Le Guin's "Coming of Age in Karhide" has a similar feeling: "As I had in the Fastness, I felt the familiar reassurance of being part of something immensely older and larger than myself, even if it was strange and new to me. I must entrust myself to it and be what it makes me" ("Coming of Age in Karhide," *New Legends*, ed. Greg Bear and Martin H. Greenberg [New York: Tor, 1995], 102. [subsequently collected in *The Birthday of the World and Other Stories* (New York: HarperCollins Publishers, 2002), 1–22]).

42. Michael Holquist, *Dialogism: Bakhtin and his World* (London and New York: Routledge, 1990), 69; hereafter cited in text as 1990.

43. We should take this opening piece as we do the first few paragraphs of *The Lathe of Heaven* (New York: Charles Scribner's Sons, 1971) in which the condition of the main character, George Orr, is offered to us through the metaphor of the jellyfish who is caught up in the "violence and power of the whole ocean, to which it has entrusted its being, its going, its will" (1). They each serve as metaphors for the books they begin.
44. We might extend this to women as well. In "Another Story," the main character, Hideo, makes an observation about his mother, and all women, that has a lot to do with what it takes to live with the Kesh or read *Always Coming Home*: "'Hideo,' said my mother, in the terrifying way women have of passing without interval from one subject to another because they have them all present in their mind at once, 'you haven't found any kind of relationship?'" (Ursula K. Le Guin, "Another Story," *A Fisherman of the Inland Sea: Science Fiction Stories* (New York: Harper Prism, 1994), 170). In this way we could say that women, artists, children, and young adults all "churten" by nature.

And there is a place in another Le Guin tale where comfort is taken simultaneously with pain. In "Coming of Age in Karhide," Sov says during a walk with a childhood friend that they "exchanged and compared symptoms [or puberty] for a mile or so. It was a relief to talk about it, to find company in misery, but it was also frightening to hear our misery confirmed by the other" (96).

Lastly, George Orr's experience in *The Lathe of Heaven* parallels the child-like experiences of reading a non-linear text: "There were by now so many different memories, so many skeins of life experiences, jostling in his head, that he scarcely tried to remember anything. He took it as it came. He was living almost like a young child, among actualities only. He was surprised by nothing, and by everything" (125).

Chapter 6

1. Jill Paton Walsh, "The Writers in the Writer: A Reply to Hugh Crago," *Signal* 40 (1983) 4; Katherine Paterson, *Gates of Excellence: On Reading and Writing Books for Children* (New York: Elsevier/Nelson Books, 1981) 47, 50; P. L. Travers, "On Not Writing for Children," *Reflections on Children,* ed. Francelia Butler and Richard Rotert (Library Professional Publications, 1984) 63; Mollie Hunter, *Talent is Not Enough* (New York: Harper & Row, 1976), 12; Barbara Bottner, "William Steig: The Two Legacies," *The Lion and the Unicorn* 2.1 (1978): 4; hereafter cited in text.
2. Barbara Wall, *The Narrator's Voice: The Dilemma of Children's Fiction* (New York: St. Martin's Press, 1991), 30; hereafter cited in text.
3. Peter Hollindale, *Signs of Childness in Children's Books* (Stroud, Glos: The Thimble Press, 1997), 31.
4. For a thorough, clear, and in all ways, useful discussion of the narrative relationships between authors (implied and real) and audiences (implied and real) in children's literature, see Barbara Wall's *The Narrator's Voice.*
5. Aidan Chambers warns us to "be wary of using as evidence in criticism what an author says about himself, publicly or privately: a caution we have not sufficiently taken to heart in talking about children's books" (Aidan Chambers, "The Reader in the Book," *Children's Literature: The Development of Criticism,* ed. Peter Hunt [New York: Routledge, 1990], 98). While this is good advice, authorial commentary gives us insight into the different ways authors think about their relationship(s) to their texts, audiences, and genre(s). Finding paradox or contradiction in the ways any one author talks about audiences and books can serve our understanding of how all writers continue to construct and complicate the notion of "childhood," as well as "children's literature."
6. C. S. Lewis, "On Three Ways of Writing for Children," *The Riverside Anthology of Children's Literature,* ed. Judith Saltman, 6th ed. (Boston, MA: Houghton Mifflin Company, 1985) 1075; hereafter cited in text.
7. Zohar Shavit, *The Poetics of Children's Literature* (Athens: University of Georgia Press, 1986), 66.

8. Writing "to the child" can also be dangerously close to writing "for the child"—the latter being potentially a less dialogic act and more a monologic "gift" of a text. Children's literature writers and critics, however, do not make a careful distinction between "for" and "to" in this sense. Walsh (1983, 4), Paterson (47, 50), Travers (63), Hunter (12), and Steig (Bottner, 4) directly point to themselves as at least a partial audience—the self-as-child—in their discourse on the creative process in children's literature; this phenomenon might encourage critics to pay closer attention to the use of "to" and "for" in the future.

9. Peter Hunt, "Necessary Misreadings: Directions in Narrative Theory for Children's Literature," *Studies in the Literary Imagination* 18 (1985): 108. This article is one of several useful treatments of narrative theory in children's literature to be found in "Narrative Theory in Children's Literature," ed. Hugh T. Keenan. *Studies in the Literary Imagination* 18 (Fall 1985); a more recent journal issue devoted to narrative theory and children's literature is *Children's Literature Association Quarterly* 28.1 (2003).

10. Roderick McGillis cites Hunt in support of his own audience-based theory of narrative (Roderick McGillis, "The Embrace: Narrative Voice and Children's Books," *Canadian Children's Literature* 63 [1991]: 26), and Margaret Higonnet claims that her own theory of narrative fragments "is itself fragmentary if it fails to address the question of the reader" (Margaret Higonnet, "Narrative Fractures and Fragments," *Children's Literature* 15 [1987]: 51). Maria Nikolajeva moves from both audience and genre in her recent book, *From Mythic to Linear: Time in Children's Literature.* She employs the chronotope as her critical lens in order to understand children's literature. She says that it allows her to "disregard, among other things, the traditional, and in my view rather obsolete, division of children's novels into realism and fantasy" (Maria Nikolajeva, *From Mythic to Linear: Time in Children's Literature* [Lanham, MD: The Children's Literature Association & Scarecrow Press, Inc., 2000], 3). I take a similar approach in the third essay of this volume and ask that we think of Le Guin's work across age-based genre in terms of the chronotopes she employs. However, genre is still a huge influence on authors, readers, and critics alike. Both structural approaches are clearly useful.

11. Jacqueline Rose, *The Case of Peter Pan, or The Impossibility of Children's Fiction* (Philadelphia: University of Pennsylvania Press, 1993), 10, 70; hereafter cited in text.

12. Roni Natov and Geraldine DeLuca, "An Interview with John Gardner," *The Lion and the Unicorn* 2.1 (1978): 117.

13. Claudia Mills, "The Ethics of the Author/Audience Relationship in Children's Fiction," *Children's Literature Association Quarterly* 22.4 (1997–1998): 181.

14. See John Goldthwaite, *The Natural History of Make-Believe; A Guide to the Principal Works of Britain, Europe, and North America* (Oxford: Oxford University Press, 1996) for a recent discussion of Lewis's questionable literary morality.

15. Jill Paton Walsh, "The Writer's Responsibility," *Children's Literature in Education* 10 (1973): 32; hereafter cited in text. Wayne Booth indirectly points to someone like Walsh when he observes that "most who have rejected ethical criticism . . . [claim] that authors must not be burdened with worries about the reader's ultimate welfare if they are to serve their art properly" (Wayne C. Booth, *The Company We Keep: An Ethics of Fiction* [Los Angeles: University of California Press, 1988] 127; hereafter cited in text).

16. Sandra L. Beckett, "Crosswriting Child and Adult in France: Children's Fiction for Adults? Adult Fiction for Children? Fiction for All Ages?" *Transcending Boundaries: Writing for a Dual Audience of Children and Adults,* ed. Sandra Beckett (New York: Garland Publishing, Inc., 1999), 32.

17. Mitzi Myers, "Canonical 'Orphans' and Critical *Ennui*: Rereading Edgeworth's Cross-Writing," *Children's Literature* 25 (1997), 120.

18. Susan Wood, "Introduction," *The Language of the Night: Essays on Fantasy and Science Fiction,* ed. Susan Wood, rev. ed. Ursula K. Le Guin (New York: HarperCollins, 1989), 8.

19. Larry McCaffery and Sinda Gregory, "An Interview with Ursula Le Guin," *The Missouri Review* 7 (1984): 82; hereafter cited in text.

20. Ursula K. Le Guin, "Introduction," *A Fisherman of the Inland Sea: Science Fiction Stories* (New York: HarperPrism, 1994), 4–5.

21. Ursula K. Le Guin, "The Child and the Shadow," *The Language of the Night: Essays on Fantasy and Science Fiction,* ed. Susan Wood and Ursula K. Le Guin, rev. ed. (New York: HarperCollins, 1989), 65; hereafter cited in text as 1989c.

22. Ursula K. Le Guin, "Introduction to *City of Illusions,*" *The Language of the Night: Essays on Fantasy and Science Fiction,* ed. Susan Wood and Ursula K. Le Guin, rev. ed. (New York: HarperCollins, 1989), 141.

23. Ursula K. Le Guin, "Introduction to *The Word for World Is Forest,*" *The Language of the Night: Essays on Fantasy and Science Fiction,* ed. Susan Wood and Ursula K. Le Guin, rev. ed. (New York: HarperCollins, 1989), 146.

24. Letter to the author. 26 November 1995.

25. William Walsh, "I Am A Woman Writer: I Am A Western Writer: An Interview with Ursula Le Guin," *The Kenyon Review* 17.3–4 (1995): 203.

26. Ursula K. Le Guin, *Steering the Craft* (Portland, OR: The Eighth Mountain Press, 1998), x.

27. Ursula K. Le Guin, "Where Do You Get Your Ideas From?" *Dancing at the Edge of the World: Thoughts on Words, Women, Places* (New York: Harper & Row, 1989), 197.

28. Ursula K. Le Guin, "Dreams Must Explain Themselves," *The Language of the Night: Essays on Fantasy and Science Fiction,* ed. Susan Wood and Ursula K. Le Guin, rev. ed. (New York: HarperCollins, 1989), 42; hereafter cited in text as 1989f.

29. Ursula K. Le Guin, *Earthsea Revisioned* (Cambridge, U. K.: Green Bay Press, 1993), 10; hereafter cited in text.

30. Victor Reinking and David Willingham, "Interview: A Conversation with Ursula K. Le Guin," *Paradoxa: Studies in World Literary Genres* 1.1 (1995), 57.

31. Here consider, for instance, Ursula K. Le Guin's *A Visit from Dr. Katz* (illus. Ann Barrow [New York: Atheneum, 1988]). It is only in the juxtaposition of the written and visual texts that the reader can really understand the imaginative game being played by mother and daughter in the story. Although the pictures reveal one clear, realistic setting, the words describe a slightly different realistic (though slightly odd) set of circumstances. In short, the "Dr. Katz" described in the text is really revealed by the pictures to be Marianne's two cats who have made a visit to her sick bed. Although no division is absolute, especially in Le Guin's work, this strong generic trend in her body of works is striking.

32. Peter Hollindale, "Ideology in Children's Literature," *Signal* 55 (1988): 9.

33. Ursula K. Le Guin, "National Book Award Acceptance Speech," *The Language of the Night: Essays on Fantasy and Science Fiction,* ed. Susan Wood and Ursula K. Le Guin, rev. ed. (New York: HarperCollins, 1989), 52.

34. Ursula K. Le Guin, "Do-It-Yourself Cosmology," *The Language of the Night: Essays on Fantasy and Science Fiction,* ed. Susan Wood and Ursula K. Le Guin, rev. ed. (New York: HarperCollins, 1989), 122.

35. Ursula K. Le Guin, "From Elfland to Poughkeepsie," *The Language of the Night: Essays on Fantasy and Science Fiction,* ed. Susan Wood and Ursula K. Le Guin, rev. ed. (New York: HarperCollins, 1989), 79.

36. Ursula K. Le Guin, "A Citizen of Mondath," *The Language of the Night: Essays on Fantasy and Science Fiction,* ed. Susan Wood and Ursula K. Le Guin, rev. ed. (New York: HarperCollins, 1989), 25.

37. Ursula K. Le Guin's official website (www.ursulakleguin.com/Biblio2001.html) lists *Gifts,* due out in September of 2004, with *The Beginning Place* as her other fantasy novel. Harcourt lists the book under its teen/young adult titles. It would seem, then, that the book is a YA fantasy novel, though it isn't yet available for review.

38. Gerard Genette, *The Architext: An Introduction,* trans. Jane E. Lewin (Berkeley: University of California Press, 1992), 65.

39. See chapter seven on Le Guin's thoughts on poetry for children.

40. Maureen Thum, "Misreading the Cross-Writer: The Case of Wilhelm Hauff's *Dwarf Long Nose,*" *Children's Literature* 25 (1997): 3.

41. Brian Attebery, *The Fantasy Tradition in American Literature: From Irving to Le Guin* (Bloomington: Indiana University Press, 1980), 165; hereafter cited in text.

42. David Galef, "Crossing Over: Authors Who Write Both Children's and Adults' Fiction," *Children's Literature Association Quarterly* 20.1 (1995): 29.

43. Perry Nodelman, *The Pleasures of Children's Literature,* 2d ed. (New York: Longman, 1995), 145.
44. Ursula K. Le Guin, *The Dispossessed* (New York: Avon, 1974); *Always Coming Home* (New York: Harper & Row, 1985); *A Ride on the Red Mare's Back* (New York: Orchard Books, 1992).
45. Ursula K. Le Guin, *A Wizard of Earthsea* (New York: Bantam, 1975 [orig. publ. 1968]).
46. Maria Nikolajeva, *Children's Literature Comes of Age: Toward a New Aesthetic* (New York and London: Garland Publishing, Inc., 1996): 7.
47. Ursula K. Le Guin, "The New Atlantis," *The Compass Rose* (New York: Bantam Books, 1982), 12–40; "Vaster than Empires and More Slow," *The Wind's Twelve Quarters* (New York: Bantam Books, 1976), 166–199; "Mazes," *The Compass Rose* (New York: Bantam Books, 1982), 169–174.
48. Tzvetan Todorov, *Genres in Discourse* (Cambridge: Cambridge University Press, 1990), 13.
49. Adena Rosmarin, *The Power of Genre* (Minneapolis: University of Minnesota Press, 1985), 7.
50. Robert Scholes, *Textual Power: Literary Theory and the Teaching of English* (New Haven, CT: Yale University Press, 1985), 117.
51. Francine Prose, "Herself a Multitude," review of *Unlocking the Air,* by Ursula K. Le Guin *The New York Times Book Review,* 3 March 1996, p. 10.
52. U. C. Knoepflmacher and Mitzi Myers, "'Cross-Writing' and the Reconceptualization of Children's Literary Studies," *Children's Literature* 25 (1997): xi; hereafter cited in text.

Chapter 7

1. Patricia MacLachlan, *Sarah, Plain and Tall* (New York: HarperCollins, 1985).
2. This is possibly a reference to Sandra Lindow, "Trauma and Recovery in Ursula K. Le Guin's *Wonderful Alexander*: Animal as Guide through the Inner Space of the Unconscious," *Foundation: The International Review of Science Fiction,* 70 (Summer 1997): 32–38.
3. Karl Kroeber, *Retelling/Rereading: The Fate of Storytelling in Modern Times* (Camden: Rutgers University Press, 1992).
4. Tom Shippey, *J. R. R. Tolkien* (New York: Houghton Mifflin Co., 2002).
5. Ursula K. Le Guin had already read a draft of the essay in this volume on *Always Coming Home* before this interview.
6. Robert Harvey, *Liberators: Latin America's Struggle for Independence, 1810–1830* (Woodstock: Overlook Press, 2000).
7. The Kesh novel is titled *Dangerous People* by Wordriver and "is a pretty good example of a Valley novel" (Ursula K. Le Guin, *Always Coming Home* [New York: Harper & Row, 1985], 337). Only chapter two is printed in *Always Coming Home.* Presumably, the second chapter of the novel was chosen because it was "exemplary of its kind" (337).
8. Here Le Guin alludes to my article "Purposeful Movement Among People and Places: The Sense of Home in Ursula K. Le Guin's Fiction for Children and Adults," *Extrapolation* 41.4 (2000): 338–350.

Bibliography

Primary and Secondary Works by Ursula K. Le Guin

Le Guin, Ursula K. *The Adventures of Cobbler's Rune*. New Castle, VA: Cheap Street, 1982.

_____. "All Happy Families." *Michigan Quarterly Review* 36.1 (1997): 43–46.

_____. *The Altered I: An Encounter with Science Fiction*. Carlton, Victoria, Austraila: Nostrilia Press, 1976.

_____. *Always Coming Home*. New York: Harper & Row, 1985.

_____. "American SF and the Other." In *The Language of the Night: Essays on Fantasy and Science Fiction*. Rev. ed. Edited by Susan Wood and Ursula K. Le Guin. New York, NY: HarperCollins, 1989: 93–96.

_____. "Another Story." *A Fisherman of the Inland Sea: Science Fiction Stories*. New York: HarperPrism, 1994: 147–91.

_____. "The Barrow." *Orsinian Tales*. New York: HarperCollins, 1976: 7–17.

_____. *The Beginning Place*. New York: Harper and Row, 1980.

_____. "Betrayals." *Four Ways to Forgiveness*. New York: HarperPrism, 1995: 1–34.

_____. "Bill Weisler." *Searoad*. HarperCollins, 1991: 59–72.

_____. "The Bones of the Earth." *Tales from Earthsea*. New York: Harcourt, Inc., 2001: 143–62.

_____. "Brothers and Sisters." *Orsinian Tales*. New York: HarperCollins, 1976: 85–127.

_____. *Buffalo Gals and Other Animal Presences*. New York: Penguin, 1990.

_____. "Buffalo Gals, Won't You Come Out Tonight." *Buffalo Gals and Other Animal Presences*. New York: Penguin, 1990: 17–51.

_____. "The Carrier Bag Theory of Fiction." *Dancing at the Edge of the World: Thoughts on Words, Women, Places*. New York: Harper & Row, Inc., 1989: 165–70.

_____. *Changing Planes*. New York: Harcourt, Inc., 2003.

_____. "The Child and the Shadow." In *The Language of the Night: Essays on Fantasy and Science Fiction*. Rev. ed. Edited by Susan Wood and Ursula K. Le Guin. New York, NY: HarperCollins, 1989: 54–67.

_____. "A Child Bride." *Unlocking the Air and Other Stories*. New York: HarperCollins, 1996: 141–43.

_____. "A Citizen of Mondath." In *The Language of the Night: Essays on Fantasy and Science Fiction*. Rev. ed. Edited by Susan Wood and Ursula K. Le Guin. New York: HarperCollins, 1989: 20–25.

_____. *City of Illusions*. New York: Ace Books, 1967.

_____. "Coming of Age in Karhide." *New Legends*. Edited by Greg Bear and Martin H. Greenberg. New York: Tor, 1995: 89–105. [Subsequently collected in *The Birthday of the World and Other Stories*. New York: HarperCollins, 2002: 1–22.]

_____. "Conversations at Night." *Orsinian Tales*. New York: HarperCollins, 1976: 37–72.

_____. "Crosswords." *Searoad*. New York: HarperCollins , 1991: 111–18.

_____. *Dancing at the Edge of the World: Thoughts on Words, Women, Places*. New York: Harper & Row, Inc., 1989.

_____. "Dancing to Ganam." *A Fisherman of the Inland Sea: Science Fiction Stories*. New York: HarperPrism, 1994: 107–45.

_____. "Darkrose and Diamond." *Tales from Earthsea*. New York: Harcourt, Inc., 2001: 107–42.

_____. "A Description of Earthsea." *Tales from Earthsea*. New York: Harcourt, Inc., 2001: 267–96.

_____. "The Direction of the Road." *The Wind's Twelve Quarters*. New York: Bantam Books, 1976: 244–50.

_____. *The Dispossessed*. New York: Avon, 1974.

_____. "Do-It-Yourself Cosmology." In *The Language of the Night: Essays on Fantasy and Science Fiction*. Rev. ed. Edited by Susan Wood and Ursula K. Le Guin. New York: HarperCollins, 1989: 118–22.

_____. "Dragonfly." *Tales from Earthsea*. New York: Harcourt, Inc., 2001: 197–265.

_____. "Dreams Must Explain Themselves." In *The Language of the Night: Essays on Fantasy and Science Fiction*. Rev. Ed. Edited by Susan Wood and Ursula K. Le Guin. New York: HarperCollins, 1989: 41–51.

_____. *Earthsea Revisioned*. Cambridge, U.K.: Green Bay Press, 1993.

_____. "Ether, OR." *Unlocking the Air and Other Stories*. New York: HarperCollins, 1996: 95–123.

_____. "The Eye Altering." *The Compass Rose*. New York: Bantam Books, 1982: 154–68.

_____. *The Eye of the Heron*. New York: Harper & Row, 1983 [originally published by Delacort Press, 1978].

_____. "Foreword." *The Birthday of the World and Other Stories*. New York: HarperCollins Publishers, 2002: vi-xiii.

_____. "Forgiveness Day." *Four Ways to Forgiveness*. New York: HarperPrism, 1995: 35–92.

_____. "Geezers." *Searoad*. New York: HarperCollins, 1991: 37–46.

_____. *Gifts*. New York: Harcourt, Inc., 2004.

_____. *The Farthest Shore*. New York: Bantam, 1975 [orig. publ. 1972].

_____. "The Finder." *Tales from Earthsea*. New York: Harcourt, Inc., 2001: 1–106.

_____. "The Fisherwoman's Daughter." *Dancing at the Edge of the World: Thoughts on Words, Women, Places*. New York: Harper & Row Publisher, Inc., 1989: 212–37.

_____. "Foreword." *Tales From Earthsea*. New York: Harcourt, Inc., 2001: xi-xv.

_____. "The Fountains." *Orsinian Tales*. New York: HarperCollins, 1976: 1–5.

_____. "From Elfland to Poughkeepsie." In *The Language of the Night: Essays on Fantasy and Science Fiction*. Rev. ed. Edited by Susan Wood and Ursula K. Le Guin. New York: HarperCollins, 1989: 78–92.

_____. "Hand, Cup, Shell." *Searoad*. New York: HarperCollins, 1991: 15–36.

_____. "Hernes." *Searoad*. New York: HarperCollins , 1991: 123–93.

_____. "Horse Camp." *Buffalo Gals and Other Animal Presences*. New York: Penguin, 1990: 143–47.

_____. "The House." *Orsinian Tales*. New York: HarperCollins, 1976: 175–87.

_____. "Ile Forest." *Orsinian Tales*. New York: Harper Collins, 1976: 19–35.

_____. "In and Out." *Searoad*. New York: HarperCollins, 1991: 47–58.

_____. Introduction to *Buffalo Gals and Other Animal Presences*. New York: Penguin, 1990: 9–13.

_____. Introduction to *A Fisherman of the Inland Sea: Science Fiction Stories*. New York: HarperPrism, 1994: 1–11.

_____. "Introduction to *City of Illusions*." In *The Language of the Night: Essays on Fantasy and Science Fiction*. Rev. ed. Edited by Susan Wood and Ursula K. Le Guin. New York: HarperCollins, 1989: 140–43.

_____. "Introduction to *Rocannon's World*." In *The Language of the Night: Essays on Fantasy and Science Fiction*. Rev. ed. Edited by Susan Wood and Ursula K. Le Guin. New York: HarperCollins, 1989: 129–33.

_____. "Introduction to *The Word for World Is Forest*." In *The Language of the Night: Essays on Fantasy and Science Fiction*. Rev. ed. Edited by Susan Wood and Ursula K. Le Guin. New York: HarperCollins, 1989: 144–49.

_____. *The Lathe of Heaven*. New York: Charles Scribner's Sons, 1971.

_____. "Legends for a New Land." *Mythlore* 56 (1988): 4–10.

_____. *The Left Hand of Darkness*. New York: Ace Books, 1969.

_____. *Malafrena*. New York: Berkley-Putnam, 1979.

_____. "A Man of the People." *Four Ways to Forgiveness*. New York: HarperPrism, 1995: 93–144.

_____. "May's Lion." *Buffalo Gals and Other Animal Presences*. New York: Penguin, 1990: 179–88.

_____. "Mazes." *The Compass Rose*. New York: Bantam Books, 1982: 169–74.

_____. "The Mind Is Still." *Hard Words and Other Poems*. New York: Harper & Row, 1981: 9.

_____. "Myth and Archetype in Science Fiction." In *The Language of the Night: Essays on Fantasy and Science Fiction.* Rev. ed. Edited by Susan Wood and Ursula K. Le Guin. New York: HarperCollins, 1989: 68–77.

_____. "National Book Award Acceptance Speech." In *The Language of the Night: Essays on Fantasy and Science Fiction.* Rev. ed. Edited by Susan Wood and Ursula K. Le Guin. New York: HarperCollins, 1989: 52–3.

_____. "The New Atlantis." *The Compass Rose.* New York: Bantam Books, 1982: 12–40.

_____. "A Non-Euclidean View of California as a Cold Place to Be." *Dancing at the Edge of the World: Thoughts on Words, Women, Places.* New York: Harper & Row, Inc., 1989: 80–100.

_____. "Old Music and the Slave Women." *Far Horizons.* Edited by Robert Silverberg. New York: Avon Books, 1999: 7–52. [Subsequently collected in *The Birthday of the World and Other Stories.* New York: HarperCollins, 2002: 153–212.]

_____. "The Ones Who Walk Away from Omelas." *The Wind's Twelve Quarters.* New York: Bantam Books, 1976: 251–59.

_____. "On the High Marsh." *Tales From Earthsea.* New York: Harcourt, Inc., 2001: 163–96.

_____. *The Other Wind.* New York: Harcourt, Inc., 2001.

_____. "Pathways of Desire." *The Compass Rose.* New York: Bantam Books, 1982: 175–207.

_____. *Planet of Exile.* New York: Ace Books, 1966.

_____. "Preface to the 1989 Edition." In *The Language of the Night: Essays on Fantasy and Science Fiction.* Rev. ed. Edited by Susan Wood and Ursula K. Le Guin. New York: HarperCollins, 1989: 1–5.

_____. "Quoits." *Searoad.* New York: HarperCollins, 1991: 99–110.

_____. "The Road East." *Orsinian Tales.* New York: HarperCollins, 1976: 73–84.

_____. *Rocannon's World.* New York: Ace Books, 1966.

_____. "The Rule of Names." *The Wind's Twelve Quarters.* New York: Bantam Books, 1976: 73–84.

_____. "Science Fiction and Mrs. Brown." In *The Language of the Night: Essays on Fantasy and Science Fiction.* Rev. ed. Edited by Susan Wood and Ursula K. Le Guin. Rev. ed. New York: HarperCollins, 1989: 97–117.

_____. "Semley's Necklace." *The Wind's Twelve Quarters.* New York: Bantam Books, 1976: 1–22.

_____. "She Unnames Them." *Buffalo Gals and Other Animal Presences.* New York: Penguin, 1990: 194–96.

_____. "The Ship Ahoy." *Searoad.* New York: HarperCollins, 1991: 3–13.

_____. "The Shobies' Story." *A Fisherman of the Inland Sea: Science Fiction Stories.* New York: HarperPrism, 1994: 75–106.

_____. "Sleepwalkers." *Searoad.* New York: HarperCollins , 1991: 89–98.

_____. "Some Thoughts on Narrative." *Dancing at the Edge of the World: Thoughts on Words, Women, Places.* New York: Harper & Row, Inc., 1989: 37–45.

_____. *Steering the Craft.* Portland, OR: The Eighth Mountain Press, 1998.

_____. "Tabby Lorenzo." *Buffalo Gals and Other Animal Presences.* New York: Penguin, 1990: 152.

_____. *Tehanu: The Last Book of Earthsea.* New York: Atheneum, 1990.

_____. *The Telling.* New York: Harcourt, Inc., 2000.

_____. "Texts." *Searoad.* New York: HarperCollins, 1991: 119–22.

_____. "Text, Silence, Performance." *Dancing at the Edge of the World: Thoughts on Words, Women, Places.* New York: Harper & Row, Inc., 1989: 179–87.

_____. *The Tombs of Atuan.* New York: Bantam, 1975 [orig. publ. 1970].

_____. "A Trip to the Head." *The Wind's Twelve Quarters.* New York: Bantam Books, 1976: 159–65.

_____. "True Love." *Searoad.* New York: HarperCollins, 1991: 73–88.

_____. "Unlocking the Air." *Unlocking the Air and Other Stories.* New York: HarperCollins, 1996: 125–39.

_____. "Vaster than Empires and More Slow." *The Wind's Twelve Quarters.* New York: Bantam Books, 1976: 166–99.

_____. *Very Far Away from Anywhere Else.* New York: Bantam Books, 1976.

_____. "A Week in the Country." *Orsinian Tales*. New York: HarperCollins, 1976: 129–54.

_____. "Where Do You Get Your Ideas From?" *Dancing at the Edge of the World: Thoughts on Words, Women, Places*. New York: Harper & Row, Inc., 1989: 192–200.

_____. "The Wife's Story." *Buffalo Gals and Other Animal Presences*. New York: Penguin, 1990: 67–71.

_____. *Wild Oats and Fireweed*. New York: Harper & Row, 1988.

_____. "Winter's King." *The Wind's Twelve Quarters*. New York: Bantam Books, 1976: 85–108.

_____. *A Wizard of Earthsea*. New York: Bantam, 1975 [orig. publ. 1968].

_____. "A Woman's Liberation." *Four Ways to Forgiveness*. New York: HarperPrism, 1995: 145–208.

_____. *The Word for World Is Forest*. New York: Berkley Publishing Co., 1976.

_____. "The Word of Unbinding." *The Wind's Twelve Quarters*. New York: Bantam Books, 1976: 65–72.

Le Guin, Ursula K., and Alicia Austin, illus. *Solomon Leviathan's Nine Hundred and Thirty-First Trip Around the World*. New York; Philomel Books, 1983.

Le Guin, Ursula K., and Ann Barrow, illus. *A Visit from Dr. Katz*. New York: Atheneum, 1988.

Le Guin, Ursula K., and Susan Seddon Boulet, illus. *Buffalo Gals Won't You Come Out Tonight*. San Francisco: Pomegranate Artbooks, 1994.

Le Guin, Ursula K., and James Brunsman, illus. *Leese Webster*. New York: Atheneum, 1979.

Le Guin, Ursula K., and Julie Downing, illus. *A Ride on the Red Mare's Back*. New York: Orchard Books, 1992.

_____. *Tom Mouse*. Brookfield, CT: Roaring Brook Press, 2002.

Le Guin, Ursula K., and Laura Marshall, illus. *Fire and Stone*. New York: Atheneum, 1989.

Le Guin, Ursula K., and S. D. Schindler, illus. *Catwings*. New York: Scholastic, 1990.

_____. *Catwings Return*. New York: Scholastic, 1991.

_____. *Wonderful Alexander and the Catwings*. New York: Orchard Books, 1994.

_____. *Jane on Her Own*. New York: Orchard Books, 1999.

Le Guin, Ursula, K., and Patrick Wynne, illus. *Fish Soup*. New York: Atheneum, 1992.

Other Works Cited

Anderson, Kristine J. "Places Where a Woman Could Talk: Ursula K. Le Guin and the Feminist Linguistic Utopia." *Women and Language* 15.1 (spring 1992): 7–10.

Attebery, Brian. *The Fantasy Tradition in American Literature: From Irving to Le Guin*. Bloomington, IN: Indiana University Press, 1980.

Auden, W. H. "After Reading a Child's Guide to Modern Physics." In *W. H. Auden: Selected Poems*, edited by Edward Mendelson. New York: Vintage Books, 1979: 246–48.

Bakhtin, Mikhail M. *The Dialogic Imagination: Four Essays*, translated by Michael Holquist and Caryl Emerson, and edited by Michael Holquist. Austin, TX: University of Texas Press, 1981.

_____. *Problems of Dostoevsky's Poetics*, translated and edited by Caryl Emerson. Minneapolis: University of Minnesota Press, 1984.

Bal, Mieke. *Narratology*. 2nd ed. Toronto: University of Toronto Press, 1997.

Beckett, Sandra L. "Crosswriting Child and Adult in France: Children's Fiction for Adults? Adult Fiction for Children? Fiction for All Ages?" In *Transcending Boundaries: Writing for a Dual Audience of Children and Adults*, edited by Sandra Beckett. New York: Garland Publishing, Inc., 1999: 31–62.

_____. Introduction to *Transcending Boundaries: Writing for a Dual Audience of Children and Adults*, edited by Sandra Beckett. New York: Garland Publishing, Inc., 1999: xi-xx.

Bittner, James W. "Persuading Us to Rejoice and Teaching Us How to Praise: Le Guin's Orsinian Tales." *Science Fiction Studies* 5 (1978): 215–42.

_____. "Chronosophy, Aesthetics, and Ethics in Le Guin's *The Dispossessed: An Ambiguous Utopia*." *No Place Else: Explorations in Utopian and Dystopian Fiction*. Edited by Eric S. Rabkin et al. Carbondale, IL: Southern Illinois University Press, 1983: 244–70.

Blanchard, Jay. "Anthropomorphism in Beginning Readers." *Reading Teacher* 35.5 (February 1982): 586–91.

Bloom, Harold, ed. Introduction to *The Left Hand of Darkness: Modern Critical Interpretations.* New York: Chelsea House Publishers, 1987: 1–10.

Blount, Margaret. *Animal Land: The Creatures of Children's Fiction.* London: Hutchinson & Co., 1974.

Booth, Wayne C. *The Company We Keep: An Ethics of Fiction.* Los Angeles: University of California Press, 1988.

Bottner, Barbara. "William Steig: The Two Legacies." *The Lion and the Unicorn* 2.1 (1978): 4–16.

Brigg, Peter. "The Archetype of the Journey in Ursula K. Le Guin's Fiction." *Ursula K. Le Guin,* edited by Joseph Olander and Martin Harry Greenberg. New York: Taplinger Publishing Company, 1979: 36–63.

Bucknall, Barbara J. *Ursula K. Le Guin.* New York: Frederick Ungar Publishing Co., 1981.

Byars, Betsy. "Writing for Children." *Signal* 37 (1982): 3–10.

Cadden, Mike. "Purposeful Movement Among People and Places: The Sense of Home in Ursula K. Le Guin's Fiction for Children and Adults." *Extrapolation* 41.4 (2000): 338–50.

_____. "The Irony of Narration in the Young Adult Novel." *Children's Literature Association Quarterly* 25.3 (2000): 146–54.

Chambers, Aidan. "The Reader in the Book." *Children's Literature: The Development of Criticism,* edited by Peter Hunt. New York: Routledge, 1990: 91–114.

Chang, Margaret A. "Heroism Revisioned: Girls, Wildness, and Mothers in Ursula K. Le Guin's Recent Writing." Ursula K. Le Guin panel, MLA Convention, Grand Hyatt Regency Hotel, Chicago, IL. December 27, 1995.

Chaston, Joel D. "If I Ever Go Looking for My Heart's Desire: 'Home' in Baum's 'Oz' Books." *The Lion and the Unicorn* 18.2 (December 1994): 209–19.

Clausen, Christopher. "Home and Away in Children's Fiction." *Children's Literature* 10 (1982): 141–52.

Cogell, Wayne. "The Absurdity of Sartre's Ontology: A Response by Ursula K. Le Guin." *Philosophers Look at Science Fiction,* edited by Nicholas D. Smith. Chicago: Nelson Hall, 1982: 143–51.

Cohn, Dorrit. *Transparent Minds: Narrative Modes for Presenting Consciousness in Fiction.* Princeton, NJ: Princeton University Press, 1984.

Crow, John H., and Richard D. Erlich. "Words of Binding: Patterns of Integration in the Earthsea Trilogy." In *Ursula K. Le Guin,* edited by Joseph D. Olander and Martin Harry Greenberg. New York: Taplinger Publishing Company, 1979: 200–24.

Cummins, Elizabeth. "The Land-Lady's Homebirth: Revisiting Ursula K. Le Guin's Worlds." *Science Fiction Studies* 17.2 (1990): 153–65.

_____. *Understanding Ursula K. Le Guin.* Columbia, SC: University of South Carolina Press, 1990.

Dietz, Frank. "'Home Is a Place Where You Have Never Been:' The Exile Motif in the Hainish Novels of Ursula K. Le Guin." *The Literature of Emigration and Exile,* edited by James Whitlark and Wendell Aycock. Lubbock, TX: Texas Tech University Press, 1992: 105–13.

Dunn, Thomas P. "Theme and Narrative Structure in Ursula K. Le Guin's *The Dispossessed* and Frederik Pohl's *Gateway.*" *Reflections on the Fantastic: Selected Essays from the Fourth International Conference on the Fantastic in the Arts,* edited by Michael R. Collins. New York: Greenwood Press, 1986: 87–95.

Erlich, Richard. "From Shakespeare to Le Guin: Authors as Auteurs." *Extrapolation* 40.4 (1999): 341–50.

_____. *Coyote's Song: The Teaching Stories of Ursula K. Le Guin.* A Science Fiction Research Association Digital Book, 2001. Available from http://www.sfra.org/Coyote/Coyote Home.htm

Esmonde, Margaret. "Beyond the Circle of the World: Death and the Hereafter in Children's Literature." *Webs and Wardrobes: Humanist and Religious World Views in Children's Literature,* edited by Joseph Milner O'Beirne and Lucy Floyd Morcock O'Beirne. Lanham, MD: University Press of America, 1987: 34–45.

Franko, Carol. "Self-Conscious Narration as the Complex Representation of Hope in Le Guin's *Always Coming Home*." *Mythlore* 57 (1989): 57–60.

_____. "Acts of Attention at the Borderlands: Le Guin's *The Beginning Place* Revisited." *Extrapolation* 37.4 (1996): 302–15.

Galef, David. "Crossing Over: Authors Who Write Both Children's and Adults' Fiction." *Children's Literature Association Quarterly* 20.1 (1995): 29–35.

Gallant, Roy A. "Pitfalls of Personification." *Science and Children* 19.2 (October 1981): 16–17.

Genette, Gerard. *Narrative Discourse: An Essay in Method*, translated by Jane E. Lewin. Ithaca, NY: Cornell University Press, 1980.

_____. *The Architext: An Introduction*, translated by Jane E. Lewin. Berkeley: University of California Press, 1992.

Gevers, Nick. "Driven By a Different Chauffeur: An Interview with Ursula K. Le Guin. SF Site Interview." November/December 2001. Available from http://www.sfsite.com/03a/ ul123.htm

Harvey, Robert. *Liberators: Latin America's Struggle for Independence, 1810–1830*. New York: Overlook Press, 2000.

Hatfield, Len. "From Master to Brother: Shifting the Balance of Authority in Ursula K. Le Guin's *Farthest Shore* and *Tehanu*." *Children's Literature* 21 (1993): 43–65.

Higonnet, Margaret R. "Narrative Fractures and Fragments." *Children's Literature* 15 (1987): 37–54.

Hollindale, Peter. "Ideology in Children's Literature." *Signal* 55 (1988): 3–22.

_____. "The Adolescent Novel of Ideas." *Children's Literature in Education* 26.1 (1995): 83–95.

_____. *Signs of Childness in Children's Books*. Stroud, UK: The Thimble Press, 1997.

Holquist, Michael. Introduction to *The Dialogic Imagination: Four Essays*, translated by Michael Holquist and Caryl Emerson, and edited by Michael Holquist. Austin, TX: University of Texas Press, 1981: xv-xxxiv.

— *Dialogism: Bakhtin and His World*. London and New York: Routledge, 1990.

Hostetler, Margaret. "'Was It I That Killed the Babies?:' Children as Disruptive Signifiers in Ursula K. Le Guin's *Always Coming Home*." *Extrapolation* 42.1 (2001): 27–36.

Hunt, Peter. "Necessary Misreadings: Directions in Narrative Theory for Children's Literature." *Studies in the Literary Imagination* 18 (1985): 107–21.

Hunter, Mollie. *Talent Is Not Enough*. New York: Harper & Row, 1976.

Hull, Keith N. "What Is Human? Ursula Le Guin and Science Fiction's Great Theme." *Modern Fiction Studies* 32.1 (1986): 65–74.

Jacobs, Naomi. "Beyond Stasis and Symmetry: Lessing, Le Guin, and the Remodeling of Utopia." *Extrapolation* 29.1 (1988): 34–45.

Jose, Jim. "Reflections on the Politics of Le Guin's Narrative Shifts." *Science-Fiction Studies* 18 (1991): 180–97.

Khanna, Lee Cullen. "Women's Utopias: New Worlds, New Texts." *Feminism, Utopia, and Narrative*, edited by Libby Falk Jones and Sarah Webster Goodwin. Knoxville, TN: University of Tennessee Press, 1990: 130–40.

Kilby, Clyde S., ed. *An Anthology of C. S. Lewis: A Mind Awake*. New York: Harcourt Brace Jovanovich, 1968.

Knoepflmacher, U. C., and Mitzi Myers. "'Cross-Writing' and the Reconceptualization of Children's Literary Studies." *Children's Literature* 25 (1997): vii-xvii.

Kroeber, Karl. *Retelling/Rereading: The Fate of Storytelling in Modern Times*. New Brunswick, NJ: Rutgers University Press, 1992.

Kuznets, Lois. "'High Fantasy' in America: A Study of Lloyd Alexander, Ursula Le Guin, and Susan Cooper." *The Lion and the Unicorn* 9 (1985): 19–35.

Lewis, C. S. *The Magician's Nephew*. New York: HarperTrophy, 1955.

_____. "On Three Ways of Writing for Children." *The Riverside Anthology of Children's Literature*, edited by Judith Saltman. 6th ed. Boston: Houghton Mifflin Company, 1985: 1075–81.

Levy, Michael. "Re: Tales from Earthsea." Online posting. June 28, 2001. Child_Lit Homepage. Available at http://www.rci.rutgers.edu/~mjoseph/childlit/about.html

Lierop-Debrauwer, Helma van. "Crossing the Border: Authors Do It, but Do Critics? The Reception of Dual-Readership Authors in the Netherlands." *Transcending Boundaries: Writing for a Dual Audience of Children and Adults*, edited by Sandra Becket. New York: Garland Publishing, Inc., 1999: 3–12.

Lindow, Sandra. "Trauma and Recovery in Ursula K. Le Guin's *Wonderful Alexander*: Animal as Guide through the Inner Space of the Unconscious." *Foundation: The International Review of Science Fiction* 70 (summer 1997): 32–8.

Lutwack, Leonard. *The Role of Place in Literature.* Syracuse, NY: Syracuse University Press, 1984.

MacLachlan, Patricia. *Sarah, Plain and Tall.* New York: HarperCollins, 1985.

Magee, William H. "The Animal Story: A Challenge in Technique." *Only Connect: Readings on Children's Literature*, edited by Sheila G. Egoff, T. Stubbs, and L. F. Ashley. 2nd ed. Toronto: Oxford University Press, 1980: 221–32.

Markowsky, Juliett Kellogg. "Why Anthropomorphism in Children's Literature." *Elementary English* 52.4 (April 1975): 460–2.

Martin, Wallace. *Recent Theories of Narrative.* Ithaca, NY: Cornell Univestiy Press, 1986.

McCaffery, Larry, and Sinda Gregory. "An Interview with Ursula Le Guin." *The Missouri Review* 7 (1984): 64–85.

McCallum, Robyn. *Ideologies of Identity in Adolescent Fiction: The Dialogic Construction of Subjectivity.* New York: Garland, 1999.

Mermelstein, David. "Detours to Broadway." *New York Times*, 5 January 1997: 36.

Mills, Claudia. "The Ethics of the Author/Audience Relationship in Children's Fiction." *Children's Literature Association Quarterly* 22.4 (1997–1998): 181–87.

Morgenstern, John. "The Rise of Children's Literature Reconsidered." *The Children's Literature Association Quarterly* 26.2 (summer 2001): 64–73.

Morson, Gary Saul, and Caryl Emerson. *Mikhail Bakhtin: Creation of a Prosaics.* Palo Alto, CA: Stanford University Press, 1990.

Myers, Mitzi. "Canonical 'Orphans' and Critical *Ennui*: Rereading Edgeworth's Cross-Writing." *Children's Literature* 25 (1997): 116–36.

Nadel, Alan. "Roethke, Wilbur, and the Vision of the Child." *The Lion and the Unicorn* 2.1 (1978): 65–72.

Natov, Roni, and Geraldine DeLuca. "An Interview with John Gardner." *The Lion and the Unicorn* 2.1 (1978): 94–113.

Nelles, William. "Beyond the Bird's Eye: Animal Focalization." *Narrative* 9.2 (May 2001): 188–94.

Newman, Anne Royall. "Images of the Bear in Children's Literature." *Children's Literature in Education* 18.3 (fall 1987): 131–38.

Nicol, Charles. "The Very Different Worlds of Ursula Le Guin." Review of *Unlocking the Air*, by Ursula K. Le Guin. *The Chicago Tribune*, 25 February 1996: 5.

Nikolajeva, Maria. *Children's Literature Comes of Age: Toward a New Aesthetic.* New York and London: Garland Publishing, Inc., 1996.

_____. *From Mythic to Linear: Time in Children's Literature.* Lanham, MD: The Children's Literature Association and Scarecrow Press, Inc., 2000.

_____. "Imprints of the Mind: The Depiction of Consciousness in Children's Fiction." *Children's Literature Association Quarterly* 26.4 (winter 2001–2002): 173–87.

Nodelman, Perry. *The Pleasures of Children's Literature.* 2nd ed. New York: Longman, 1995.

_____. "Reinventing the Past: Gender in Ursula K. Le Guin's *Tehanu* and the Earthsea 'Trilogy.'" *Children's Literature* 23 (1995): 179–201.

_____. "Pleasure and Genre: Speculations on the Characteristics of Children's Fiction." *Children's Literature* 28 (2000): 1–14.

_____. "Bibliography of Children's Literature Criticism." January 29, 2003. Available from http://www.uwinnipegca/~nodelman/resources/allbib.htm

Paterson, Katherine. *Gates of Excellence: On Reading and Writing Books for Children.* New York: Elsevier/Nelson Books, 1981.

Prince, Gerald. *A Dictionary of Narratology.* Lincoln, NE: University of Nebraska Press, 1987.

_____. "Introduction to the Study of the Narratee." *Narratology: An Introduction*, edited by Susana Onega and Jose Angel Garcia Landa. New York: Longman, 1996: 190–202.

Prose, Francine. "Herself a Multitude." Review of *Unlocking the Air,* by Ursula K. Le Guin. *The New York Times Book Review,* 3 March 1996: 10.

Pullman, Philip. "Carnegie Medal Acceptance Speech." Online posting. 2000. Available from http://www.randomhouse.com/features/pullman/philippullman/speech.html

Rees, David. *The Marble in the Water: Essays on Contemporary Writers of Fiction for Children and Young Adults.* Boston: The Horn Book, Inc., 1980.

Reid, Suzanne Elizabeth. *Presenting Ursula K. Le Guin.* New York: Twayne Publishers, 1997.

Reinking, Victor, and David Willingham. "Interview: A Conversation with Ursula K. Le Guin." *Paradoxa: Studies in World Literary Genres* 1.1 (1995): 42–57.

Rochelle, Warren G. *Communities of the Heart: The Rhetoric of Myth in the Fiction of Ursula K. Le Guin.* Liverpool, UK: Liverpool University Press, 2001.

Rose, Jacqueline. *The Case of Peter Pan, or The Impossibility of Children's Fiction.* Philadelphia: University of Pennsylvania Press, 1993.

Rosmarin, Adena. *The Power of Genre.* Minneapolis: University of Minnesota Press, 1985.

Ross, Jean W. "Interview with Jean Ross." *Contemporary Authors.* 32 (1999): 251–54.

Sale, Roger. *Fairy Tales and After: From Snow White to E. B. White.* Cambridge, MA: Harvard University Press, 1978.

Sanders, Scott Russell. *Staying Put: Making a Home in a Restless World.* Boston: Beacon Press, 1993.

Scheiding, Oliver. "An Archeology of the Future: Postmodern Strategies of Boundary Transitions in Ursula K. Le Guin's *Always Coming Home.*" *Amerikastudien* 41.4 (1996): 637–56.

Schneekloth, Lynda K. "Plants: The Ultimate Alien." *Extrapolation* 42.3 (2001): 246–54.

Scholes, Robert. *Textual Power: Literary Theory and the Teaching of English.* New Haven, CT: Yale University Press, 1985.

Selinger, Bernard. *Le Guin and Identity in Contemporary Fiction.* Ann Arbor, MI: UMI Research Press, 1988.

Senior, W. A. "Cultural Anthropology and Rituals of Exchange in Ursula K. Le Guin's *Earthsea.*" *Mosaic* 29.4 (1996): 101–13.

Sharefkin, Belle D., and Hy Ruchlis. "Anthropomorphism in the Lower Grades." *Science and Children* 11.6 (March 1974): 37–40.

Shavit, Zohar. *The Poetics of Children's Literature.* Athens, GA: University of Georgia Press, 1986.

_____. "The Double Attribution of Texts for Children and How it Affects Writing for Children." *Transcending Boundaries: Writing for a Dual Audience of Children and Adults*, edited by Sandra Becket. New York: Garland Publishing, Inc., 1999: 83–98.

Shippey, Tom. *J. R. R. Tolkien.* New York: Houghton Mifflin Co., 2002.

Sinclair, Karen. "Solitary Being: The Hero as Anthropologist." *Ursula K. Le Guin: Voyager to Inner Lands and to Outer Space*, edited by Joe De Bolt. London: Kennikat Press, 1979: 7–13.

Slusser, George E. *The Farthest Shores of Ursula K. Le Guin.* San Bernadino, CA: Borgo Press, 1976.

_____. "The Earthsea Trilogy." *Ursula K. Le Guin*, edited by Harold Bloom. New York: Chelsea House Publishers, 1986: 71–84.

Sobat, Gail Sidonie. "The Night in Her Own Country: The Heroine's Quest for Self in Ursula K. Le Guin's *The Tombs of Atuan.*" *Mythlore* 81 (1996): 24–32.

Spivack, Charlotte. *Ursula K. Le Guin.* Boston: Twayne Publishers, 1984.

Stephens, John. "Maintaining Distinctions: Realism, Voice, and Subject Position in Australian Young Adult Fiction." *Transcending Boundaries: Writing for a Dual Audience of Children and Adults*, edited by Sandra Becket. New York: Garland Publishing, Inc., 1999: 183–200.

Stott, Jon C. "Running Away to Home-A Story Pattern in Children's Literature." *Language Arts* 55.4 (1978): 473–77.

Stott, Jon C., and Christine Doyle Francis. "'Home' and 'Not Home' in Children's Stories: Getting There—and Being Worth It." *Children's Literature in Education* 24.3 (1993): 223–33.

Swinfen, Ann. *In Defence of Fantasy: A Study of the Genre in English and American Literature Since 1945.* London: Routledge & Kegan Paul, 1984.

Thum, Maureen. "Misreading the Cross-Writer: The Case of Wilhelm Hauff's *Dwarf Long Nose*." *Children's Literature* 25 (1997): 1–23.

Todorov, Tzvetan. *Genres in Discourse.* Cambridge: Cambridge University Press, 1990.

Travers, P. L. "On Not Writing for Children." *Reflections on Children,* edited by Francelia Butler and Richard Rotert. Library Professional Publications, 1984: 58–65.

Trites, Roberta Seelinger. *Disturbing the Universe: Power and Repression in Adolescent Literature.* Iowa City: University of Iowa Press, 2000.

Tschachler, Heinz. "Ursula K. Le Guin: Ethnic Fantasy as Political Parable." *Literature, Culture and Ethnicity: Studies on Medieval, Renaissance and Modern Literatures*, edited by Jurak Mirko. Ljubljana, Slovenija: Uene Delavnice, 1992: 99–106.

_____. "What If Arlington, Texas *Is* Utopia? Ursula K. Le Guin, Postmodernism, and (In)determinacy." *Postmodern Studies* 11 (1995): 251–94.

_____. "How to Walk with My People: Ursula K. Le Guin's Futuristic Frontier Mythology." *Western American Literature.* 3.3 (fall 1998): 254–72.

_____. *Ursula K. Le Guin.* Boise, ID: Boise State University Printing and Graphic Services, 2001.

Waddey, Lucy E. "Homes in Children's Fiction: Three Patterns." *Children's Literature Association Quarterly* 8.1 (1983): 13–15.

Walker, Jeanne Murray. "Rites of Passage Today: The Cultural Significance of *A Wizard of Earthsea*." *Mosaic* 13.3–4 (1979): 179–92.

Wall, Barbara. *The Narrator's Voice: The Dilemma of Children's Fiction.* New York: St. Martin's Press, 1991.

Walsh, Jill Paton. "The Writer's Responsibility." *Children's Literature in Education* 10 (1973): 30–36.

_____. "The Writers in the Writer: A Reply to Hugh Crago." *Signal* 40 (1983): 3–11.

Walsh, William. "I Am a Woman Writer: I Am a Western Writer: An Interview with Ursula Le Guin." *The Kenyon Review* 17.3–4 (1995): 192–205.

Watson, Ian. "The Forest as Metaphor for Mind: *The Word for World Is Forest* and 'Vaster Than Empires and More Slow.'" *Ursula K Le Guin,* edited by Harold Bloom. New York: Chelsea House Publishers, 1986: 47–56.

Webb, Sarah Jo. "Culture as Spiritual Metaphor in Le Guin's *Always Coming Home*." *Functions of the Fantastic: Selected Essays from the Thirteenth International Conference on the Fantastic in the Arts.* Westport, CT: Greenwood Press, 1995: 155–60.

White, Donna. *Dancing with Dragons: Ursula K. Le Guin and the Critics.* Columbia, SC: Camden House, 1999.

Wolf, Virginia L. "From the Myth to the Wake of Home: Literary Homes." *Children's Literature* 18 (1990): 53–67.

Wood, Susan, ed. "Introduction." *The Language of the Night: Essays on Fantasy and Science Fiction.* Rev. ed. Edited by Susan Wood and Ursula K. Le Guin. New York: HarperCollins, 1989: 6–14.

Zanderer, Leo. "Popular Culture, Childhood, and the New American Forest of Postmodernism." *The Lion and the Unicorn* 11.2 (1987): 7–33.

Index